THE CHARDON PRESS SERIES

Fundamental social change happens when people come together to organize, advocate, and create solutions to injustice. Chardon Press recognizes that communities working for social justice need tools to create and sustain healthy organizations. In an effort to support these organizations, Chardon Press produces materials on fundraising, community organizing, and organizational development. These resources are specifically designed to meet the needs of grassroots nonprofits—organizations that face the unique challenge of promoting change with limited staff, funding, and other resources. We at Chardon Press have adopted traditional techniques to the circumstances of grassroots nonprofits. Chardon Press and Jossey-Bass hope these works help people committed to social justice to build mission-driven organizations that are strong, financially secure, and effective.

Kim Klein, Series Editor

The Power of Legacy and Planned Gifts

HOW NONPROFITS AND DONORS WORK TOGETHER TO CHANGE THE WORLD

Kevin Johnson

JOSSEY-BASS
A Wiley Imprint
www.josseybass.com

Published by Jossey-Bass
A Wiley Imprint
989 Market Street, San Francisco, CA 94103-1741—www.josseybass.com

Jossey-Bass books and products are available through most bookstores. To contact Jossey-Bass directly call our Customer Care Department within the U.S. at 800-956-7739, outside the U.S. at 317-572-3986, or fax 317-572-4002.

Jossey-Bass also publishes its books in a variety of electronic formats. Some content that appears in print may not be available in electronic books.

Chapter 1: Excerpt from "Donors Learn How to Be Effective by Seeing a Charity's Real Challenges" by Mark Kramer, *Chronicle of Philanthropy,* Nov. 23, 2006. p. 39. http://philanthropy.com/.

Chapter 2: Excerpt from *Management: Tasks, Responsibilities, Practices* by Peter F. Drucker. Copyright © 1973, 1974 by Peter F. Drucker. Reprinted by permission of HarperCollins Publishers.

Chapter 4: Excerpts from Rees Johnson, © 1999–2009 Rees C. Johnson. Reprinted with permission.

Resources; The Model Standards from Partnership for Philanthropic Planning (formerly National Committee on Planned Giving). Model Standards of Practice for the Charitable Gift Planner. Revised April 1999.

Library of Congress Cataloging-in-Publication Data

Johnson, Kevin, 1954–
  The power of legacy and planned gifts : how nonprofits and donors work together
to change the world / Kevin Johnson. — 1st ed.
      p. cm. — (The Chardon Press series)
  Includes bibliographical references and index.
  ISBN 978-0-470-54136-4 (paper/website)
  1. Deferred giving. 2. Fund raising. 3. Nonprofit organizations—Finance. I. Title.
  HV41.2.J62 2010
  658.15′224—dc22
                                                            2010003897

Printed in the United States of America
FIRST EDITION
PB Printing   10 9 8 7 6 5 4 3 2 1

TABLE OF CONTENTS

LIST OF EXERCISES, EXHIBITS, FIGURES, AND TABLES

We are a story-telling culture. Humans evolved relying upon stories to survive, to learn how to feed our families, to create and build enduring cultures. The stories we tell about ourselves, family, work, favorite dogs, or adventures define us as individuals and as a culture. Sometimes stories help us tell the world what is important to us; at other times, the telling of the story enables us to discover something more about our own life and the world at large.

This book seeks to showcase how growing numbers of Americans are creating and telling their own stories that demonstrate what matters most to them. An integral part of this trend is how they express their lifetime values and make them real—by planning charitable gifts in the form of bequests directed to small and mid-size nonprofits. These gifts support their positive visions and hopes for society and community. Every gift is an inspirational story about the value of the work of nonprofits and visions of a better tomorrow.

Often a bequest—a legal term to describe the act of giving something through a will or larger estate plan—is viewed by nonprofit leaders as a fundraising tool. A bequest is a tool for donors too. The impact of a bequest—how the gift is used—is the real reason anyone would make such plans. Acknowledging that outcomes are most important, I often call such bequests "legacy gifts" to better describe their value. Such gifts can also provide nonprofits with a powerful moral compass or guide for the future.

Many readers of this book will be volunteers or staff leaders of nonprofit groups seeking to bolster their resources. Other readers may simply seek to better understand and support their favorite nonprofits. Unlike other guides that address the topic of bequests and planned giving, this is written specifically for the perspective of a nonprofit leader or board member of a small or mid-size nonprofit. Approaches used in large nonprofit institutions, such as universities, hospitals, or large public broadcasting stations, often fail when scaled down to the level of small and mid-sized nonprofits.

A restructured economy also means that legacy gift practices used successfully in the 1980s and 1990s may falter now. Many such tactics may no longer account for the dramatic shifts that occurred in attitudes and needs of donors, the evolving roles of professional advisors such as attorneys and financial planners, and the impact of the proliferation of commercial philanthropic services and products.

Although this book is written with a focus on the unique perspective and needs of a small or mid-size nonprofit, you will find useful real-life examples, exercises, homework questions, and strategy guides to enable a nonprofit leader, of any scale group, to get to work immediately.

Over the years, I've worked with several hundred nonprofit organizations, ranging from animal protection groups, land trusts, social service organizations, private colleges, and regional hospitals to advocacy groups of many stripes. In conversations with their donors and board members, I often heard about issues that were most important to them. A few years ago, I began to notice a disturbing phenomenon.

Often these passionate donors spoke eloquently, telling stories describing the positive impact of the small and mid-sized nonprofits that they supported or helped as volunteers. Yet, when it came time to make plans for the future, instead of including bequests to these special small and mid-sized groups, they instead made plans to include national or large institutional charities. I began to wonder why such discontinuity existed between their expressed passions and actual behavior.

I became more interested in how small and mid-sized groups could demonstrate to their donors that they are appropriate legacy gift destinations. As a consultant, I see the tremendous impact that legacy gifts—from retired teachers, small-business owners, government employees, and lawyers—make in the work and financial stability of small and mid-sized groups. The value the thousands of small and mid-size nonprofit groups contribute to our communities is inestimable. People do want them to succeed and thrive.

Seeking to understand this larger question, when speaking to a group of nonprofit donors, I posed this discussion question: "How much more endowment does Yale University really need? They have more than $22 billion now. Why not give instead to local small and mid-sized groups?"[1] Since bequests are often directed toward endowments of larger groups, the question was intended to spur thought and raise questions about the impact of bequest giving. It sparked much conversation.

Afterward, a man and a woman in their early 50s walked across the room to me and announced, "Both my wife and I went to Yale. Yale is in both our wills." I paused, involuntarily bracing for what I feared would come next. "But," he continued, "our gift won't be millions of dollars. We're still going to give something to Yale, but we've decided to give most of our estate to local nonprofit groups where our gifts will be big enough to make a real difference." His wife nodded emphatically in agreement. Gifts such as these will truly make a difference.

DON'T COMPARE NOTES WITH LARGE INSTITUTIONS: SMALL AND MID-SIZE NONPROFITS *ARE* DIFFERENT

Planned giving, bequest, or legacy gift fundraising techniques that work well with big institutions possessing many development staff and large databases don't translate well into the world of small and mid-size nonprofits. Yet small and mid-size nonprofits constitute the majority of nonprofits in our urban and rural communities.

I was slow at arriving at this conclusion when it came to planned giving and bequest fundraising techniques. My introduction to planned giving and bequest fundraising came as a planned giving officer of a large, national organization. Later, as a consultant, I used the tactics that seemed to produce results when I was a planned giving officer. Often they didn't seem to "take" or to produce big results. I began to adapt my thinking and observe what worked and why. The result is this book.

Conventional wisdom asserts that to have a credible planned giving program the nonprofit organization should have a full-time planned giving person, along with an assistant and a healthy marketing budget. Although this is certainly a relevant recommendation for any large organization that wishes to make a credible planned gift effort, for the small and mid-size organization it is a luxury few could ever afford.

The reality for many groups in the small and intermediate range is that they do not have the resources to start and operate a *separate* planned giving program. Not surprisingly, attempts to emulate what works on the scale of a large institution but without comparable resources and scale, often fails to live up to expectations. This book will focus on how leaders of small and mid-size nonprofits can use their strengths, including their relative size, for effective legacy gift fundraising.

WHAT YOU WILL FIND

The purpose of this book is to enable nonprofit leaders and donors of small and mid-size nonprofit organizations to create their own unique path to building a stream of future income from bequests. The time is ideal to encourage, promote, and seek bequests. The collective age of our population, distribution of wealth, and increasing interest in leaving a legacy of good work are all reasons small and mid-size groups could fare well and receive substantial numbers of bequest gifts in coming years.

The average age of donors to many nonprofits continues to increase. Viewed one way, many key donors will soon no longer be with us to continue making their significant gifts. Who will replace them? Encouraging and actively seeking bequests today may ultimately provide critical funds for groups to continue to evolve and sustain their mission. Even a handful of bequests could transform any single small or mid-size group by, for example, making a reserve fund possible, or by increasing working capital and overall financial resiliency, providing thoughtful expansion of services, providing a fund for special projects or opportunities, or even creating an endowment to support core operations in years to come.

In Part One, Chapters 1 through 5, you will find an overview of some of the assumptions and ways of thinking that can stop or get in the way of nonprofit leaders seeking to encourage legacy gifts. There is also some basic information about what exactly is a bequest and how it can be used in personal financial planning. I hope by the time you finish Part One you will have a new level of comfort and quiet confidence about the topic.

Part Two, Chapters 6 through 10, focuses on a series of steps you can take to discover the potential for legacy gifts and begin to realize that opportunity for your nonprofit group. These steps are intended to help you, other nonprofit staff, and volunteer leaders identify the important characteristics that uniquely make the case for why someone would make plans to direct a legacy gift to your organization. It's been my experience that there are often very interesting discoveries carrying out these steps that have additional, positive impact in your current fundraising.

Part Three, Chapters 11 through 14, include discussions about professional advisors such as lawyers and financial planners and their roles, as well as ethics and transparency questions.

In an Association of Fundraising Professionals survey[2] that one of the bright spots is gifts in the form of bequests. It is my hope you will be able to put what you learn to work immediately and continue to use it in your day-to-day work.

ABOUT THE FORMAT OF THIS BOOK

For most of the book, the writing is addressed to a staff or volunteer leader of a nonprofit group. In some instances, I intentionally shift the reader's focus and assume the viewpoint of a prospective donor or someone planning a bequest for the purposes of helping nonprofit leaders better understand the personal factors that go into making a decision to complete a bequest to a nonprofit group.

In the many workshops, training sessions, and conference presentations I have conducted on these topics, the highest audience evaluations are linked to interactive exercises. This reflects that adults learn more through asking questions and interactive discussion rather than by lecture or presentation. As a result, this book includes a series of questions, exercises, and suggestions about how you can bring this interactive process to life in your own organization to help your staff and volunteers to learn. You can do many of these on your own or use them in groups of varying sizes.

TRUE STORIES

Throughout this book are a number of quotations and stories about people and many nonprofit groups. They are all true stories. The gifts, successes, and failures all happened with real people and real small and mid-size nonprofit groups. I do not identify people or organizations by name because I did not want to violate confidentiality or unintentionally embarrass anyone. I often intentionally changed a minor detail or two so that a group or individual could not be identified.

I am grateful to all the nonprofit leaders quoted and the many groups with whom I have had the privilege to work. As a former news reporter, I took many contemporaneous notes over the years throughout many client engagements and speaking events, but of course, being human, I undoubtedly made some mistakes or errors of omission.

WORDS AND DEFINITIONS

The world of charitable gift planning is filled with jargon and a collection of legal terms combined with words that may have a different common-sense definition. Throughout this book I have tried to use words and terms of art in ways that reflect common-sense meanings and that also reflect the ways I have heard donors often use them in conversations about gift planning. As a result, at times I may have sacrificed an exact, technical, or legal definition. I apologize in advance for the imprecision.

For example, a will is a specific legal document. Leaving a bequest in a will is technically different from using an IRA plan beneficiary designation form to direct that the IRA be transferred to a nonprofit or other heir. Yet both could be described in casual conversation as a bequest. Using precise language while focusing on what are the most important factors in making a decision is a challenge we will all face. In this book, I use the word *bequest* in a more general way to describe a gift included in a will or any other part of estate planning that is completed after a person passes away. That's broader than the legal definition— but it captures the spirit of how many people think about the word. An estate plan would address the questions of who should receive a bequest and how or what form the bequest would take.

I also encourage you to use the Glossary as you read; it's not just something to read after you finish everything else. Donors and professional advisors (and writers like me) often use specialized vocabulary without making sure terms are understood by everyone involved the glossary will help you.

REMINDER: WHY DONORS MAKE BEQUESTS

It's been my experience that donors place most value on the impact of their gift, and far less on the mechanical details required to execute it. The key drivers to most gift planning decisions are often emotional and based on personal lifetime values, not the highly technical details of how to actually complete a gift as part of overall estate planning. Planning details are, of course, critical in executing any functional estate or gift plan. However, ultimately charitable intent will be the driver throughout the entire planning process. Without that driving intent, no gifts or planning will be completed. This book will focus on how to work with donors to help them discover the overlap between their personal values and the work of your nonprofit. It is at this intersection that the potential for legacy gifts will be realized.

DISCLAIMER

Although this book provides general educational information, it cannot give you legal or tax advice on a specific matter or about the laws in the state in which you reside. In planning your personal and organizational affairs, please consult an attorney or tax expert about your own specific situation.

UNDERSTANDING WHERE WE STARTED

Personally, I often skip book introductions and get right to the heart of the book. You could do that here, too. But, may I politely suggest you actually read this introduction? Revealed here might be reasons why some planned giving and legacy gift techniques, or "best practices" may be more a product of history or habit than anything else. Understanding how the current state of planned giving evolved may help you pick out the most useful and right-sized thinking for your organization and its unique collection of donors.

A BRIEF HISTORY OF CHARITABLE BEQUESTS AND PLANNED GIFTS

Many assume that bequests to charity are primarily the province of the wealthy. We recall the publicized legacies of Carnegie, Ford, and Rockefeller. We also note local newspaper headlines heralding multi-million-dollar gifts to a nearby museum or a college.

There is a long history of bequests to charity in United States. One of the earliest prominent bequest gifts in the United States occurred in 1831, when Philadelphia banker Stephen Girard died, leaving $7.5 million to charity. At the time of his death, he was the wealthiest man in America. He gave almost all of his fortune away in the form of gifts through his will to a number of charitable and municipal institutions, including a boarding school for poor male orphans.

Throughout the 19th century there was popular support for such giving. Philanthropy historian Robert Bersi writes: "In view of the popular prejudice against ostentatious enjoyment of riches, the luxury of doing good was almost the only extravagance the American rich of the first half of the nineteenth century could indulge in with good consciences. Even the bequeathing of large estates to one's children was frowned on. Horace Mann declared 'a fortune left to children is a misfortune, since it takes away the stimulus to effort, the restraints from indulgence.'"[1]

Although there is a long, documented history of such large bequests, no longer are charitable bequests only for the wealthy. Today, 9.4 percent of the population of charitable donors have included a nonprofit in a will or another part of their estate plan and the numbers are growing.[2] Another 30 percent to 40 percent of the population reports they are willing to make or to consider making a charitable bequest. According to researchers, "The average bequest (circa $30–40,000) comes from the estate of a retired woman, who either has no living children or feels they have enough money of their own."[3]

Returning to consult the history books for perspective, it was in the late 1800s and early 1900s that fundraisers for colleges and many other charitable causes began to focus their primary attentions on wealthy individuals rather than mass solicitation. Although fundraising techniques evolved and expanded to include many mass solicitation methodologies, this focus on the wealthy and "major gifts" continues today.[4]

Given the institutional concentration on major donors, this targeting of wealthy prospective donors was emulated in gift planning work as well. Through the mid- and late-20th century, a body of specialized knowledge developed about estate planning combined with charitable giving. For the most part, this rather arcane body of knowledge of the mechanics of charitable trusts and estate complexities remained solely in the hands of a small number of large established nonprofits.

In 1969, in response to perceived abuses, Congress provided a codified structure for deferred charitable giving. With this new legal structure more visible and now clearly described in law, the number of trusts and other deferred gifts grew. Over the decades of the 1970s, 1980s, and early 1990s, the number of (mostly) large nonprofits entering the deferred gift field grew rapidly. The new entrants often copied activities and methods of long-established programs, in particular the practice of hiring highly specialized experts.

Planned gift fundraising concepts trickled down as increased numbers of donors learned about the concepts through seminars, mailings, newsletters, and personalized visits from development officers. Some smaller and mid-size nonprofits saw an opportunity and entered the market in response to changing population demographics (increased numbers of older prospective donors) and increased numbers of wealthy individuals.

These smaller nonprofits tended to copy approaches used by large institutions, reflecting a bias toward wealthy donors in combination with a focus on specialized techniques and legal arrangements. They hired staff with job descriptions emphasizing the technical aspects and promotion of charitable trusts, gift annuities, and pooled income funds. By the end of the 1990s, thousands of groups had self-described "planned giving programs" and dedicated full- or part-time planned giving staff.

Reflecting the growth and interest in planned giving in 1988, a national organization was created to support the planned giving profession. The National Committee on Planned Giving (NCPG) "grew by more than 1,000 new planned giving council members every year throughout the 1990s, without any organized recruitment effort. It seemed that there really might be a dedicated planned giving specialist in every charitable organization, from small to large. [In this same period] *Working Woman Magazine* and *U.S. News & World Report* both identified 'planned giving officer' as a hot career prospect. Fifteen years later, philanthropy and fundraising practices have changed."[5]

Along with this explosion in interest during the past 10 to 15 years, large institutional nonprofits invested millions of dollars and countless hours to educate the broad marketplace of prospective donors about the concept of giving through estate planning and planned gift tools. As the marketplace expanded, the label of "deferred gift" fit less well to describe this category of gift; the newer phrase "planned gifts" soon became part of nonprofit and donor vocabularies.

Professional advisors—lawyers, CPAs, financial planners—in large numbers followed interests of their clients, many beginning to advertise and promote charitable planning as part of their day-to-day offerings. An array of commercial products with philanthropic components also arrived on the market. The most visible of these philanthropic product providers[6] is the Fidelity Charitable Gift Fund.

The overall result is real and substantial growth in the knowledge base of prospective donors and their advisors combined with a wide array of philanthropic products available to donors at all gift size and income levels. With the exception of some existing large institutional programs, far fewer donors now expect or need detailed legal and tax-oriented advice from nonprofit staff. Instead, donors appear to be more focused on the impact and legacy of their gift. This shift in donor needs has profound implications for how gifts are marketed, what gifts should be promoted, and how gifts of all types will be managed in the future.

Nonprofits of all sizes copied the techniques (planned giving committees, gift vehicles and arrangements, and promotional methods) seeking to emulate the fundraising success of the older, more established institutional players. Few stopped to examine the actual market and ask the equivalent of the question Where's the money? Even for most of the well-established planned giving programs at prominent institutions, a predominant proportion of the dollars raised in any given year come in the form of simple bequests through wills or living trusts. Exhibit 1.1 and Table 1.1 describe some of the research revealing who makes bequest gifts.

One director of development of a mid-size nonprofit described the shift this way: "Many nonprofit organizations with staff focus a lot on the tools of planned

Exhibit I.1 Who Makes Bequests?

Average household income is $75,000, but 36 percent of bequest donors earn less than $50,000.

79 percent of the bequest donors have some affiliation or past connection with the charitable beneficiary.

43 percent of bequests are made by people younger than 55 years of age; 44 is the average age at which a will or living trust is made, and 49 the average age when the first charitable bequest is made.

Bequest donors tend to be married, living in one- or two-member households without children under 18.

Source: National Committee on Planned Giving. 2001.

TABLE I.1	
Percentage of Charitable Bequest Donors by Ages	
Age	**Percentage**
18–34	3
35–44	14
45–54	26
55–64	22
65–74	20
75+	15

Source: National Committee on Planned Giving. 2001.

giving. In other words, the complex gifts, the charitable trusts, income funds, gift annuities, and so on. To some extent it's because they can. But from our perspective we're never going to have a full time staff person who's going to be an expert. Many of our donors are not going to wake up and say, 'I should call _____ (my nonprofit) to talk about the details of my charitable trust.' That's not going to happen. But they might wake up and say, 'Their work is really important to me. I'd like to make a difference, how can I do that?' So that's where the story becomes a conversation we can have with the donor about a legacy—I AM an expert at that kind of conversation."

IMPORTANT POINTS TO CONSIDER

- A dramatic shift in how donors receive information about planned gifts has occurred—the model of a planned gift expert is no longer an expectation on the part of many donors.

- There is increasing awareness and growing interest among the community of financial and legal professions about the inner workings of planned gifts, along with expanded offerings to their clients related to charitable gift planning. Professional advisors look less and less to charities for help with planned gifts, with the result that small and mid-size nonprofits don't need planned giving experts on staff.

- Donor expectations are shifting toward focus on the impact and outcomes of their gifts—of all kinds. Every nonprofit is an expert about its own mission.

- More than 90 percent of gifts in the category of deferred or planned gifts are simple bequests (within which I also include retirement plan designations or gifts through living trusts). Ten percent or less of the money to nonprofits comes through the more complex trust or life income vehicles most often emphasized in large institutional marketing. Follow the money if you wish to be successful.

Part
One

Loyal Donors and the Path to Nonprofit Sustainability

Would a gift of $90,000, $150,000, or perhaps $1 million be treasured by your small or mid-size nonprofit?

Such gifts are not idle speculation. A gift of $90,000 was made to a small advocacy group by a local dentist; a $150,000 gift was made to a small-town land trust by a retired teacher; and a $1 million gift was made by a single woman to benefit a group serving low-income people. It's worth noting that the group that received the million-dollar gift had been in existence for less than a year at the time it received the gift. All three of these gifts were directed to the nonprofit with few or no strings attached.

Legacy gifts like these could be transformational for almost any small or mid-size nonprofit receiving them. Can you imagine what would happen if, over the next decade, your nonprofit organization periodically received gifts like that? What difference would that make in the day-to-day operations of your nonprofit organization? What difference would it make in your ability to plan and to increase the impact of your mission? It would make much possible—it's the stuff that dreams are made of, isn't it?

For small and mid-size nonprofit organizations, there is a compelling reason to focus on bequests as a tool for fundraising. In the United States, bequests from individuals account for 156 percent more than total corporate charitable giving, or about $22.6 billion in a recent year.[1]

BEQUESTS CAN SAVE AND BOLSTER SMALL AND MID-SIZE GROUPS

How long will difficult economic times last? At the time of this writing in early 2010, a number of economists are suggesting years of sluggish or sputtering economic performance for the United States. They predict no "recovery," but rather a slow emergence of a new economy. Such a new economy will have implications for fundraising work and require changes in how we work. Shifts in donor perceptions, expectations, and giving patterns have already started. In a recent survey, one fundraiser lamented, "We did everything just like we did last year, but it didn't work this year."

Now, and in the coming years, nonprofits will be forced to expand fundraising opportunities with donors in order to maintain their own financial viability. The smart nonprofits will focus on the larger goal of long-term sustainability. A key part of building a model for sustainable funding in the coming decade will be collaborating with their most loyal donors to construct a stream of future income in the form of expected bequests or legacy gifts.

Over the years, large bequests have transformed a number of institutions in the United States. Some of these bequests were spent immediately or over a short period of time; many others were used to start or expand endowments, to establish special programs, or to undertake new endeavors.

New cash infusions from bequests can also make the difference in continued, basic financial resiliency. One nonprofit director put it this way: "We have been talking about bequests now for about six years and are starting to see reliable returns." His organization applied consistent effort and is starting to see consistent results. "Bequests saved our bacon," is how he phrased it to a group of peers.

Legacy gifts have been described as an "ultimate" gift: a final, nonrecurring expression of donor commitment and values. What is important for the executive director or board president to know about these gifts? He or she must understand legacy gifts from two perspectives: that of the organization and that of the donor. From the viewpoint of the organization, how can these gifts, which are often in the tens or even hundreds of thousands of dollars, be used strategically to build the strength of the organization? From the viewpoint of the donor, how can a donor match gifts with lifetime values and how can a donor be confident that the gifts will be used well?

CONVERGING TRENDS DRIVE BEQUEST PLANNING

Events in the lives of donors are a primary driver when it comes to making estate- and financial planning decisions. When using the word "drivers " or "events," I mean the experiences of donors that often spur a decision to make or complete estate plans. Each time someone starts to work on or revisits their estate plans, an opportunity exists to include a nonprofit in that plan.

As an example of what I mean by such events, when I was working with The Nature Conservancy, I received a call from a woman in Prescott, Arizona, to tell me that her younger sister had unexpectedly passed away. Now she had two houses in town and could live in only one. She had just received a newsletter with my name and phone number in it. When she began to think about her new situation, she thought of my organization and picked up her phone to call. Could we talk about how she could plan a gift now and through her estate, she asked? There are many other such events that trigger planning decisions of individuals and couples.

Other trigger or driver events include a reaction to witnessing the poor handling of a friend's estate or an argument among surviving children, changes in health, changes in laws or financial circumstances, birth of grandchildren, and many others. How many people do you know who have updated their will before traveling internationally?

Four converging trends will help drive and encourage an increasing number of prospective donors to make decisions about estate planning. As a result, the coming years hold great potential with regard to bequest fundraising and tremendous opportunity for small and mid-size groups.

1. "The golden age of bequests" is now upon our society. Research strongly suggests that unprecedented numbers of people who will pass away in the next several decades will transfer significant wealth in record amounts.

In this case, the changing needs and psychological stages of aging represent important "event" drivers. Despite recent economic shocks, the potential and opportunity for legacy gifts continues to be vast.

2. Estate tax laws are changing. Regardless of specific legislative outcomes at the federal and state levels, continued change is predictable. This dynamic will prompt an increased volume of tax planning for personal estates. Every time an estate plan is reviewed or created, there is an opportunity for a charitable gift to be included.

3. Large nonprofit institutions have invested countless hours and millions of dollars promoting the concepts of planned gifts and bequests to their donors. Since donors to small and mid-size groups are often donors to larger groups as well, this promotion has helped build a much wider awareness about the tools of giving. Someone else has already worked hard to create this awareness and educated donor base; small and mid-size groups can put this to work in their favor now.

4. In recent times, many people experienced dramatic changes in their economic position—both real and imagined. This visceral shock prompted many to reevaluate long-range plans for themselves, family, and philanthropy. When life and estate plans are reevaluated, there is an opening and opportunity for donors to implement or expand charitable plans.

Current legal and economic factors, combined with an aging population, mean that the coming years present a unique opportunity for small and mid-size nonprofits to make a case for why they are appropriate destinations for bequests, both large and small. This coming period may represent a kind of (positive) perfect storm driving donors' gift planning decisions. Any nonprofit serious about intermediate and long-term sustainability must be proactive now if they wish to set up a pattern or stream of expected bequests to be received over many years to come. Will your nonprofit be ready?

THE GOLDEN AGE OF BEQUESTS

Over the past 40 years, charitable bequests have grown at a faster rate (4.5 percent) than any other category of giving, such as corporate, foundation, and individual giving (Table 1.1). Work done by researchers at Cornell and Boston

TABLE 1.1	
Growth Rate of Giving over the Past 40 Years	
Type of Giving	**Increase**
Bequest	4.5%
Foundation	4.4%
Individual	2.8%
Corporate	2.7%

Source: GivingUSA 2009. *The Annual Report on Philanthropy for the Year 2008.* Glenview, IL: GivingUSA Foundation.

College[2,3] suggests that, over periods of 20 years and 55 years, respectively, more than $1.4 trillion, perhaps as much as $6 trillion, will be transferred to charitable causes.[4] We are about 18 years into the first period of the transfer study, and only about $320 billion has been reported.

These general study predictions may come to pass for the long term but not perhaps for the initial 20-year projections.[5] Even if trends don't quite match expectations, there is still a phenomenal amount of money on the move. How many five- or six-figure bequests would it take to transform the work of a small or mid-size organization? The answer is only a few—in some cases, only one. Table 1.2 shows the total amount of bequest gifts in recent years.

Examining the social implications of generations and demographics in their book *The Fourth Turning*, William Strauss and Neil Howe describe the generation born in the 1920s: "Long a reliable generation of donors, the Silent will be legendary philanthropists in their final years. This will reflect a last urge to set things right, like the club that passes on members' Social Security checks to needy young people."[6] People want to help, to make a difference, to leave a legacy. How will your organization enable them to accomplish their dreams? The graying of America continues, which means that every day more and more people are planning their estates.

ESTATE TAX LAW CHANGES

Over the past decade, there have been persistent attempts to eliminate the estate tax. The current tax has a long history dating back to 1916 and the Progressive

TABLE 1.2
Bequest Gift Totals by Year

Year	Bequests (billions of dollars)
1998	12.98
1999	17.37
2000	19.88
2001	19.88
2002	20.9
2003	18.19
2004	18.46
2005	23.45
2006	21.65
2007	23.15
2008	22.60

Source: GivingUSA 2009. *The Annual Report on Philanthropy for the Year 2008.* Glenview, IL: GivingUSA Foundation.

Era, when people such as Theodore Roosevelt and Andrew Carnegie advocated for the estate tax as a reaction, in part, to what they saw as a concentration of wealth in America. Today, people like Bill Gates, Sr., Warren Buffett, David Rockefeller, Jr., and George Soros, all quite wealthy, advocate in favor of keeping an estate tax.

Current estate tax law requires that a federal estate tax form be filed for every deceased citizen with an estate value of at least $3.5 million. Based on current law (2009), in effect the first $3.5 million of an individual's estate would not be subject to federal estate tax (the amount would be double, or $7 million, for a couple). Further changes are expected once the current law expires.

The amount exempt from estate tax means that very few people will be subject to the tax. Bill Gates, Sr., and Chuck Collins write: "The indisputable fact is that the estate tax is paid only by multimillionaires and billionaires, the top one-half of one percent of the wealthiest households in the U.S."[7]

Warren Buffet, appearing before a Senate committee on November 14, 2007, described his view on the value of an estate tax, saying, "Dynastic wealth, the enemy of meritocracy, is on the rise. Equality of opportunity has been on the decline. A progressive estate tax is needed to curb the movement of a democracy toward a plutocracy." Bill Gates, Sr., the father of Microsoft's Bill Gates, agrees. He describes the estate tax as "a commonwealth recycling program. It is an appropriate levy to pay back the commonwealth, that helped create the wealth in the first place."[8]

Opponents of the tax have attempted to shift the emphasis of debate on the issue by labeling it as a "death tax" and suggested (but failed to document) that the estate tax hurts farmers and small businesses.[9]

Research suggests that if the tax were eliminated, overall charitable giving would decrease. The Congressional Budget Office estimated that elimination of the estate tax might cause a decrease in lifetime giving of perhaps 6 percent to 12 percent and in charitable bequests of 16 percent to 28 percent; that could translate into $13 billion to $25 billion per year less for charitable causes.[10] It is in the interest of nonprofits to advocate in favor of the tax both from a practical, as well as a larger social, perspective.[11]

Regardless of arguments for or against an estate tax or about a specific level of tax, I would argue that simply the existence of the tax contributes to increased numbers of estate gifts directed to nonprofits. It's been my observation that the mere existence of an estate tax encourages many to begin and complete estate planning processes. During estate planning sessions, a question professional advisors increasingly pose to clients is one to discover charitable interests. For many people, this can be an important opening to encourage charitable bequests.

WIDER KNOWLEDGE AMONG DONORS

For decades, the detailed knowledge about the many tools of charitable gift planning beyond the simple bequest was the sole province of the charitable gift planner. Such planners were, in turn, employed by only a handful of the largest nonprofits: universities, the biggest hospitals, and national organizations.

In the past decade, there has been a complete reversal of this picture as large numbers of professionals advising clients (or prospective donors, from the viewpoint of the nonprofit) actively entered the market. These estate and tax lawyers, accountants, financial planners, brokers, insurance professionals, trust officers, and even some real-estate brokers increasingly represent themselves as able to help clients (your potential donors) make charitable plans and execute a variety of planned gifts. (See Table 1.3 for an overview of shifts.)

TABLE 1.3
Shifts in Gift Tools and Markets

When	Who (Donors)	Who (Nonprofits)	Why (and How)
1950s through the 1970s	Only the most wealthy	Big, sophisticated institutions	Trusts of all sorts often used for tax avoidance, newsworthy bequests
1980s	Mostly the wealthy	Regional and leading charities	CRTs, PIF for investments and diversification; sale of real estate
Early 1990s	The above plus the upper middle class	The above plus virtually every large charity and leading intermediate-size groups	CRTs, PIF, CGA for diversification of assets
Mid-1990s	The above plus middle class	The above plus many intermediate-size groups	CGA for investment and fixed income
Today	Everyone or almost anyone	The above plus groups of all sizes and shapes	Bequests (including gifts from living trusts and retirement plans)

CGA = charitable gift annuity; CRT = charitable remainder trust; PIF = pooled income fund.

Charitable gift planning has become a regular topic at legal and financial services conferences and continuing education training. Advisors see increased involvement in this area as a way to help them expand relationships with clients, to continue to manage assets instead of passing them to a community foundation or charity, as well as a way to establish a legacy for clients and possibly open up the next generation of family members as possible clients.

Coupled with an explosion of new and continued interest among professional advisors, money managers at all levels have become active in offering an array of products that have charitable components. In fact, in recent years, the amount of money flowing into commercially operated, philanthropically oriented businesses placed several into the top categories of new "funds raised" as compared with the largest national nonprofits.

Reflecting on these trends in a report of the Strategic Directions Task Force of the National Committee on Planned Giving:

- Information about charitable planned giving has proliferated, and it is now easily accessible to all.

- There is heightened charitable awareness and receptivity among donors.

- Planned giving officers have less control now than in the past over donors' gift planning processes and are not the only source of information and advice for donors.

- Models for planned giving operations based upon the ability to control and manage the information are no longer effective.[12]

All of these changes favor small and mid-size nonprofits and begin to encourage loyal donors to complete legacy gifts.

A NEW CLIMATE CHANGE: ATTITUDES ABOUT WHAT IT MEANS TO GIVE

Economists use the term *structural break* to describe the point at which the relationship of trends and patterns change. While I cannot yet point to hard research to support what I am about to write, I have observed—in interviews with donors and in a number of nonprofit fundraising efforts—what I believe is a fundamental shift in the thinking and actions of donors.

What is this "break" that is about to become more apparent? A shift in philanthropy away from a primary focus on "the gift" to a focus on "the impact" has been occurring. Previously, the emotional benefit from giving was often derived from the act itself. More givers now are putting focus on and becoming emotionally connected to the *impact,* or outcome, of the gift. This shift in perspective has profound implications for how nonprofits interact with their donors as established patterns change and new ones emerge.

"Philanthropists and donors may be told daily by appreciative development officers that they are 'making a difference.' But for all the money they give and time they spend, they will not have understood the problem nor seen any change result from their efforts. And they will often feel a certain hollowness in the whole exercise that saps their commitment and diminishes their generosity," writes Mark Kramer, describing a research study of donors.[13]

He continues, "We have created a black hole in philanthropy, capable of absorbing endless amounts of money without demonstrating impact. Until they see results, however, donors don't shift away from giving modest sums to reaching deep and engaging personally in solving social problems. Educating donors, therefore, is not about books or conferences. It is about how nonprofit groups themselves perform, and the opportunities they provide for their major donors to experience the problems and see the solutions they have financed first hand."[14]

To many experienced development or foundation professionals, these donor concerns will not be a surprise. A focus on outcomes has long been an integral part of the cultivation and solicitation of major gifts or in more sophisticated grant-making processes. What's new is the spread of such expectations to a wider audience.

IMPORTANT POINTS TO CONSIDER

- The legacy gift marketplace for 2010 and the years immediately following will be quite different from the period of 1968 to the mid-1990s, when many of the marketing techniques and approaches for planned gifts and bequests that are used today were developed and described in articles and books. The rules have changed. Your organization must acknowledge, reflect upon, and respond to these changes in donor expectations and needs if you are to be successful in securing gifts.

- Four converging trends will help drive and encourage prospective donors to make decisions about estate planning. As a result, the coming years hold potential with regard to bequest fundraising, and there will be a tremendous opportunity for small and mid-size groups. These trends include:

    1. Researchers predict "the golden age of bequests," which is based on age and wealth distribution in the population.

    2. Estate tax laws are in flux and changing. Changes drive review or creation of new estate plans. Every time an estate plan is reviewed or created, there is a new opportunity for someone to include a charitable gift to a nonprofit.

3. Large nonprofit institutions have invested countless hours and millions of dollars promoting the concepts of planned gifts and bequests to their donors. Small and mid-size nonprofits can put this donor knowledge to work in their favor.

4. In recent times, many people experienced dramatic changes in their economic position—both real and imagined. This visceral shock prompted many to reevaluate long-range plans for themselves, family, and philanthropy. When life and estate plans are reevaluated, there is an opening and opportunity for donors to implement or expand charitable plans.

Transforming Old Habits into New Strategies

" I read the books. I went to the planned giving seminars. I tried it all. It didn't work." These are the words of a competent nonprofit executive with more than 17 years of fundraising experience. At the time, her organization had 14 staff, a $1.3 million annual budget, and a positive history with supporters. Sadly, too many small and mid-size groups have similar experiences. Ultimately, it should not be a surprise that the methods that produce results when used with large mailing lists of 50 years' worth of detailed alumni relationship data, or half a million grateful patients, don't perform for groups with 1,000 members.

The concept of a planned giving program is adopted by many small and mid-size groups more out of habit than from the result of careful examination of what their donors need and expect. Viewing legacy gift work through the single lens of a "program" will not serve most small and mid-size groups. Rather, a conscious effort to make legacy gifts a part of the culture or DNA of your nonprofit has great promise for success.

EVERY DONOR COUNTS

Many how-to and reference books on legacy or planned gifts were written from the perspective of development staff working in large institutions possessing double- or triple-digit–sized development staffs, institutional marketing budgets, and large constituencies. The authors appropriately describe what they experienced: specialized planned giving programs in big institutions with big budgets.

For a time in the late 1990s and early 2000s, it appeared as though scaled-down models of large institutional programs might produce solid results for smaller groups. It seemed a reasonable assumption to observe what large institutions did successfully and then adjust for size. I served as a planned giving officer with a large national organization and used these same assumptions when starting consulting work with small and mid-size groups. Over time the fundamental differences in how small organizations function, when compared with large nonprofits, and how donors to smaller groups experience and express their relationships, became more clear. A primary difference for a small or mid-size nonprofit is that every name, every donor, must count. One director of development wrote to me, describing his group's experience this way: "We get several gifts a year, and primarily it's based upon a pretty personal relationship with the organization." *Every donor must count* represents a fundamental difference that will drive your messages, marketing, and work plans in regards to seeking legacy gifts.

Methods large groups rely on are often based on mass-marketing techniques whose success depends on very big numbers. Direct mail is one such example. For a large group, a fraction of a percent return on a mailing can translate into hundreds of responses and keep a full-time planned giving officer very busy. Playing the odds works for large groups but similar success is much less certain for smaller nonprofits.

Yet, when faced with a task, everyone likes an ordered checklist. The idea of carrying out a list of tasks and getting a "planned giving program" in return is quite appealing. Based on my observations of many groups over the past 15 years, I would assert that, for the most part, program results for many were more often a function of luck or chance, not completion of a checklist. These checklist-oriented efforts collected and counted a small number of the most loyal or true believers/donors—people who would likely have made bequest commitments in almost any event because of their passionate connection to the cause.

Checklist performance can lead to a false sense of security. The organizational culture needed to keep legacy gift awareness and interest alive and meaningful among donors, staff, and volunteers never reaches a critical mass; legacy gift awareness and related behaviors are never integrated into how staff and board members think and behave with donors. As a result, efforts labeled a "program" often start with a spurt and then are forgotten as staff and volunteers change roles and time passes: few or no gifts arrive.

Exhibits 2.1 and 2.2 tell the story of one organization over a period of about a dozen years. I followed their journey through stories and observation. I hope you will learn from their experience. Buttonholing legacy gifts into the narrow definition of a "program," or by making strategic decisions burdened with unexamined, false assumptions is common and avoidable. (More about assumptions in the next chapter.)

IT'S NOT A PROGRAM: IT'S A CULTURE

I often deal with CEOs and board chairs who say with emphasized assurance that they understand how important legacy giving is to their institution. Their actions often tell different stories.

"What question can I ask my donors that will get them to give a legacy gift? We know our donors really well," one executive director asked. It was true he maintained friendly, warm relationships with donors—holiday cards were even exchanged among families. As the conversation continued, it became clear he might not have known his donors as well as he believed. What was the "tell," as an observant card player might ask? His questions focused on what he could do to manipulate those same "friends" by discovering the magic question or silver bullet to turn annual gifts into "big" bequests.

Such thinking might be described in the form of this three-sentence tale: "Winter is coming. The roof on our building leaks. Let's get some donations to fix it before the heavy rains start and leak gets worse." In effect, this fundraising and marketing "plan" is a reaction to immediate need; the plan has little anchor in a long-term narrative or strategic direction. It's urgent: Fix the roof! Many groups build their fundraising efforts based on the urgent. If groups led by such executives get bequests, it may be more a credit to earlier leaders or passionate board members than to any current vision.

EXHIBIT 2.1 Start, Stop, Fade Away, Start, Stop. . . .

I was referred to Mary, the executive director of a program that provided social services throughout a large metropolitan area. (As in other stories and real-life examples throughout the book, identifying details are changed to preserve confidentiality.) She told me the story of that nonprofit's struggle with bequests and planned giving.

Three years before our conversation, the group had received a foundation grant to start a planned giving program. A staff person was promptly hired, and he dutifully followed the steps prescribed for starting a planned giving program including creating a policy, starting a planned giving committee, creating brochures to educate donors about planned giving opportunities, running stories in the newsletter, getting a gift annuity license, and using direct mail regularly to solicit gifts.

After a year or so, he took another job. Nothing more was heard about the program until about a year and a half later, when a new director of development, Martha, found the planned giving manual hidden on an office shelf in an unmarked, white binder. Martha quickly recognized the potential of planned gifts for their many older donors, senior volunteers, and clients. She decided it was time to re-create the program. Along with a consultant, Martha began to put together a new plan. But the executive director left and, shortly after his departure, Martha departed too.

In the meantime, cutbacks in public-sector support for their work resulted in difficult financial times for this organization. Several of their most prominent donors passed away as well during this time, leaving minimal or no charitable bequests directed to the group.

Over the next five years, I followed their progress as an observer. The effort she began not long after we met quickly faded once Mary and her coworkers completed the checklist of things to do (advertise annuities with mailings, send mailers, declare a name for a heritage society, and so on). Not long ago, the next new development director also realized that in recent years, many volunteers, clients, and donors had passed away and their charitable estate gifts, for the most part, had been directed to other local and national charities. Just last year, he decided it was time to "start a program" again.

While the details vary, many organizations make an attempt at planned giving, follow the directions, attend the workshops, read the books, and then end up with programs that subsequently fade into obscurity.

EXHIBIT 2.2 Through the Looking Glass: Examining Board Member Perspectives

Let's imagine ourselves at a board meeting. This meeting took place about midpoint in their story, and is based on actual comments made by the board members of the organization in Exhibit 2.1 at one of their meetings.

The director agreed that bequests and planned gifts could be important. He placed a slot on the agenda for a short presentation about planned giving. The day of the meeting, the speaker provided an overview of types of planned gifts and why planned gifts should be an important part of their overall fundraising strategy. After all, with the transfer of wealth approaching and the relatively low cost per dollar of funds raised through planned gifts, why wouldn't a board embrace the concept?

Let's review a few of the responses of the members of the board:

John, a successful attorney, has colleagues who are estate planning attorneys. Their practice focuses on individuals with a high net worth, with estates often in excess of $5 million—some have significantly more. This is the planned giving market from his perspective: a small number of individuals with high net worth who are already known donors, whose names appear on the patron lists of any number of local, regional, or even national nonprofits.

He supports a program in concept, but doesn't see value in doing anything more. After all, while he considers himself successful—able

(Continued)

to send his children to private school and to afford special family vacations—his wealth is just not in the same league as those who are the clients of his estate planning attorney colleagues. Besides, there's plenty of time later in the year to think about these things. John looks at the existing donor list, thinks about the number of prominently wealthy who are on it (or mostly those who are conspicuously absent), and then makes a considered conclusion. "Our organization just doesn't have the kind of donors we need to have a planned giving program. It's a good idea—just not for us right now."

Mike is a midlevel corporate attorney. His firm specializes in complex corporate issues. He is to the point and very task-oriented. He earns a good income and can easily make a $1,000 gift. He is a very busy person—very passionate about the mission of the group, but almost perfunctory in his approach to the board operations. Mike is interested in being what he would describe as a responsible fiduciary. In other words, he wants a balanced budget, to be proud of his affiliation, and to see that the costs are kept very low. "Isn't planned giving a job for specialists?" he asks himself. He comments, "My college has some really sharp staff—but that's just not for a social services group like us. Having a specialist on board is just too expensive."

Mary is a securities broker for a national firm. She's mentioned charitable lead trusts as a great planned giving tool and suggested a number of times that the charity should really be promoting such gifts, since "this is the perfect time because interest rates are just right." Her unspoken hope is that if the charity promotes lead trusts, a few high-net-worth prospects might turn up and she'll have a chance to connect with them. Of course, there would be nothing unethical about the connection, but business relationships have to start somewhere.

Marcia is retired. She had a career, working with the county government for most of her life. She got involved with the group some years earlier as a volunteer. She is frugal, lives in her home in a recently revived part of the city, and gets the maximum level of public employee pension income, which almost equals the full-time salary she had when she was employed. She's still a little worried about her retirement income and is uncomfortable when other board members talk about fundraising. They have big incomes and nice houses, she thinks. "I don't want to talk about estate gifts—that's something for the wealthy," she said at the board meeting. "I think it would be hard to ask for bequests. Our donors and volunteers just don't have any money," she remarks.

The board chair asks a question that demonstrates he has not been listening to every word and has other things on his mind. The speaker is thanked and excused; no formal action is taken; the board moves on to other important business: reviewing the results of the fall direct mail campaign and a reviewing last month's expenditures.

The executive director, seeing little enthusiasm among board members, decided to go ahead and implement some basic planned giving activities internally. He had come to this organization from a larger, national organization that received millions of dollars in bequest donations. He had seen legacy gift giving work. His model—that of the national organization with dozens of state and metropolitan affiliates—was the basis for his experience. He observed that a direct mail education program, combined with one or more professional planned giving staff, a committee composed of local estate planning professionals, and donor seminars were the key to success. He looked at some of the nitty-gritty, nuts-and-bolts mechanics and perhaps he thought, "This is all there is to planned giving. We can do that too."

The planned giving brochure that had been written several years earlier was revised. The hundreds of extra (and now outdated because of specific references to tax law provisions) brochures were sent to be recycled. But weeks passed, then months, and the revised brochure was never printed.

This start–stop pattern is one I have observed many times. These otherwise well-run organizations that provide important community services suffer from myopia. By focusing singularly on current donations, they ignore their futures. When asked to explain that dynamic, one excellence-award–winning executive director said honestly "I'll be retired by then. It's the next director's problem."

What if simply talking about legacy gifts is the beginning of a cultural change for your organization? That is a bold assertion, I know, but pursuing legacy gifts often raises fundamental questions from board members, volunteers, and staff. One director of development described the challenge facing his group, saying, "I want to learn about setting up our organization so that people are comfortable in thinking of us in the long term and leaving (legacy) gifts for us. Part of our challenge is having people think of us as doing long-term work. Part of that is cultural in the organization, but it's also about learning to tell our story." In this case, a focus on legacy gifts sparked an effort to recast the story of their day-to-day work and connect it with long-term values.

Stories we tell can often describe a culture. For groups that regularly receive bequests, the stories that staff and donors tell are grounded in the values and strengths of their institution. The stories tell how the institution will continue to be true to its heritage and stay the course and demonstrate how it will be a wise steward of gifts. There will be a plan describing how this will be accomplished today and an outline of what will happen in years to come. Faithful execution of the principles of such a plan can do much to secure a nonprofit's financial future—one in which leaky roofs will be of small import.

What Is "Culture"?

The definition of *culture* is "the ideas, customs, and art of a particular society" or "the predominating attitudes and behavior that characterize the functioning of a group or organization." The *Merriam-Webster Dictionary* defines it in part as "the set of shared attitudes, values, goals, and practices that characterizes an institution or organization."

Starting a conversation about a legacy gift invites examination of the reasons why someone would (or would not) make a bequest to benefit your organization. Such a conversation may quickly arrive at big questions about the value and impact of your work, trust in the leadership and board, or transparency and accountability.

A successful conversation about a bequest will focus on personal values and the overlap between the donor's values and those of the organization. It will not be focused on the tools of giving. One board member described it by saying, "A legacy gift is a perfect way to describe your confidence in the future." It's not always an easy discussion, and one executive director describes his experience this way: "It's fun to talk to people about this but it's sometimes uncomfortable—it's a great lesson to understand that this is a wonderful kind of discussion."

Asking Questions Now to Better Understand Your Legacy Gift Future

While helping a group create a plan to integrate legacy gifts into their long-term financial/business strategies, I scheduled a series of research interviews with long-time donors to seek advice. One of those loyal donors was described by the deputy director as a "true believer." As proof, he then reeled off an impressive list of accomplishments and contributions made by this particular retired businessman. The meeting with the long-time donor went differently than expected.

One of the first things this 81-year-old donor said was, "My wife and I are not going to even think of leaving this group a bequest. They just don't run themselves like a business that is going to be around for the long haul." He continued, "They don't even have enough working capital to grow. We've made plans to include a large national group and the church in our will." I was stunned. But his comments made complete sense as he explained them.

We talked for another hour about how he and his wife had come to their conclusions. In a positive, thoughtful way, they had examined their beliefs and passions, distilling their lifetime experiences to choose two nonprofit groups they wished to receive gifts through their estate.

He was not the only donor to have concerns about the business side of this nonprofit. Not long after that conversation, the board took bold action to restructure their operations with the goal of growth and sustainability in mind. Some months later the donor described above, unprompted, announced at a public event that he and his wife had changed their will to include this group in their estate plans.

A bequest conversation that began with a simple question, "Have you ever considered including this nonprofit in your will?" drove a discussion of larger, valuable questions about the future of the organization. Five years later this same group has recruited an all-star board, has dramatically expanded its staff, and is embarking on a major fundraising campaign that would once have been unimaginable. The decisions spurred by a single legacy gift conversation enabled this group to thrive and grow.

This experience, and others like it, prompted me to shift my perspective from that of a fundraiser using fundraising tools to one more akin to a facilitator or matchmaker matching the interests and needs of an organization to donors who desire to make a positive difference in their communities.

Researchers suggest that the reason small and mid-size groups don't get bequests is that they don't ask.[2] But perhaps the most hindering factor is that fundraisers for small groups don't understand the motives or determinants of their prospective donors of legacy gifts, with the result that their efforts don't match donor interests or needs.[3] (See Exhibit 2.3 for a story about how nonprofit donors might view your nonprofit.)

Peter Drucker describes this perspective in a slightly different way when he writes:

> The final question needed in order to come to grips with the business purpose and business mission is: "What is value to the customer?" It may be the most important question. Yet it is the one least often asked. One reason is that managers are quite sure that they know the answer. Value is what they, in their business, define as quality. But this is almost always the wrong definition. The customer never buys a product. By definition the customer buys the satisfaction of a want. He buys value. . . . What a company's different customers consider value is so complicated that it can be answered only by the customers themselves. Management should not even try to guess at the answers—it should always go to the customers in a systematic quest for them.[1]

Imagine rereading this passage and substituting "donor" for "customer."

Building a reliable pipeline of bequest gifts is not the predictable result of executing a checklist culminating in a direct solicitation. Rather, it is creating a culture embraced by staff, donors, and volunteer leaders in which there is a clear path of understanding about the value and impact of legacy gifts on both the financial sustainability of the group, and its larger social impact.

EXHIBIT 2.3 A Vision for the Future Translates into a Legacy Gift

I was puzzled. While meeting with a long-time donor to one of my nonprofit clients, he told me about his plans for bequests to several large nonprofits—but not to the one we were meeting to talk about.

I inquired, "You speak so passionately about this local group, why not make a bequest or planned gift that benefits their work? What's preventing you?" One of several follow-up questions I asked was, "Why not put your resources where your heart is?"

"I never thought about it," came one reply. "They never asked," was another. "I never thought about them in that way—they seem so focused on the immediate challenges, I didn't think about what they might be doing 10 or 20 years from now," he continued.

"They don't seem to have a plan for the future—it's just about this year or the next big thing. They're always sending me letters about some crisis or another. When I think about a bequest, I want to create something—not react to something."

This story illustrates what I have heard over the course of several hundred conversations with donors throughout the western United States: that many small and mid-size nonprofit groups are not connecting with their donors when it comes to legacy gifts. Donors do not view many groups as able to accept bequests or as worthy of legacy gifts. Sometimes, in addition to estate gifts, this perception is expanded to include large current gifts.

When donors tell me about their decision to include a nonprofit in their estate plan, their story often includes a description of the kind of world or impact they wish to encourage. After describing that vision for the future, there is often an emotional conclusion that might sound something like, "as a result, I decided to include them in my will. I made a bequest to them."

IMPORTANT POINTS TO CONSIDER

- Many how-to and reference books on legacy or planned gifts are written from the perspective of development staff working in large institutions with resources that small and mid-size groups may never have.

- Too many small and mid-size groups follow checklist approaches to create a planned giving program that often quickly fades away. The result is missed gifts or, worse, increased donor doubts and concerns about the organization's ability to manage legacy gifts when they observe the program fade away.

- Focusing on legacy gifts from the perspective of the donor's interest can prompt hard discussions about the value and nature of your day-to-day work. Be prepared.

- Successful legacy gift efforts become part of the organizational culture or its DNA.

Assumptions That Mean Success or Failure

O ver the years, I have observed some small and mid-sized non-profits become quite successful in securing legacy gifts; others enjoyed much less success. Why the difference? When I look back at the many groups and individuals with which I have worked, two important differences appear to be the primary reasons for success or failure: (1) the perspectives about legacy gifts they embraced mattered and (2) key leaders made their own legacy gifts first. Based on my observations about what successful groups do as compared with those that are less successful, this may be the most important chapter in the book.

There are many embedded assumptions about small and mid-size groups and the planning of legacy gifts; most are false or misleading. This chapter describes some of the more deadly versions. I have seen many attempts at building legacy gift awareness scuttled by well-meaning people applying out-of-context or inaccurate assumptions with the result that their organization's legacy gift efforts die in confusion.

Using exercises like those in this chapter to explore assumptions will enable you and your colleagues to identify these issues and talk about them as perspectives or viewpoints—not absolute truths. The resulting discussions will contain far less emotion and more facts. By taking time to discover hidden assumptions, you make it possible to later address concerns carefully, accurately, and tactically. You will increase your overall chances of success in creating or expanding a stream of legacy gifts for your nonprofit.

This chapter concludes with a series of exercises you can do as a reader or use with nonprofit colleagues. If you are serious about building a stream of legacy gifts for your organization, I strongly urge you to take the time, using these exercises, to explore some assumptions your staff, board, and volunteers have about these kinds of gifts. Engaging assumptions early often means they won't surface later in convoluted forms at the wrong time and place. By removing some of the fears and concerns, what's left is excitement about the potential of legacy gifts.

WHAT ARE YOUR PERSPECTIVES? DO THEY HELP OR HINDER?

As I prepared this book, I came across several agendas and session notes from training sessions I delivered between 1999 and 2001. As I looked at the names of nonprofit groups and their leaders, I was pleased to reflect on the success of many. Over a small number of years, they received a significant number of bequests totaling millions of dollars.

In one case, a small group, which at the time of its first workshop had an annual budget of $104,000, has since received more than $1,250,000 in cash and real estate in legacy gifts, with a like amount expected over the next few years. These gifts enabled them to create a savings account for the future, to run a successful campaign for a large, special project, and to start an endowment to support work in future years. The resulting financial resiliency carried them through difficult recent economic times and an executive-director transition.

In sad contrast, several groups from those same sessions, as far as I know, have yet to receive a bequest. One group ended up dissolving despite its 100 years of history; another mid-size group continues to struggle from year to year, and all the while a number of their long-time donors receive public congratulations for making large estate gift commitments to other, larger organizations.

Why the difference among groups and their success? When I reflected on their relative successes and failures, one important difference between them was rooted in the perspectives their leaders embraced as they began their focus on legacy gifts. Equally important were the assumptions they did not embrace or consciously rejected.

Perspectives from the Donor's Point of View

Donors have assumptions about your group and about legacy gifts just as you have many about them. Those assumptions range from how they perceive or rank their wealth, to social comparisons about whether they are "the kind of people" that make bequests, to what kinds of groups "should" get estate gifts.

Often stereotypes donors hold may overlap with those held by nonprofit staff, board members, or volunteers. On the surface, donor concerns do sound similar to those held by nonprofit leaders, but the way they affect decisions or perceptions can be different. Listed below are a few of the more common assumptions from the perspective of a donor. Can you imagine a donor to your nonprofit saying or thinking the following?

- Only the wealthiest make bequests. I am not wealthy enough to be able to make such a large gift.
- Only very old people make bequests. I am nowhere close to ending things or winding down. I plan on living a long time.
- Planned gifts generate some sort of income, don't they? What do I get, what's the deal here? Should I shop around for the best deal?
- They are wealthy and should do it (referring to someone socially or economically prominent).
- I don't have time for planned gifts, maybe next year. I am too young to plan. (I once heard an 80-year-old say this.)
- I plan to live long enough to spend all my assets before I die; I plan to die broke.

The quiz in Exercise 3.1 is a quick way to uncover some of the perspectives you may have regarding legacy gifts. Consider using it as a staff or board meeting exercise.

	Exercise 3.1

Quick Quiz

You could use this as an exercise with staff, volunteers and board members.

Legacy Giving: True or False

1. Donors to my nonprofit organization already know about bequests and other forms of planned gifts.

   True ____ False ____

2. Bequest and estate gift fundraising is too complicated for my organization to get involved.

   True ____ False ____

3. I have heard about planned giving and charitable bequests, but I am not an expert. We need an attorney or tax planner.

   True ____ False ____

4. Bequest giving should be separated from other fundraising and development.

   True ____ False ____

5. Promoting bequest gifts will "cannibalize" the annual gift campaign and divert big gifts.

   True ____ False ____

6. Only elderly widows or 90-year-olds are good prospects for bequests.

   True ____ False

7. Once we decide who will manage our endowment, like a money manager or a community foundation, "our work is done."

   True ____ False ____

8. Bequests will solve all of our problems.

   True ____ False ____

9. My organization doesn't have the time or the resources to get started seeking bequest gifts.

   True ____ False ____

SOLUTIONS

1. **Donors to my nonprofit organization already know about bequests and other forms of planned gifts.** False. Many donors do not immediately think of small and mid-size groups as the place to direct their charitable bequests. But more and more donors know about the general power and impact of bequests.

2. **Bequest and estate gift fundraising is too complicated for my organization to get involved.** False. You only have to listen and know a few short, simple questions to plant the seeds for a legacy gift. One of the most powerful and effective questions is "What would you like to accomplish with your gift?"

3. **I have heard about planned giving and charitable bequests, but I am not an expert. We need an attorney or tax planner.** False. You know why your work is so important. That's what is most important to the donor, too. Donors' professional advisors can take care of the details—in fact they often insist on that. But you are *the* expert on the impact of legacy gifts and how the gifts will ultimately be used, and that is one of the most important parts of any donor's planning decision.

4. **Bequest giving should be separated from other fundraising and development.** False. It should be fully integrated into all your activities—program and development alike. Treat it separately and it will languish over time.

5. **Promoting bequest gifts will "cannibalize" the annual gift campaign and divert big gifts.** False. Cultivating bequest giving often increases current giving and opens up new, bigger gift opportunities. Research shows that annual donors who have made charitable bequest plans give 200 percent more; in the case of wealthy donors, it is 450 percent more annually.

6. **Only elderly widows or 90-year-olds are good prospects for bequests.** False. Any committed donor or volunteer can be a bequest donor. Increasing numbers of staff are making charitable bequests, too. However, it is true that women tend to outlive their husbands; thus, a bequest more often arrives when the wife—the second of the two—passes away.

7. **Once we decide who will manage our endowment, like a money manager or a community foundation, "our work is done."** False. People give to people. You and your board can best represent your mission, and that is a function no money manager, even one in a community foundation, will ever

be able to perform on your behalf. It is important to acknowledge that the reason you select the services of a money manager is so that you and the board are freed to do what you can do best and on to focus on what matters most: build trusting donor relationships. I have observed some nonprofit boards who hire a money manager (such as a community foundation, bank trust department, or prominent investment advisor) to manage their investments with the expectation that those same managers will help attract new planned gifts. This is a false assumption. Those advisors may offer advisory services to prospective donors, but that is not the same as building a long-term, mission-based relationship. It's been my experience that virtually no new gifts result from the expectation of fundraising help from money managers, despite hopes or promises to the contrary.

8. **Bequests will solve all of our financial problems.** False. Or, perhaps, True. Bequest gifts coupled with the wise use of those gifts could help stabilize your organization's finances. However, it takes persistence and patience to build a stream of gifts that can contribute to your financial sustainability and strength. It will also take careful planning today to make sure that donors have confidence how their gifts will be used tomorrow. Bequests will not automatically arrive. Each organization will have to invest time and resources to receive them.

9. **My organization doesn't have the time or the resources to get started seeking bequest gifts.** True OR False. It's up to you. Today.

Worst Fears

Another way to uncover some of your own perspectives about legacy gifts is to complete this sentence: My worst fear about planned giving or talking about charitable bequests is. . . . My worst fear was talking about death (see Exhibit 3.1).

Here are some responses from a range of nonprofit leaders and volunteer board members of small and mid-sized groups when asked this same question in legacy gift training sessions I have conducted over the past few years. Are your worst fears on this list?

- Alienating donors.
- Talking about death—it's awkward.

Exhibit 3.1 Being Hit by Lightning and Learning to Talk about Death

In the mid-1990s, while working as a planned giving officer with The Nature Conservancy, I happened to be at one of its Arizona preserves located in a remote canyon near Sedona in the midst of a summer thunderstorm. Storms were common that time of year, but the one this early August evening seemed more dramatic than any I had experienced. Lightning not only came down from the clouds, it made cross-hatched patterns in the sky.

All of a sudden, everything around me began to shine and became very, very white, then velvety black. It was still and quiet. I only later became aware I had been hit by lightning. Some undetermined amount of time later, there was a clear moment of choice: live or not. The moment I made a choice, awareness flooded my body and I awoke in a fetal position. There were burn marks on stones by me, nearby small pieces of metal had melted, and the smell of fire and smoke was sharp in the air. Murphy the yellow Labrador retriever was peering at me intently.

The next day I kept an appointment with a prospective donor for the purposes of discussing a bequest gift. As we talked about his plans, hopes, and wishes for the future, I realized that I was not afraid of dying. The realization was profound, yet almost matter of fact in its discovery. The experience of being hit by lightning left me with a different clarity about both life and dying. As I told the donor the story, I noticed a surprising shift in our conversation. It was as though the donor had been released or given a new kind of permission to talk about his feelings about making a bequest and the emotion that goes into making end-of-life choices. There was a freedom in the conversation I had never experienced with a donor before, because it was true for him as well.

What became clear to me after that experience was that recognizing my own emotions and focusing on the donor (instead of me)

(Continued)

> could shift a routine conversation into a life-changing exchange between two people.
>
> No one wants to die. But everyone will die. It is our task to live life in the fullest possible way. That will be different for each person. I look at my work with donors as someone who helps them discover what that way might be for them. There is value in recognizing your own fears. Sometimes naming them enables you to park them at the door, so to speak. When you can do that, your friends/donors can think more clearly about their own situation.

- Not knowing enough.
- Making a legal mess.
- Uncertainty about who should do what.
- Convincing others of the value of planned giving.
- Getting started—there's tension about how to mix the needs of the long term with immediate needs.
- The possibility of getting (or giving) bad advice.
- Asking too soon.
- Pushing the boundary of a friendship or relationship.
- People seeing my approach as a manipulation of our relationship, and it affects the future of our relationship.
- Rejection/failure.
- They may be disappointed in us for asking (because they know us as program staff).
- Resentment of being asked to give.
- They will say "no."

How would you complete this sentence: "We have not done more to systematically encourage bequest gifts because...." Here are some responses from a range of nonprofit leaders and volunteer board members of small and mid-sized groups:

- I don't have the answers to their next questions.
- There's not enough time to build relationships.

- There is a lack of capacity to follow through with the relationship.
- I don't know how to sell something that's "way up there."
- There are no deadlines for it, therefore it never happens.
- It's too technical.
- I'm not comfortable.
- Our organization is too small.
- We have only a few wealthy donors.
- We don't know who should do what.
- I have to convince others of the value of planned giving first.
- If they say "no," it feels personal.
- If I raise big money, I wonder if the organization will do the right thing in following through.
- I am not comfortable with a conversation about estate gifts.

It's not out of the ordinary to have such concerns. In workshops I have conducted, participants have owned up to one or more of those biases. On occasion someone confesses to having almost every concern.

An assumption that may be true for you personally may not be shared by your donors. This is particularly true when there is a difference in age and life experience. By way of example, in the book *The Seven Faces of Philanthropy*, the authors describe seven types of donors.[1] Each has their own particular world views. There is value in recognizing that people give for different reasons. When I reflect on mistakes I have made in fundraising work, virtually every major one was because I assumed the donor would think or act like me. I was wrong on all counts. I could have been more observant and focused on their needs and interests, and a little less on mine.

Fear: Will You Alienate Donors?

One of the most charged concerns nonprofit leaders have about legacy gifts is the fear they will alienate donors. It's been my experience that this is an unfounded fear.

A donor in Utah once told me that being asked by a development officer for a legacy gift changed her life. It opened up new possibilities and helped her to appreciate her life and her circumstances and to celebrate what she had accomplished. That kind of experience is the sort that happens with friends. Asking for a gift can be the act of a friend, not a salesman, not a manipulator; it's the act of a friend who cares.

Regardless of the specific reasons for which people make bequests, there is great willingness to consider such gifts. There have been a number of studies conducted in the United States and Canada that report notable levels of interest in including charitable groups in wills and estate plans. A collection of surveys suggests that 8 percent of the population probably already include a nonprofit in their plan, another 14 percent are considering it without being asked, and another 30 percent would include one if asked.[2] Given such high levels of interest, another survey posed the question to nonprofit supporters as to whether it would be OK to ask them for a bequest. More than 76 percent of respondents said yes, asking for a bequest is OK.[3]

On more than one occasion, a donor has expressed their disappointment to me that their favorite nonprofit has not asked them. "I guess they aren't able to use a large gift," one donor sadly told me as we talked about one of his favorite nonprofits. Is he right about your group? You may offend donors by *not* asking. You may also miss gifts if you don't make an effort. Is your nonprofit "able to use a large gift"?

Fears: Not Knowing Enough or the Possibility of Getting Bad Advice

One assumption that stops many groups is that one must know a lot about the ins and outs of estate planning, combined with the variety of planned giving tools, often referred to as "life income gifts" (the alphabet soup of gifts: CRTs—trusts of many forms, CGAs—annuities). In the case of small and mid-size groups and bequest fundraising, this is no longer true.

Large numbers of professional advisors now have working knowledge about the more complex charitable gifts. Coupled with their intimate knowledge of their clients' situations, they may be the best resources to assist their clients (your donors) when implementing specific charitable gift planning choices.

It's likely your donors already rely to varying degrees on an array of professional advisors, including lawyers, accountants, financial planners, insurance professionals, and brokers. Often the advisor the donor trusts most will assume a primary role.

However, these advisors will *never* be experts on the work of any individual nonprofit group. That will remain your sole province and specialty. By focusing on the impact of the gift and the connection with the donor's personal values, you will always be considered an expert in the right subject at the right time.

You will never know enough about any donor's personal situation for the purposes of detailed estate planning, nor should you. You are not his legal or financial advisor. It is important for you to state that clearly to the donor. Instead you *are* the expert on how their gift will be put to its ultimate, good use.

Assumption: Only Very Old People Make Bequests

In a large national survey of those who reported they had included a charity in their will, 43 percent were younger than 55 years old. Forty-nine is the average age at which a charitable bequest is first included in a will/estate plan.[4] Research suggests that donors between the ages of 40 and 60 are prime prospects for bequests because increasing numbers of younger people are actively making wills and estate plans. Whenever people engage in planning, there is the opportunity for a nonprofit group to be included in that plan.[5]

One of my client nonprofits received a $90,000 bequest from a former board member who died early in life from cancer. Another received a $1.5 million bequest for conservation work from a 35-year-old who unexpectedly passed away. A serviceman about to leave for a tour of active duty in Iraq notified one group it was now the beneficiary of his military life insurance policy if he were "to fall in harm's way."

Market research in the United States and Canada[6] shows high interest and willingness in the adult population to include charitable groups in their wills and to make charitable bequests. Estimates range from 30 percent to 50 percent who say they have already taken action, are considering it, or would consider including a charity in their will if asked.

Assumption: We Have Only a Few Wealthy Donors (Therefore We Have No Legacy Gift Potential)

The facts: Bequest donors tend to have a household income of about $75,000, but 36 percent earn less than $50,000.[7] The average bequest varies by organization. By way of example, Table 3.1 shows the number of bequests and average amount for just three categories of groups. Many groups that have actively promoted bequest giving experience much higher averages.[8]

TABLE 3.1
Average Size of Legacy Gifts

Category	Medium-Size Groups		Small Groups	
	No. of Bequests	Average	No. of Bequests	Average
Arts	4	$27,968	4	$500,051
Environment	4	$102,992	2	$90,613
Human services	13	$48,048	3	$11,821

Source: GivingUSA 2007. *The Annual Report on Philanthropy for the Year 2006.* Glenview, IL: GivingUSA Foundation.

The most reliable source of information about giving by charitable bequests is provided in *Giving USA*, the annual fact book on philanthropic giving in the United States.[9] It reports data from its surveys on giving, including bequests, each year. In one detailed report, they describe the size and number of bequests for groups in categories of large, moderate, medium, and small size (Table 3.1).

Imagine if your group invested time with your loyal donors and, over a small number of years, you reached a point at which the gifts you received averaged 13 gifts of $48,000 each? 13 × $48,000 = $624,000.

Assumption: It's Too Technical

Large institutions and national organizations have invested much effort promoting life income gifts and these types of gifts are most often labeled "planned gifts." What are these gifts or gift tools? They are called variously charitable trusts, CRTs, unitrusts (all three of these are actually the same thing legally), charitable gift annuities, pooled income funds, or lead trusts, along with several others. These tools provide a mix of income or tax advantages, or both. (For an expanded list, please see the Glossary.)

Early promoters of gift annuities marketed them like financial products. Some still do today and, for example, emphasize "competitive" rates on gift annuities. This approach to marketing readily taps into our consumer mindset. Many planned giving programs focus on these life income gifts, promoting them much like a business would sell or market a product. This is not a productive direction for small and mid-size groups to pursue. You may have donors who wish to use these tools and direct the ultimate charitable use of the gift to your organization.

But for most small and mid-size groups, you will find your investment of money and attention better spent focusing on simple bequests in the form of a provision in a will or living trust, or being named as the beneficiary of a retirement plan or an existing life insurance policy.

Assumption: Only the Wealthiest Make Bequests

Of course, we would all like to receive the $20 million bequest. But would you settle for an IRA worth $45,000, a house worth $276,000, a percentage of an estate worth $10,000, or what's left over after all bequests have been paid (in one instance, this resulted in a $600,000 gift from a man who did not have a taxable estate)? One nonprofit leader described her experience this way: "The one thing that has really struck me through the past few years is that it's almost always the most unlikely person—someone of modest means—that can give us the biggest gift."

Most groups consider major donors to be their best prospects for bequests. Lawrence Henze of Target Analytics writes: "the majority of planned giving prospects will never consider a major cash gift. These prospects are found among your organization's most loyal donors and constituents and are often ignored as significant prospects because of their past low level of support."[10] Many nonprofits have trouble getting bequests, Henze asserts, because they are focused on the wrong prospects and don't keep their appeals simple or personalized enough.

Research conducted by Target Analytics (a Blackbaud company),[11] which included more than 100,000 planned gifts of all sizes and types, clearly shows that although major donors do make planned gifts, they are not alone: The $20-a-month donor or the donor who has given faithfully for 15 years is much more likely to make a bequest. There are many, many smaller bequests of all sizes from people who were teachers, small-business owners, forklift operators, janitors, and restaurant cooks.

Almost every experienced planned giving fundraiser can tell you stories (that word is intentionally plural) of people who appeared to have no assets or little visible means making bequests in the tens or hundreds of thousands, even millions, of dollars.

"I knew him and I had no idea," the development professional exclaimed. She was referring to an announcement that a local man had just passed away and left $11.4 million to charity, some of which went to help children.

"I remember seeing him picking up cans along the highway to recycle. He would chase kids off his property. I never had any idea." A local paper ran a picture of the donor's house: it had broken-down porch rails, almost no paint, and an unkempt yard.

Sometimes this stereotype still gets in my way. When a prospective donor arrived for his appointment with me wearing a much-worn sweatshirt, beat-up shoes, and worn ball cap, my first thought was that I had wasted my time. Ten minutes later, I had completely reversed my opinion. It turned out that he had a 12 rental houses, most held free and clear. He wanted to create an estate plan to donate most of them to charity. He had come to talk about how his future gift would be used. (Update: My first encounter with this person was in 2003. In 2009, while writing this chapter, I read in one nonprofit newsletter about this same person making yet another large estate gift commitment. I still remember the sweatshirt and beat-up shoes from our first meeting.)

Fears: I Don't Have Enough Information; It's Too Technical

The complexity of planned gifts is often stated as a concern, but it's not one to fear. Here's an example of how a development director with no planned giving experience turned a complex gift conversation dominated by tax regulations into a million dollar gift—including cash today and a gift in the future.

Mark approached me after a presentation I had made to a group of about 90 executive and development directors. "I have a problem," he began. "I'm working with a donor and his tax advisor has told him . . . ," and he continued on to describe a messy situation. What became apparent was that Mark also didn't know that the advisor was not only giving the donor the wrong information, but he was also making any attempted gift conversation needlessly complex. The result was that Mark was in a difficult position.

I asked Mark if he knew what the donor wanted to accomplish with the gift. He paused and said, "I'm not really sure. I know he cares a lot about children and really admires the work our staff does with children. But no, I have to admit I don't know."

The conversation Mark was having with the donor and the advisor was, shall we say, off the road and into the weeds. It was all about the technical aspects related to a specific asset, in this case the donor's retirement account. How could he get back on track?

Would you suggest that Mark, in his role as a fundraiser and representative of a nonprofit, seek better tax advice? Perhaps he should look for a board member with tax and legal skills? Maybe he should wait for the donor and his advisor to sort things out? Perhaps a visit to the donor, accompanied by a well-known expert, to take on the advisor would be the right thing?

If your answer is "none of the above," you are on the right track. Instead, Mark called the donor and did something very easy. He asked the donor these three questions:

- What are your dreams for this work?
- What do you want to accomplish with your gift?
- What difference do you want to make with your gift?

A short time after Mark and I talked about his dilemma, he reported back to me (actual quote with the donor's name changed): "Kevin, you were correct about my conversation with the donor moving into the weeds. We stepped off the merry-go-round and just talked about dreams. Robert made a $1 million commitment to our endowment campaign: $240,000 over 6 years in cash and he committed another $760,000 in a simple bequest, and he is SO happy about it. Thanks for your help in all dimensions of this gift."

All I did was suggest that Mark ask easy questions, starting with: "What are your dreams for this gift?" Simple, right?

Marianne had been a faithful donor for many years—almost 20 years in a row, in fact. During a conversation, I had the opportunity to ask her whether she had included any charities in her estate plans, and she had.

I then asked if she had ever considered including the organization about which we were talking. There was a long pause during which I thought I must have said something wrong and offended her. Since I didn't have real evidence of any offense, I remained quiet and waited. It seemed forever, but then she replied in a breathless voice, "I am chagrined to say that I haven't." Pausing, she then continued, "But on the basis of this conversation, I will." Though she thought highly of the accomplishments of this organization, and its work was close to her heart, she had never considered them as a candidate for an estate gift. But the moment she considered it, her immediate answer was "yes." Is she alone in her thinking? How many loyal donors might your organization have like Marianne?

EXERCISES AND PERSPECTIVES

I suggest experimenting with different perspectives as a way to start identifying some of yours and those of your colleagues. After completing exercises such as those in Exercises 3.2 and 3.3, some nonprofit leaders have told me they look at bequest fundraising and their relationships with donors very differently and with greater interest. You can use this process as a way to explore these issues within staff or volunteer groups, or simply as an exercise for yourself.

Exercise 3.2

What's Stopping Us?

This exercise can be done with a small group or several small groups as part of a larger group including staff, volunteers, or board members. You can also use the results from one group to spur discussion of this topic with another group gathered at another time or place.

- First, pose three questions to the group (see Initial Questions below). Ask each person to write the answers to these three questions on a sheet of paper.

- Second, break up into groups of two or three people with the assignment that each small group will take 5 to 6 minutes to talk about their responses.

- Third, reconvene as a large group and ask someone from each of the small break-out groups to report on their discussion.

Initial Questions

1. My worst fear about planned giving or talking about charitable bequests is _____.

2. We have not done more to systematically encourage bequest gifts because _____.

3. I would feel confident enough to talk to donors about bequest gifts if _____.

Large Group Discussion Questions

1. What trends do you see here?

2. What do you notice about the words and reasons you see written on the board? What's behind that? Did anything surprise you?

3. What conclusions would you draw from these responses?

4. What opportunities appear with regard to bequest fundraising for your organization? With regard to donors?

5. What should you do next with regard to bequests and building a pipeline of future gifts?

Exercise 3.3

Fears and Causes for Celebration

Part One: Worst Fears

This exercise can be done alone, with partners, or in groups of three people. Moving around the room does make a positive difference in the experience of the exercise.

1. Pick four to six of the worst fears listed earlier in this chapter. You will likely know which ones would work best for you and your team in this exercise. Write out the phrase describing each on a separate card or piece of paper.

2. Put these individual pieces of paper in different places in your office or in the meeting room.

3. To begin, stand up, or move to a different place in the room if you are already standing, and move to the first card. If you have a larger group, you can pair up or even move about in groups of three.

(Continued)

4. Read what the card says to yourself. You might wish to close your eyes and imagine: What would your world look like if you lived constantly with this perspective as your primary focus? Take 3 to 4 minutes to imagine what this would feel like. If you are in a group, exchange your thoughts.

5. When you have a sense of what your world would feel like if this worst fear was your primary perspective, answer the following questions with that perspective in mind:

   a. "What does a meeting with a donor feel like with this perspective?"

   b. "What would be the experience of your friend, the donor, if you approached your next conversation with this perspective?"

   c. "What does this feel like to you?"

   d. "Is there some value or benefit to you to have or hold on to this attitude? What does it get you? What do you lose by keeping it?"

6. Now the group should come together to report on the most interesting things they observed or learned.

Part Two: Cause to Celebrate

1. Use the following items (or add some of your own based on positive donor experiences), and write out the phrase describing each on a separate card or piece of paper. Here are some examples:

   • The smile on the face of a donor when he or she tells you about the decision to make a bequest

   • The experience that a donor trusts you and your organization

   • The peace of mind for you (or a donor) after arriving at a considered conclusion of bequest gifts and focusing on the organizations that you (or a donor) feel truly make a difference in the world

   • A relationship with honor, respect, and confidence

   • The joy of knowing the gift will have important impact

2. Put these individual pieces of paper in different places in your office or in the meeting room.

3. To begin, stand up, or move to a different place in the room if you are already standing, and move to the first card.

4. Read the card to yourself. You might wish to close your eyes and imagine: What would your world look like if you lived constantly with this perspective as your primary focus? Take 3 to 4 minutes to imagine what this would feel like. If you are doing this in a group, partners of two or three persons per group might ask each other open-ended questions such as:

   a. "What difference did you notice with your experience with this set of statements as compared with the first group?"

   b. "How would you like to be treated as a prospective donor?"

   c. "What did you learn about bequests and your donors?"

   d. "What might you like to learn more about with regard to the wishes and interests of your donors?"

   e. "What surprised you?"

   f. "What will you do differently when you meet with donors in the future?"

5. Now the group should come together to report on the most interesting things they observed or learned. What does this learning mean for your legacy gift endeavors?

IMPORTANT POINTS TO CONSIDER: ASSUMPTIONS THAT MEAN SUCCESS OR FAILURE

Even if you are convinced that the right thing to do now is to start to build a stream of future gifts in the form of bequests, you will encounter speed bumps along your journey. Often these come in the form of the opinions of others. I have observed many efforts to encourage bequest gifts falter or fail because their advocates are challenged by questions or assumptions of others. This can be avoided by remembering the following:

- Take the time to encourage and help your allies and colleagues understand their own perspectives, biases and fears related to bequests, estate planning, and stereotypes about planned gifts.
- Worst fears can be faced and may be worse if not faced.
- Simple questions can be a positive solution to many situations.
- Upon reflection and the light of day, many fears and inaccurate assumptions may melt away.
- For assumptions that still remain, keep notes, because activities in later chapters will present opportunities to convert skeptics and worriers.

It's Valuable to Make Your Own Plans First

An experienced fundraiser will advise anyone who plans to ask for money to make his or her own gift first. This is equally true when it comes to legacy gifts: make your own gift plans first.

Most of this book is addressed to nonprofit staff and volunteer and board leaders. The point of view contained in this chapter and the next is intentionally different. Both chapters are written imagining that the reader is someone who has a will (or living trust) or is planning for one and that they are considering including some nonprofit group in those plans—perhaps it will be your organization. If you have not already taken some time to include a nonprofit group in your plans, this chapter and the next are also addressed to you. This chapter will focus on estate planning more generally and the next on how to choose a nonprofit to include in your plans.

Completing your own plans and including a provision for a nonprofit group will help you to discover and answer some of the questions—and real or imagined fears—you may have about the entire topic of estate planning and charitable bequest gifts. If you take notes during your journey, you will also come away with a story you can share that can be a powerful tool in your later work with donors.

FREEDOM AND CONTROL: THE POWER OF MAKING AN ESTATE PLAN

I had avoided making a will for a long time. It's done now. After completing it, I experienced a combined sense of relief, choice, and even a degree of expanded freedom. It enabled me to look to the future with a new level of confidence and optimism.

For me, a will was the primary estate planning document. But that is not always the case. "To many people, estate planning means nothing more than having a will. They incorrectly assume that a will is all that is necessary to get their financial affairs in order, and that once it is signed, they can file it away and forget about it," writes estate planning attorney Rees Johnson. "While a will is central to many estates, for many individuals, a living trust has become the central document. Signing the documents, however, is merely one step in a process that starts with an analysis of your property and debts. This process may involve assistance from a number of different professional advisors, including a lawyer, an accountant, a trust officer, a life insurance agent, and an investment counselor."[1]

STARTING YOUR JOURNEY

Before making a will, one of the first things I did was to learn more about the process of estate planning. From my public library, I checked out one of the many handbooks about how to do a will in my state. There is likely one written for your state, too. The book described the process of planning and some of the pitfalls. It also contained useful suggestions about how to prepare for a visit to an attorney to actually complete an estate plan and will.

I also asked friends and professional colleagues for names of attorneys they had used when making their wills. A bonus to that process was that each time I asked the question, I heard an interesting story about estate planning—or why it was being avoided. I learned much from them about what had worked well (and in some cases, about pitfalls to avoid).

With this list of suggested attorneys in hand, I talked with several who appeared to be a good match for me. All were more than willing to talk for a few minutes and I used the opportunities to ask questions about how they approached planning and working with clients. Based on these mini-interviews, I selected an attorney who I also knew was an active volunteer with a local nonprofit. I had confidence that someone like that would understand my interest in making a charitable bequest.

In advance of our first meeting, he sent me a checklist of documents to assemble and bring to the first meeting. (A sample list similar to one I used is in the Resources section.) I found that gathering and assembling the necessary documents took time—even for my simple estate.

I don't have children, but I do have a beloved dog. What would need to be in place to make sure that Mollie the Labrador was taken care of if something were to happen to me? These were among the many questions raised as I reviewed the planning checklist provided by the attorney. It was good that there were several weeks to go before my appointment because I needed the time to think through the answers to a number of the questions.

At the first appointment he asked questions to clarify some of my answers on the planning checklist. He also raised new questions that I realized I needed to take time to consider and respond to later. There was also a review of how my assets were titled or owned. He raised the questions of medical and advance directives. Did I want them in place? I had been thinking about them for quite some time, and this was just the impetus to get them set up, too. He had the forms handy and gave me a set to review.

After our meeting he prepared a draft of a will for me to consider. I had time to time to think about some of my initial choices and to revisit them. I asked for a few changes that were easily made. A few weeks after our initial conversation, he prepared a final copy and I signed the will in his office with several witnesses to make it official.

Following the signing, I sent copies of the will and the medical directives to family members to make sure that they knew of my plans and would be able to have access to the documents when the time came. I also notified the nonprofits named as a beneficiaries of one of my retirement plan accounts that they were included.

"Is anything the matter?" my father wrote in an e-mail just after receiving a copy of the directives and will. "No, nothing is wrong," I replied during a telephone call. "I am just planning." "OK, then," he replied, clearly sounding relieved.

A primary reason to plan your estate is to preserve your choices and to exercise control over what happens when the time comes. Even if you don't think you have much, there is great value in taking care of your affairs for the benefit of your family, friends, and community. Exhibit 4.1 shows a list of activities describing what you might expect as you go through your own planning process.

IT'S NEVER TOO EARLY TO PLAN

Over lunch with a board member of a large children's organization, the board member asked his friend Bob if he had any plans in place. Bob, 70 years of age, owned a number of apartment buildings that he still actively managed. He was in great health; in fact, he was heading out for a duck-hunting trip later that day.

"It's too early to plan," he said. His friend responded, "Bob, what if there's a hunting accident? What about Marilyn?" Bob's facial expression markedly changed when his wife's name was mentioned. Although he was in robust health and looked forward to a long life, he realized that accidents could happen.

At that moment, he decided it was time for him to stop avoiding planning because "he didn't need it." He decided to plan to take care of his wife Marilyn and his family—not because he was giving up on life or because he was giving in to fears about the future. Rather, he could see now that it was the act of a responsible husband and provider—and he was very much that kind of husband.

There are other ways to address the topic. In southern California, one group of aging business partners refused to talk about estate plans or the prospect of dying. However, they were very interested in making sure that they had a succession plan in place just in case they were all in the van at the same time going to a Thanksgiving event and "there was a freeway wreck." Such crashes are rare, yet common enough in southern California to be included in a practical business-succession plan designed to provide for business continuity.

One of the barriers to completing a legacy gift or bequest designation is a hesitation to plan. As a nonprofit leader you may hear such comments as "It's not time," "I don't know how to talk about it," "I am afraid of the issues it brings up," or "I am afraid to talk about it with my spouse." Often what prompts action is an unexpected event or a change in life plans: the passing of a sister; the family arguments that resulted after a friend without good plans passed away and left a mess; a friend's accident; as well as driving forces discussed earlier.

LET'S CHECK IN: IF BEQUESTS MAKE YOU UNCOMFORTABLE AT FIRST, KEEP MOVING FORWARD

I'm wondering whether about this time you are noticing a vague feeling of hesitation or unease while reading. Creating a will can be a very practical activity, a "what if" sort of plan that answers a question or addresses a possible, future problem. What if something happens while traveling: who will take care of the kids? Or, what if my business partners get in a freeway wreck: how do we figure out what we will do with the company? Or, if I don't plan, then someone in my family whom I absolutely do not trust with money will get what I have worked hard to save—I want to make sure that doesn't happen.

Beyond the problem-solving aspects of creating a will, consciously choosing who will get what assets and possessions can raise some expected and unexpected emotions. Making a tally of what you own can be liberating or depressing depending upon how you judge and value money and the things you own. It's baggage like this that can weigh someone down, stalling the process of completing a will or stifling the conversation about who or what should get a bequest.

I have noticed people who, because of fears or worries, make it a burden. I have also observed people at this stage in life approach planning with the intent to create something positive and meaningful.

Helen Nearing, at age 91, describes her approach to living and thinking about death in her book entitled *Light on Aging and Dying:*

> The whole of our lives so far has been our message. What now, in the time still available? We can deepen our awareness; we can fulfill ourselves and help others by imparting what we may have learned from the high and low phases of our existence. In that way we can find completion at the end of our lives. It is here and how that we make the conditions of any future life. It does not matter much if we continue as our present personal entities. More important is what we have learned and what we have contributed to the general welfare. The more aware we become, the more we participate productively, the more lessons we can learn—the more we enhance the whole.[2]

Anatole Broyard described his optimistic approach to planning, writing, "If we face now the reality, at 63, or 70, 75, 80 or 90, that we will indeed, sooner or later, die, then the only big question is how are we going to live the years we have left, how many or few they be? What adventures can we now set out on to make sure we'll be alive when we die? Can age itself be such an adventure?"[3]

THE MANY FORMS OF A BEQUEST

In a will or living trust, you might describe and direct a specific gift, such as a house, or a percentage amount of the entire estate to an heir or nonprofit. Another form a bequest could take is a beneficiary designation for a retirement plan, such as an individual retirement account (IRA). Or perhaps the asset may transfer to someone else because of the way the legal title was arranged in advance. Another method is to use a "payable on death" (POD) designation for a bank account. All are gifts completed or transferred after someone passes away.

There are a number of ways to approach planning a bequest. Sometimes there are specific things you may wish to direct by leaving detailed instructions. For example, grandfather's hunting rifle will go to a certain grandson. Beloved land might be given to a local land trust. Family heirloom furniture may be divided among the children. A collection of antique silver could be directed to a local museum to add to its silver collection.

Another approach is to use percentage or proportional division. For example, heirs might get 50 percent of the value of the estate and several favorite nonprofit groups would receive the other 50 percent. In this example, it would be up to the executor or personal representative to dispose of the assets and ultimately write a check to each beneficiary representing their proportional share of the estate.

Approaches can be combined too. For example, the family farm might go to a local land trust; other assets might be divided in equal proportions or percentages among children or other heirs. An example of a phrase one might include in a will or living trust to direct a bequest to a nonprofit is: "I give, bequeath and devise the sum of $50,000 to the ABC Nonprofit, with the current business address of 123 Main Street, Portland, Oregon, and Federal Tax ID Number of 94-12345."

Of course, how assets are titled and their legal and tax status should play a role in your planning, too. For example, if you are planning a gift to a nonprofit, one of the best assets to use is a retirement plan. (See Exhibit 4.4 for a discussion about income tax benefits of IRA gifts.) Your professional advisors can help make sure you accomplish your plans in a way that best fits your own unique situation.

THE POWER OF A PERSONAL STORY

One of the most effective ways to bring up the topic of planning is to be able to tell your own story describing your experience in planning. Sharing a story gives permission for the donor to learn from it and provides an opening for them to share theirs with you. I have also noticed that every time I tell my story to a donor or nonprofit leader, I learn something new about myself, my gift, and my own motivations (and that's useful to me, too).

When you tell your own story, it does not have to contain personal details. It should be about your experience, the emotions you went through in making your choices; these are the things every human being can share or understand. It will also enable you to speak with authority about the emotions you experienced.

Keep notes about your own journey to plan and create a legacy gift. It will serve you for years to come. In the words of one executive director: "I realized for years that I needed to get my will done. Now that I will be going on a trip to Africa soon, I finally just did it. It was surprisingly easy. Changing the designation on my IRA form was straightforward too. Now I can tell our donors, 'I've done this—I have plans in place and several nonprofits are included.'" Exhibits 4.1, 4.2, 4.3, and 4.4 describe different aspects of planning and list some of the things you can do to get to work immediately on your own plans.

Exhibit 4.1 Start with YOU, Then Seek the Help of Others: Five Steps to Estate Planning

First: Talk to family members and friends now and decide how to handle your financial and medical affairs if you become incapable of making your own decisions.

Second: Take time to consider exactly what is important to you. What values do you want to pass on to family and community? What kind of a legacy do you want to leave?

Third: Start working with professional advisors—especially an attorney—now. Make sure you have the documents in place so that your property will be distributed according to your wishes after you

(Continued)

die. Start with where you are today: Make a list of property and debts. This step includes reviewing the many documents describing insurance, mortgages, deeds, and other things you own. Include in your list your qualified retirement plans as well. With each asset, note how each is owned or titled. The kind of ownership title can be critical in tax and estate planning.

Fourth: Make the important decisions now. Don't burden loved ones with financial troubles when you can no longer provide for them. Answer the question: Who is the beneficiary of these assets? Determine who will receive your property and make sure the legal designations are accurate and in place. Set goals. Once you have an initial plan in place, what goals are important to accomplish in the future about these plans?

Fifth: Implement your goals. Your goals and decisions may require changes in documents, financial matters, or other arrangements.

Keep your plans up-to-date as life moves forward and circumstances change. Periodically review your plans and goals to see that they live up to your expectations.

Exhibit 4.2 Planning Your Will

Rees C. Johnson, Attorney at Law

Your right to dispose of your property at death is a valuable incident of ownership of your property. This has been described by one court as a "sacred and inviolable" right of your absolute dominion over your property. As part of that right, you are entitled to give your property to whomever you please and without regard to the natural or legitimate claims of your heirs.

Whether or not you exercise your right is up to you. If you do not exercise your right, then the state exercises it for you and directs how your property will be disposed of at your death. If you die without a will, then you die "intestate" and your estate passes by "intestacy." Such laws are known as the laws of "intestate succession" or "descent and distribution."

Not surprisingly, these laws direct that if you die without a will, your estate will be distributed to your closest relatives. Your state-made one-size-fits-all will, however, does not and cannot take your particular circumstances into account in making your will for you. For instance, if you have a child who has special needs and you want to place that child's share in trust or give that child a larger share of your estate than you give your other children, your state-made will cannot do it for you, because it will give your estate in equal shares to your children and with no trusts for them.

You should plan your will as if it were your last will. It can be risky to do an "interim" quick-fix will, say, just before you go on vacation, with the intent to revise it later after you have had time to reflect on how you really want to plan your estate. Too often an interim will becomes the final will because of the testator's accidental death, incapacity, or procrastination.

Your will should reflect at least two different plans for the disposition of your estate. The first plan should reflect the dispositive plan for your estate should you die a day after you sign the will. The second plan should be your long-range plan and should cover changes in circumstances which occur between the date of your will and the date of your death. It is particularly important that your will cover the possibility that one or more of the beneficiaries you name in your will die before you do, or that you may dispose of property that you specifically mention in your will.

For instance, as hard as it is to contemplate, suppose one of your children predeceased you. Would you want that child's share to go to

(Continued)

that child's children, your grandchildren, if any? Or would you prefer that the child's share go in part to the child's spouse? Or would you prefer that the child's share be distributed equally to your surviving children?

If you have only one or two children and no grandchildren, then you should also have a disaster clause covering the possibility that all your children may predecease you and your spouse. This is especially important for married couples with "mom and pop" wills leaving all your estate to each other and then to the children. If you do not cover this possibility in your wills, and the wife dies first, then if the husband outlives all your children and grandchildren, upon his death second, all your estate will be distributed to the husband's heirs. Conversely, if the husband dies first, then upon the wife's later death, all of your estate will be distributed to the wife's heirs.

One option for a disaster clause is to name charities or specific relatives from both families as beneficiaries. At a minimum, your wills should provide that if all your children and grandchildren predecease both of you, at the death of the surviving spouse, half of your estate will be distributed to the husband's heirs and half to the wife's heirs. By using such a clause, you will avoid the risk that the order of your deaths will determine which spouse's heirs will inherit your estate.

EXHIBIT 4.3 Sample Fact Sheet: About Bequest in Wills and Living Trusts

What is a bequest? A bequest is a section of your will or living trust that directs a gift from your estate to the person or institution of your choice after you die. Bequests may be used to provide gifts of money, real estate, stocks, or even works of art or jewelry.

Do I need an attorney? Your attorney should draft or review your will and/or living trust. For a bequest to a nonprofit, we suggest using wording below. Ask your attorney to review such wording before signing the will. If you already have a will, you may add a codicil providing for a charitable bequest.

A specific bequest is the simplest form of bequest. It designates a fixed dollar amount or specific property to a beneficiary (in this case, your organization). This type of bequest is appropriate when you have an item of value (stocks, bonds, real estate, works of art) or a definite dollar amount you wish to leave to a nonprofit.

Residual or proportional bequests designate either your entire estate or a percentage of your estate *after* other specific bequests are distributed. The advantage of designating a proportion of your estate to a nonprofit is that the bequest automatically adjusts in size over time along with your estate.

Contingent bequests are carried out only if circumstances make it impossible to carry out a primary bequest. For example, if all other beneficiaries are deceased, then a contingent beneficiary receives a bequest. Nonprofits are often named as a contingent beneficiary in the wills and trusts of young friends and those with children.

Bequest Wording

In general, the following language may be inserted in your will (or in a codicil to your will) to accomplish a simple bequest. In addition you may also include additional wording with more specific instructions as to how your bequest is to be used and when it is to be used.

"I give to the _____ (legal name of organization), a nonprofit corporation organized and existing under the laws of the state of _____, and with the current business address of_____, the sum of $_____ to be used in furtherance of its exempt charitable purposes."

(Continued)

OR

"all of my interest in the following described property: _____."

OR

"_____ percent or all of the residue of my estate,"

"to be used as the Board of Directors of _____ (name of organization) shall determine,"

OR

"to be used for the benefit of _____." (Examples: A field of interest, or a category such as scholarships, or an area such as a city, state, or region. Naming a specific program may be too limiting, as specific programs can change over the years.)

Additional Suggested Clause to Help as Times Change

"If in future years, the above stated purpose is no longer necessary, practical, or possible, the Board of Directors of _____ (name of organization) shall use its discretion to designate this gift for a purpose closely related to the donor's original purpose in furtherance of its exempt purposes."

Note: State law varies. Make sure you review this language with your legal counsel to make sure it meets all the specific or unique requirements of your state of residence.

EXHIBIT 4.4 Sample Fact Sheet: Retirement Plan Gift Opportunities (Including IRAs, 401(k)s, 403(b)s, and Others)

Did you know that retirement plan assets may be taxed at rates in excess of 70 percent? One of the simplest and most "tax-wise" ways to make a gift to a nonprofits is through your IRA, 401(k), 403(b), or other retirement plan. Why? Considerable taxes may result when your retirement plan is distributed directly to an estate or to heirs.

Individuals pay income taxes when they withdraw money from a retirement account; this includes heirs. When a nonprofit receives the account it can draw out the money tax-free. If you are planning a bequest, it can be tax smart to use retirement accounts first for this kind of gift.

Designating your plan is easy to do once you have made your decision. It might take 15 minutes or less. Here's how:

1. Get your account number and name of your plan administrator.

2. Go to their website and search for a form usually labeled as "beneficiary designation." This form enables you to tell the plan administrator how you would like what is left in the plan to be distributed when you are no longer here.

3. Usually the form can be downloaded or printed out. Fill it out with your name and account number.

4. Under the section for beneficiaries, put the names of the people or the nonprofits. There are often blanks to indicate percentages to enable you to give to multiple people and/or groups. (*Note:* Using percentages is the easiest; using a dollar amount can confuse plan administrators and present administration or tax problems later.)

   Critical Detail: Make sure you include the nonprofit's federal tax ID number on the beneficiary form. Nonprofits serious about bequests and legacy gifts will make it easy to find their tax ID number in the "About Us" or "Giving" tabs on their website.

5. Review the form to make sure it is complete, and then sign it.

6. Fax it to the plan administrator. I finished my own designation in less than 15 minutes. You can too.

7. Write a letter to the nonprofit group you have included as a beneficiary to tell them of your plans. That way, they can make sure to keep you up-to-date on their work and you can keep an eye on them to make sure that they stay on track. You can also tell them

(Continued)

how you wish to stay in touch—how much mail to send you or what to invite you to (or not) as well. Don't be shy about asking for information either. Your decision is an important one and that should be reflected in how they treat you in return.

Optional: Write a letter to the individuals included in your plans to tell them about your charitable bequest. Your letter could be an inspiration to others and spark meaningful conversations that benefit you and other family and friends. You put a lot of thought into your decision; this is one way to expand its impact and value to you.

CHECK WITH YOUR PROFESSIONAL ADVISORS

Every situation is different, and it is important that each person work closely with her or his own legal and financial advisors to structure their estate to best meet personal needs and objectives. A common mistake in estate planning is forgetting that the designation of a beneficiary in your plan documents, not a will, will be the one plan administrators use when they distribute it. Make sure your wishes are accurately recorded in the right place.

IMPORTANT POINTS TO CONSIDER

- Make your own plans and gifts first. Start now, because it will take some time to accomplish. What you learn along the way will help you become a more effective legacy gift fundraiser.

- Keep notes about the experiences you have in creating a legacy gift. Use this experience to craft a story you might tell others about what you learned and felt during the process.

- A sample checklist for estate planning is in the Resources section. A printable version is available on the Web.

A Reason to Give: Inspiration and the Donor Experience

Many people make gifts to charity. Far fewer make gifts through their will, living trust, or other part of their estate plan. A common reason people consider but fail to complete the act of including a nonprofit group in their will is because they have hidden doubts or unanswered questions about their decision.

There are three questions nonprofit donors often confront: (1) Is this the right group? (2) How will my gift be used? and (3) When will my gift be used? Each question must be answered in the context of a legacy gift. Often the answers will be different from what you expect.

As you read this chapter, I invite you to read it from a personal perspective. Later, as you put into practice some of the suggestions in this book and work with loyal donors to your organization, you may find it useful to return and reread it from the perspective of a nonprofit fundraiser. You may discover you have gained a new perspective about bequest giving.

DO YOU MAKE GIFTS TO NONPROFIT CAUSES?

I regularly give money to an animal welfare group, several land trusts and environmental advocacy groups, a nonprofit that helps other nonprofits be more effective, and a social service group connecting volunteers and service opportunities; I also make occasional gifts to other nonprofits. Spreading gifts around like that is quite common. In 2007, 83 percent of Americans said they had made gifts in the previous year to nonprofit organizations.[1] Many gave to multiple groups.

However, when it came time to include a nonprofit in my will, I named only one. I might add others later, but I am quite satisfied with my initial choice. When it comes to including a charitable organization in a will, many people spread gifts among several groups. I have often observed people including two, three, or four nonprofits. The most I have seen is 21.

It's common to include a charitable group to receive a bequest in a will, living trust, or as a part of other estate planning. One study published in 2009 reported that about 9.5 percent of those who donated to charity already included a nonprofit in their estate plan.[2]

Although it's relatively easy to write a small check to a good cause, when it comes to investing or choosing nonprofits in which to invest time and money, many people feel they lack the requisite knowledge to evaluate the organization's work, impact, and performance. Making the decision to include a group in your estate plan can also be an unexpectedly emotional journey.

What goes into the decision to make a gift through your estate? Perhaps you are clear as to the right group for you to include in your own plans, but now you are faced with the question of how to make the gift in a way that has the impact you want. Perhaps the question is also "How much?" A related challenge might be how to determine which group, among many doing similar work, is the right place to put your interest and support. For each person, it is a carefully considered decision.

The balance of this chapter focuses on how to make a choice about which nonprofits group to include in your estate plans.

WHEN YOU MAKE THE "RIGHT CHOICE" ABOUT YOUR GIFT, YOU'LL KNOW IT

I sat down with Susan, a university professor, to listen as she described her journey in choosing how she would direct her retirement funds—her primary asset—when she died and no longer needed what was left in the account. She began telling the story of teaching in the field of social work. She even named some of the many students she had encountered over the years, the many different professions they entered, and the differences their work made in the world. She continued saying how much she valued that work that spanned many types of organizations and geographically distant communities.

The tone of her voice and the conversation changed when she began to talk about one of her students in particular: a woman named Mary who, in her mid-30s, had returned to school after a tumultuous period in her life. Mary worked hard, and her graduation was truly a celebration of the human spirit. The power and the courage this student showed in life made a profound, lasting impact on her teacher.

Over the months during which the professor thought through how she might want her gift ultimately used, the thought of Mary returned repeatedly. Her conclusion: her gift would be directed to create a scholarship fund for women returning to school later in life. The process and learning involved in the shaping of this gift had deep emotional meaning and value for the social work professor. When she announced her choice, it was with pride, pleasure, satisfaction, resolution, and a sense of "this IS the right thing to do." And it was.

Not only must the gift be the right thing emotionally, but many also want to know that their gift really does make a difference and that it has impact. More and more donors view their relationship with a nonprofit like that of an investor: they want a social return in exchange for their gift/investment in the cause.

In this example, Susan carefully made decisions that helped establish and direct her gift. She chose the kind of impact that was important to her (helping financially struggling women who were returning to school later in life), the place (a regional school), and when her gift would be used (a portion each year).

What is it in your life that has a meaning that will help you shape the gift and legacy you want to make? Or is it time to start noticing and looking for the answer to that question?

WHEN IT COMES TO DECIDING THE TYPE OF GIFT YOU MAKE, BUSINESS IS ALMOST ALWAYS PERSONAL

After quite some time for reflection, here is how one donor answered the question: "I was barely a 'C' student then," Robert said, beginning the conversation. As he reflected on the causes of his success, he returned to the value of his college education. "But I had to work a full-time job at the same time I was a full-time student. I had no time, it seemed, for anything else. Life's been good to me and I want to give back."

In his late 50s, Robert was now a successful businessman. He had arrived at a point in his life at which he had made plans to take care of his family and financial matters to his satisfaction. "I'd like to make sure students like me could get some help, to not have to work at work as much and instead spend more time studying," he said in a slow, thoughtful way. Robert was quietly proud: this scholarship was exactly on target.

He continued to tell the story of how the process of making the decisions about who and what to include in his will began to define and describe the man he had become in a new way. He was pleasantly surprised at the personal nature of the discoveries he had made on the path to making his charitable decision.

Like Susan, in this example Robert chose the kind of impact he wanted to make with his gift ("C" students working full time to go to school), the place to make the gift (the school that had given him a start), and when the gift would be used (a fund would be set up through his will; in the meantime, he intended to start making gifts directed to this purpose to test out his gift).

Although Robert's and Susan's stories are about gifts to educational institutions, they could have named any number of important causes. What should you do as you consider making your own gifts?

Is This the Right Group?

It's been my experience that many nonprofit groups use bequest gifts wisely. Knowing that bequests may arrive in the future has also encouraged nonprofits to engage in long-range planning as well as inspired other donors to make or increase their gifts today. Sometimes, knowing that loyal donors have included a group in estate plans encouraged other donors to make gifts today to ongoing building projects. Knowing bequests are in the future, other prospective donors may give today with a greater confidence knowing that, in the years to come, there will be money to continue this work, as well as to maintain and staff the new building.

But not everyone necessarily has confidence in their gifts to nonprofits. Google.org sponsored a national survey of 8,000 donors who made more than $16 million in combined gifts and reported a wide gap between what donors thought their money was being used for and how it was actually used in the areas of both religious giving and nonreligious giving.[3] Given this gap, the question, "Is this group the right one to support or to include in my will?" becomes important to answer.

To help you determine the right group for you, my suggestion is to start with the groups that you already give money to each year and investigate each in more detail. The next several sections make suggestions about how you might test out these groups.

As a way to test out nonprofits I also regularly make "test gifts." I have found such gifts to be one of the most effective ways to literally test how the charitable organization responds to gifts. In the case of gifts to groups you wish to know better, consider designating your larger gifts to particular projects and ask the organization to report back on the results (or lack of them). Exercise 5.1 shows how you can start making your own test gifts.

Determining what groups or issues to support, and how best to accomplish that, is often an incremental process. In a study based on interviews with successful philanthropists, a clear pattern of personal growth emerged.

> [T]he effective donors began their philanthropic journeys like other benefactors: responding to those who asked them for money, unsure of how much they could afford to give, concerned about preserving their privacy, and without any direct apprehension of the difference their giving made. In fact, they were highly skeptical that philanthropy could have any significant impact. . . .
>
> They became prominent philanthropists in the communities but had not yet distinguished themselves as highly effective. Then something happened. A cause or issue came along of great personal significance and urgency. A magnificent historical landmark was about to be torn down. A child was diagnosed with a rare disease. A wilderness preserve from childhood was about to be sold to a developer. A charismatic acquaintance brought an environmental issue to life. . . . Each of these donors stepped up in a new way, often giving a far larger sum than they had ever imagined. . . . The urgency of the cause and the magnitude of their commitment forced them to roll up their sleeves and take an active hand in solving the problems they had discovered.[4]

How Will My Gift Be Used?

Often nonprofits ask for support for specific projects. You should expect their internal operations to track the use of that money for that specific work. Good nonprofits will report back on what happened and how your gift was used.

Equally often, solicitations come asking for a gift to support "our good work" (unrestricted or undirected gifts). Warren Buffett made his gift to the Gates Foundation essentially unrestricted in terms of how it would be used.[5] In an interview, he said, "I've had a chance to see what they've done, where I know they will keep doing it—where they've done it with their own money, so they're not living in some fantasy world—and where in general I agree with their reasoning."[6]

What would I do—direct my gift, or leave it up to the nonprofit? For local groups whose mission I wholeheartedly endorse and in which I have personal connections with staff and/or board, my trust in them would result in gifts to be used where the need is greatest (variously described as undesignated, general operations, or unrestricted).

But in directing your gift, there's also the hazard of assuming you know in advance what is needed. An example of assumptions is illustrated by a newspaper picture that appeared not long after Hurricane Katrina of books rotting in their boxes. The books had been sent to restock libraries damaged by the hurricane. Had well-intentioned donors asked first, they would have been told that there was no one at the libraries to store, stock, or catalog any new books. Libraries in the hurricane-damaged communities didn't need books or couldn't accommodate new books; rather, they desperately needed money first to hire librarians and staff. The lesson: Ask what's needed and why.

When Will the Gift Be Used?

Although Mr. Buffett did not restrict the Gates Foundation as to how to spend his millions, he did restrict when the dollars would be spent. He wanted his gift spent sooner rather than later, and he gave specific directions about the timing.[7] You may make a gift through your estate planning and wish it to be used immediately, over a period of years, or perhaps added to a permanent fund that generates annual revenue. Each is a legitimate choice.

In making your choice, consider the impact you wish to make. For some organizations, say a local public library, you know it will need and use support today and for many years to come. For organizations such as this, you may wish to designate your gift to be placed in a permanent endowment. An endowment gift will result in income, year in and year out, far into the future.

In other situations, a group may occasionally need large sums of money for special projects or opportunities. An example is a land trust that might have to move quickly to acquire a special piece of property or risk losing that property to other uses forever. In such a situation, you might request that your gift be put aside and used for a special project or land purchase.

For some nonprofits, the issues they work on are particularly immediate and pressing. In this case, your gift might make the biggest impact if it is used immediately. In the case of a larger gift, you might suggest that a part of the gift be spent over a period of several years. All of these considerations about the how and the when can be a bit daunting. A different approach to this conversation follows.

FINDING YOUR STORY BY HONORING YOUR TRUTH: WHAT IS YOUR STORY?

Imagine this: You are talking with a friend and she asks whether you have ever thought about including a charity in your will. What story will you tell in response?

Or imagine this: At some point many years in the future, you are reflecting on why you chose to plan a bequest the way you did. Imagine how it feels to have made the right choice. Now, describe the gift that gave you that positive, fulfilling feeling. How did it realize your intentions? How did it give you the spark or show the spirit so important to you?

If you are having some difficulty settling on exactly what your story might be, or perhaps you wish to refine or help that story evolve, I suggest you start with a few test gifts to some nonprofits. Test gifts can tell you much about how an organization operates. It can answer or raise questions that will help you discover the answer to one or more of these questions. Start with a test gift and keep notes about what happens next (Exercise 5.1). Following the test gift exercise and checklist suggestions is a list of sample due-diligence questions and related resources (Exhibit 5.1). Enjoy your journey and explorations!

Make Test Gifts First

Ask friends: Take a tip from new parents when they start evaluating schools: they ask friends, other parents, and others in the community for their recommendations—both positive and negative. What do your friends know about the charities they support, they volunteer with, or for which they serve on the board? You will be pleasantly surprised at how well networked your friends are when it comes to doing good work or knowing others who are. Who else is involved with the nonprofit? Who is on the board, and why are they donating their time for this work? Do you or your friends know any of the board members? If so, you have an opening to talk with them about why they volunteer their time and efforts to that particular group.

Start an informal giving circle: There is growing interest in giving circles. Google the phrase "giving circles" for a wealth of information on the topic. There is a good how-to checklist at: http://www.minnesotagiving.org/options/circlesteps.htm.

Ask insiders: Do you know people who work for nonprofits? Ask them about what groups they support and why. They can often inform you about the many intangible aspects as to how well gifts are leveraged and put to work.

Test drive your legacy gifts: In one instance, a couple setting up a scholarship in their will worked with the college to fund the scholarship immediately. The result was that they saw how the school would implement the gift and had the chance to see how well (or not) their scholarship criteria worked. They also had the opportunity to fine-tune it to make sure it was exactly what they wanted.

Here are some factors that may be useful to consider as you do your own due diligence on groups that are candidates to be included in your estate plan. Following each is a suggestion as to what the result might indicate or suggest:

- How quickly do you get an acknowledgment? A prompt thank you might suggest that the group has a solid infrastructure to account for and track gifts. Prompt responses also let you know your gift was received; without an acknowledgment, a donor may not know whether the gift was put to work. Nonprofits that care about their donors tend to respond promptly and accurately when they receive gifts. Did the acknowledgment tell you how the money was or will be used?

- What if you don't get a thank you? Did your gift get lost? You can verify whether your gift was received if your check got cashed or your credit card was charged. Mistakes can always happen, but they can also signal a cause for concern. If you inquire about your unacknowledged gift, what kind of response do you get? What is the tone of the response? Is it satisfying to you? Sad but true, it's been my experience that missing acknowledgments and glitches at this basic level are often symptoms of larger, internal organizational issues. So, for me, if I don't get a prompt acknowledgment, that is the last time I give to that group.

- What happens after your gift? Do you get reports about the work of the group or only a cascade of solicitations? Did the nonprofit give away or sell your name to another group? That suggests they may value you less as a donor and think of you more like an ATM. Did they ask you about how best to communicate with you? Do you get information about the impact of your gift? Is your overall experience satisfying? Why or why not?

- If you ask for certain kinds of information, what happens as a result? Did someone call you back within a reasonable amount of time? Was your inquiry handled courteously? Did you get a call or a note back?

- Does the information you receive about the group help or enable you to confirm that your gift(s) and choice of groups match your intentions?[8] Are those gifts producing the results you want in the community and the world? What is your evidence of this? What evidence do you want to see?

- As you reflect on your experience with the group, how would you describe your overall giving experience on a scale of 1 to 7, with 1 being "sadly disappointed" and 7 being "I'm impressed!" How would you describe the reason why you rated it the way you did?

- Did the nonprofit live up to the letter and spirit of the Association of Fundraising Professionals Donor Bill of Rights (a copy of which is included in the Resources section)?

Exhibit 5.1 Due Diligence

You might use some of the following questions[9] as the basis for your own list.

- What is your mission and how long have you been doing that work?

- Recognizing that much has changed in recent years, how has your mission changed or adapted?

- What are the main obstacles to the greater success of your mission?

- How do you compare with other groups doing similar work?

- How do you compare your results from year to year? How do you measure your success and impact? Why or how did you choose those measures or metrics? How do you evaluate the impact of your work and the difference it makes in the world?

- How much turnover of key staff positions have you had in the past 3 years? Which positions?

- Where does your support come from each year? What are the prospects for revenue this year?

- What are your activities (functions that directly advance your organization's mission)? If you do not spend 65 percent or more of your budget on program activities, why not?

- What are obstacles that might get in the way of the organization's success?

- Who is on your board and how long have they been board members?

- What percentage of the board has made donations to your work this year? What percentage of the board has included your organization in their will or estate plan?

- Do you hire fundraising solicitation companies for services such as direct mail, telephone, or annual fund? If so, what percentage do you receive of the donations that they produce?

- Do you have a reserve fund? How many months of expenses are in the fund?

- Do you have an endowment? How much is in it? Where and by whom is it managed?

SOME FOOD FOR THOUGHT FOR MORE QUESTIONS

Expectations: "Instead of showering hard-earned dollars on charities and hoping for the best, we need to demand clear, detailed information on the results of their efforts. We ask the government and public corporations to be transparent and accountable. Charities should meet the same standard."[10]

Impact and Results: "The main finding of the book *Forces for Good* is that the best charities often make their greatest impact outside the walls of their own organizations—suggests that foundations and philanthropists must work harder than ever to uncover charities that deserve support. The work that charities do apart from their own programs can be expensive, and it often doesn't show up as a concrete 'outcome' that can be neatly measured against the charity's budget."[11]

MORE RESOURCES

Rosenberg, Claude, Jr. *Wealthy and Wise: How You and America Can Get the Most Out of Your Giving.* Boston: Little, Brown, 1994.

Collins, Chuck, and Pam Rogers. *Robin Hood Was Right: A Guide to Giving Your Money for Social Change.* New York: Norton, 2000. It has useful checklists and examples.

There are several good guides and discussions about creating a personal giving statement, or how to discover and clarify charitable interests. One excellent resource in particular is Tracy Gary's book entitled *Inspired Philanthropy.* It's filled with exercises, practical

(Continued)

information, and questions to consider as you create your own philanthropy plan.

Guidestar is a source for the IRS financial reports nonprofit organizations must file. You can see these forms, called 990s, at http://
www.guidestar.org. You don't have to be a premium member to see
the 990s; it will just take a couple of extra clicks to work your way
to the right page.

IMPORTANT POINTS TO CONSIDER

- There are three general questions donors often raise when the consider making a legacy gift: (1) Is this the right group? (2) How will my gift be used? and
(3) When will my gift be used? How these questions fit together is illustrated
in Figure 5.1.

- Although sometimes questions may be obvious, often donors may not be
consciously aware of other questions that are equally important. Use the sample due diligence questions as a way to help discover the specific issues most
important to you and to your donors. By asking questions you can elicit hidden fears or concerns to emerge. When these concerns are named they can be
addressed. (That's the topic of the next chapter.)

- If the answers to key questions remain hidden, donors will not complete gifts.

Figure 5.1
Legacy Gift Tools

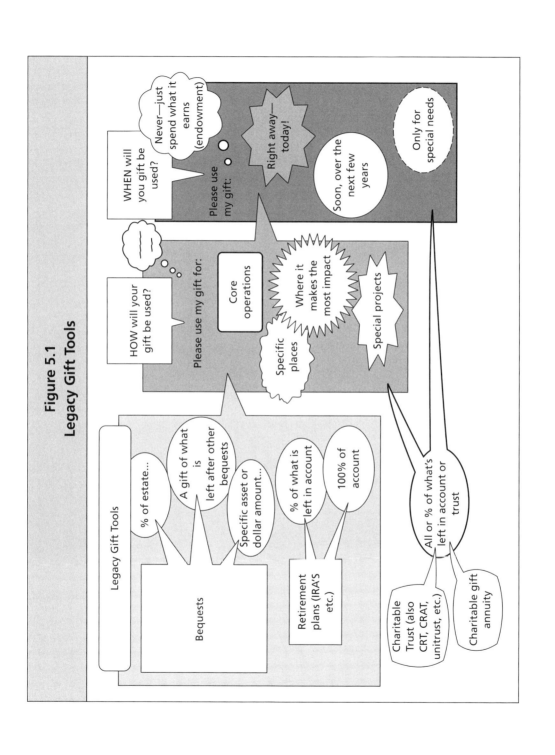

Part
Two

The Four Steps to Create a Stream of Gifts

The next four chapters describe steps to help you create a stream of future bequest gifts for your nonprofit group: (1) setting the stage for gifts; (2) building trust and credibility among your core group of loyal supporters; (3) reaching a tipping point of interest among key donors, staff, and board; and finally, (4) "going public" with your efforts, including all of your current donors as well as others who support your work.

The activities recommended are designed to engage donors, volunteers, and board members in order to build relationships with donors focused on their personal lifetime values. As these relationships grow, so will opportunities to invite them to become an important part of your nonprofit's "extended family." In turn, they may come to consider you part of their family and honor your group by planning a legacy gift.

Taking shortcuts in this process will shortchange your most loyal donors, future board members, future executive directors, and most of all the people whom your mission is to help. Taking shortcuts will also produce lackluster or somewhat middling results.

If you do these suggested activities will you get gifts? Yes. Often I have observed that nonprofits actively and sincerely engaged in these steps see increases in bequest gifts within a year of when they begin. It's also been my experience that groups not only discover new bequest gifts, but also that many donors also increase their current gifts. Although certainly an exception, in one case a mid-size group in a rural community received a million-dollar cash gift their first year. The gift was originally intended as a bequest, but in response to work the group was doing focused on legacy gifts, the donor was inspired and converted her plans for a future bequest gift into a $1 million gift for today.

STEP 1: SETTING THE STAGE

"Setting the stage" is centered around identifying your potential for gifts and building a case for future gifts. Taking the time to identify your potential will help serve as a gauge to determine how much time and effort you wish to invest in this larger effort. As part of assessing potential you will also identify prospective donors. You will seek out the advice and counsel of some of those prospective donors and construct a case for making a legacy gift that is uniquely suited to your nonprofit. Along the way you will discover and document barriers to legacy giving for your prospective donors that need correction or explanation.

This phase of setting the stage might be compared to setting the table for guests for dinner. It is a time of preparation: you have a menu, you know what you will serve, the menu is matched with a shopping list of ingredients. When I plan for dinner, I make up a timeline for the day so I don't forget anything or get out of sequence cooking. These preparations make for a successful dinner. These days, I also check in with the guests about food allergies or preferences to make sure I don't end up with wild king salmon on the table and a guest with a fish allergy.

Likewise, how you set the stage for legacy gifts will determine later success. It's been my experience that a careful process of preparation means you will get gifts sooner and that work later will be easier. But it will require patience and there will be times of frustration. You might hear, in the words of one Type A executive director, "But when can I ASK for the gift?" (It's interesting to note that the experience of donors suggests that simply bringing up the general topic of legacy gifts is in effect "an ask.")

What Is Your Potential? How Many $25-a-Year Donors Can Give $100,000?

Solid research[1] verifies that donor loyalty is one of the most reliable predictors of legacy gifts. The first place to look for loyal donors is your database. One development officer reported that a survey of donors to his nonprofit revealed that a surprising number were over the age of 65. Another discovered while researching his database that there were more than 300 donors who had been giving regularly for more than 15 years. One group conducted an informational survey as part of setting the stage, and 28 long-time donors responded that they had already included the group in their plans or that they were considering doing it soon.

Understanding potential can sometimes be accidental. In one case, an executive director and I had talked about the impact periodic bequests could have on his organization. Even though his nonprofit had been around for more than 30 years, it rarely received any bequests. The prospect of getting such gifts seemed abstract to him.

A week or two after our last conversation, I picked up the phone to hear the excited voice of the executive director of a client organization asking, "Kevin, guess what?" He paused for dramatic effect then continued, "We just got a check for $100,000! It was a bequest from a donor who had never given us more than $25. We added up all the gifts she ever gave to us and the total was less than a thousand dollars."

"How many $25-a-year donors do you have?" I asked him.

"A lot," he replied thoughtfully. "A lot." Now, he understood the potential of legacy gifts and was ready to move forward.

But there's a hazard if you wait until you get a check.

Making the Right Case for a Legacy Gift

Identifying potential is not only about taking a look at who supports you but also looking at (or evaluating?) the match between their interests and the long-term viability of your organizational mission. Do you have to be an organization that has been around for 100 years? Not at all. An organization less than a year old can have a credible conversation about why a bequest could have an important impact on their organization's future. However, a clear mission combined with demonstrated ability to implement it is also important.

We know that times change and the nature of the work of any group will have to adapt. Will the principles that guide your work now be equally applicable or powerful in years to come? If the answer is "yes," you are on the way to defining your case for someone to make a legacy gift to your organization.

As you think about some of the loyal supporters and volunteer leaders (past and present) who might consider including you in their wills, what will they need to know or understand about your work in order for them to want to move forward and include your nonprofit in their plans?

It's time to ask for donors' advice about this question. Using one-on-one interviews, spend some time with them discovering what is important to them about your work. The result of these conversations will be a document that lays out your case for giving in general and making a legacy gift in particular.

Many groups already have a "case statement." It's often a great-looking brochure with bullet points and bold statements. Unfortunately, most such case statements I have seen do *not* match (or meet) the needs of prospective legacy gift donors. These donors have different needs and interests, and you must discover what those are. Without that knowledge, any later attempt at marketing is doomed to falter (or fail).

As you discover and clarify donor needs, your board will also have to answer the questions: How would you use a bequest gift? What's your plan for the money? These are sometimes easily answered; at other times, the questions will launch several board meetings' worth of impassioned discussion and between-meeting lobbying. It's all worthwhile in the context of the larger objective of building a steady stream of future bequests.

In this phase, it's been my experience that the groups most likely to succeed involve many donors in all steps. For the Type A executive director, please be forewarned it means talking to a lot of loyal donors.

Preparing to seek and ask for legacy gifts can be somewhat abstract, until you get a check with four or five zeroes and a comma in it. At that point, most executive directors or board presidents predictably ask three questions:

"Why weren't we doing more to prepare?"

"What have we missed?"

"What do we need to do now?"

If You Wait, Are You Missing Gifts?

I remember Dorothy well. She was a small, articulate, gray-haired woman who dutifully showed up every Wednesday to take care of the garden beds in front of the old stagecoach station located in the midst of the Hassayama River preserve in central Arizona. She drove over winding mountain roads 63 miles from Prescott to the river preserve every week, year in and year out. She had a smile for everyone.

I was surprised to hear news she had passed away and left a bequest of $1,500,000 to a local college. As a fundraiser helping the preserve, I never considered her as someone who might have interest in making a gift today or in the future—and certainly not a gift of that size. After all, my reasoning went, she was just a volunteer doing some needed gardening.

Wondering what clues I had missed about Dorothy and her gift, I did some research. It turned out that none of her children attended the college to which she directed her bequest; it was not located near her home; she was not involved in any of the programs offered by the college; she never volunteered to help the college. The more I dug around and asked questions, the more the list of non-connections grew. Then I discovered the answer: the college asked her for a gift.

There were many times I saw her in the garden volunteering her time. I did not think of her as a prospective legacy donor, nor did anyone else there. Even today, I still feel we missed out on a million-and-a-half-dollar gift. When we missed the clues, did we miss the opportunity to help her make a gift that would have brought her great joy and satisfaction? Did we miss the opportunity to help her celebrate her contribution and her love of the land? Did we sell her short? Did we simply forget to include her and show her that a gift of any size could have valuable impact and meaning.

STEP 2: BUILDING TRUST AND CREDIBILITY

By this time, you have talked with a number of donors who likely consider themselves insiders or, in the words of one development officer, "true believers." You included in your interviews seeking advice about your case for legacy gifts a number of board members along with community members whose advice and inclusion added credibility to this process. You now have a draft case statement in hand—often a few pages filled with pictures and clear statements (not pages of narrative or a glossy brochure).

By now, a number of questions will have surfaced that must be addressed before donors will feel comfortable including your group in their wills. The nature and scope of these questions will vary from group to group. In one case, for example, a donor expressed concern about how some building contractors were selected for a building project of the organization that raised a larger concern about the professional conduct of the board. Behind this was the unstated concern that if there were potential conflicts of interest, how could I trust them to handle my bequest later? As a result of this expressed concern, a board conflict-of-interest policy was created, enacted, and followed.

In another case, a donor asked the question, "What if the organization goes away, what happens to the assets?" The response was to create a simple plan to provide that if the group disbanded, any remaining assets would be promptly transferred to a local community foundation along with specific instructions that the funds be used to further the same kind of work.

There may be other types of questions that arise about how you might manage future gifts or larger sums of money. There may be other questions related to good governance practices or to address fears that donors may have after hearing stories about things that happened at other nonprofits. It may also be necessary to create or develop an investment or endowment policy in response to donor questions and interest. What is needed will vary from group to group.

As you reach the end of this phase and the beginning of the next, there will be a growing sense among donors and board members that might be expressed in words like these (actual quote): "This always was a good group. I might want to do that [put them in my will]."

STEP 3: A TIPPING POINT

A "tipping point" is described as the level at which the momentum for change becomes unstoppable. The term was popularized by Malcolm Gladwell's book of the same name, *The Tipping Point.*[2] Though the phrase has become common today, it is still quite accurate in terms of what you will experience with regard to building a stream of future bequest gifts.

When you reach this point, your organization is generally and consciously recognized by donors as a worthy and appropriate place for a legacy gift. Your organization has satisfactorily answered donor questions about how their gifts will be used; donors see your group as a credible steward of gifts. There may also be several donors who serve as leading examples who have publicly announced or given permission to announce their legacy gifts. You will have a core group of volunteers, board members, or donors who assert to you that, "We need to include more people—I know they will want to do this too!" Their support and encouragement will help drive the next phase.

STEP 4: GOING PUBLIC

Up until now, your focus has been very targeted among the most loyal or visible supporters, board members, and key volunteers. Now it's time to broadcast their endorsements and use their commitment and passion to leverage even more support. It's time to "go public" and include a much greater number of people and to put in place the processes that will keep this work alive in the immediate future as well as in the years to come. Some groups will actually launch a more formal campaign for bequest gifts at this point.

No Preparation = No Gifts

We all recognize that change comes as a result of shifts in behavior over time. It's true for you and me; it's true for organizations as well. If I want to get in better physical shape, I know the path is through consistent attention over time to what I eat (or don't eat) and exercise. It does not happen overnight; it must take the form of appropriate habits practiced and maintained over long periods.

Yet often nonprofits think that writing a gift acceptance policy and checking off boxes on a to-do list will result in bequest gifts. It's a bit like saying "I wish I was 10 pounds lighter," eating well and exercising for one day, and then wondering why the weight isn't melting away. Gifts do not come from announcements or policies, no matter how well crafted or well intentioned they are.

WHAT PREDICTS SUCCESS?

Building a stream of bequests and future income will look different for each group. You will have your own path to create and follow. Observing many different types and sizes of groups create their own plans, I have noticed some common attributes of success.

- Good listening is demonstrated: Sincerely and with a sense of true curiosity, successful groups will ask the question, "Why would someone leave us all or a part of their life's work in the form of a bequest?" They will explore that question with staff, board, volunteers, and loyal donors. They will follow the answers in order to address and resolve issues from the past and create a shared vision for a positive future.

- Consistent visibility over time: Make sure you talk about how bequest gifts fit into your long-term plans, and continue to describe the impact and difference such gifts will make over time. Be persistent and consistent in talking about the potential, promise, and value of bequest gifts.

- Messages linked to the future: Your messages speak to current work, but always make sure to connect the dots to a bigger future vision.

- Culture of respect: The existence of a quality of respect for donors as partners in your work (as opposed to treating donors as cash machines or ATMs). Pitching a product or selling a plan does *not* work. Although there are many unique opportunities or special projects that lend themselves to sales-oriented techniques, encouraging bequests is not among them.

- Attention to service: Continually demonstrate that you care about how donor gifts will be used and that your organization is and will be a reliable steward of gifts today and in the years to come.

- Patience: Be consistent over a period of years with measurable activities that build donor confidence, cultivate future donors, and take good care of existing donors. One of the most useful ways to help ensure that you exhibit such persistent patience is to include activity-based metrics related to bequests and bequest donors in job descriptions (in program staff as well as administrative and development staff descriptions), in annual work plans of the staff, in board member job descriptions, and in your organization's annual plan.

IMPORTANT POINTS TO CONSIDER

- Over the years I have watched many nonprofit groups start legacy gift efforts. The ones that appear to have the best intermediate- and long-term support are those that take the time to discover how to best match the interests of their donors with the work of the nonprofit. Often nonprofit leaders discover that what may be important to donors is different from what they had assumed. For any serious effort to be successful it will be important to engage and include donors early and often.

- The four steps to building a successful legacy gift effort begin with setting the stage—a time to build a case for legacy gifts.

- The next stage you will use to answer donor questions and concerns that could otherwise delay or prevent future gifts.

- As the quantity and quality of your work with donors expands, you will experience what Malcolm Gladwell describes as a "tipping point."

- Finally, with increasing donor interest and momentum, you can expand your reach and encourage even greater numbers of gifts.

Step 1: Setting the Stage for Legacy Gifts

In our society people traditionally pass on property to family members. Including a nonprofit group in an estate plan places a nonprofit in the same category as a family member and heir. Although the stated focus of this book is fundraising using bequests as tools, it would more accurately be described as setting forth a process to initiate and expand lifelong relationships with donors—members of your nonprofit family. An expression, or measure, of that relationship will often be a legacy gift as donors include your nonprofit as part of their family.

The next several chapters will have their share of things to do. However, the focus of these activities, combined with how they can be structured and timed, will be from a perspective quite different from how many nonprofits carry out fundraising. Donors are not ATMs; fundraising is not a necessary evil. Rather, your work and these activities will focus on starting, rekindling, and deepening relationships with donors in ways that emphasize and match lifetime values held by donors and the principles that guide your nonprofit mission. As a result, you will come to count them as family and they will include you in theirs.

SETTING THE STAGE

The first step in the process of preparing for, encouraging, and receiving legacy gifts is setting the stage. Although many activities in this step will be familiar to experienced nonprofit leaders, there will be a difference in perspective in how they will be applied. Volunteers and prospective donors will be also be involved in expanded and meaningful roles. Primary goals of this first step include:

1. Identifying your prospects for bequest gifts.
2. Documenting and reporting past experiences with legacy gifts.
3. Assessing and describing your potential for legacy gifts. This will help you to choose your level of commitment and interest, as well to galvanize additional support for this work.
4. Discovering and engaging loyal donors to help you build a case statement describing or making the case as to why someone would wish to make a legacy gift to your organization.
5. Describing your initial objectives for seeking legacy gifts and creating metrics to measure progress, which will change as your plans evolve.
6. Identifying the hidden questions that get in the way of people completing legacy gifts.
7. Describing how legacy gifts fit into your future.
8. Educating, informing, and engaging your board about the potential and responsibilities associated with legacy gifts.

1. IDENTIFY YOUR PROSPECTS FOR BEQUEST GIFTS

Do-It-Yourself Identification

Donor loyalty is the single best predictor of bequest gift potential. Consistent, low-dollar-amount giving is an excellent indicator of bequest gift potential. Large-scale research and analysis of more than 100,000 planned gifts demonstrate that consistency of gifts is a much more effective indicator of this potential than gift size.[1]

How many loyal donors do you have? How far back do your reliable donor records go? The farther back the better. If you don't have a long history of data, but have a longer organizational history, perhaps there are old giving or donor records in storage or in someone's basement that may have the names of early donors that no longer appear in your computerized databases. Are any of the founding members still around who might have copies of early records or donation records?

Ideally, you will be able to generate a list of donors and their donations stretching back to the founding days of your organization. However, that's not very likely. Consider your organization truly blessed if that is the case. Even if you have terrible records, or are a younger organization, there are still things you can do to start building your list of prospective bequest donors.

Your initial goal is to identify a pool of prospects that is large enough to attract your attention and interest, but small enough for the volume of your efforts to have a significant effect. The reality is that every donor is a prospect. But some will more obvious than others.

Useful Donor Records Take Many Forms

When working with a Boys & Girls Club, we started database research to discover who might be a likely bequest prospect. Though the club was decades old, and had a rich history of widespread community support, a computer conversion a few years earlier had failed to carry forward all the years of data collected.

In addition, after the conversion, no effort was made to enter any historical records into the new system. As a result, the date of the first gift for most of the donors in the database was the same day that the new software system went live. Although this condensing of donor data saved a few dollars at the time, valuable historical data, as well as the ability to use the information to seek future gifts, was completely lost.

Faced with this "data challenge," I sought out longtime donors to ask who they remembered from their board service in earlier decades. Since the group owned multiple facilities, I also wondered whether paper records might have ended up in a storage room someplace. I asked Julio, the head of facilities, to keep an eye out for such records. A couple of weeks later, Julio told me he had found something. I followed him to a storage room, where he had unearthed a metal filing box with two long drawers holding hundreds of 4-by-6-inch cards. On the cards were handwritten donation records detailing gifts made in the 1970s and into the 1980s.

Armed with these names, we reconstructed many donor histories for longtime donors. As we reviewed the cards with board members and longtime donors, it was not uncommon to hear the comment, "He was very involved, I know he would like to know what we are doing now" or "I'd forgotten all about him, he would be proud of what we have done. Let's call him." We used these records to assemble and expand our list of legacy gift prospects.

Whether you begin with detailed records or the sparsest of notes, you can assemble a list of loyal donors. If you are a relatively new group, you might use a "passion index" to help you target your efforts. In this case you might rate the passion of supporters on a 1-to-7 high-to-low scale as a way to help narrow your focus and create a manageable prospect list. Exercise 7.1 outlines how you could create your own prospect list.

Exercise 7.1

Create Your Prospect List

For the purposes of your research, let's define *loyalty* as a function of the number of gifts over time. If you have a monthly gift program, you will have to factor in how your database tracks these gifts or you may skew results.

> How many donors do you have in your database who have been giving to you for 10 or more years? _____

> Of this group, how many have made gifts in 6 of the past 10 years?
> _____

> In what months or quarters did those donors make their gifts?
> _____

> Plot the results of your data on at least two graphs: the first showing numbers of donors by years of giving, and the second showing a pattern of the time of year of gift. _____

Of this pool of donors, consider plotting the locations of their homes on a map to discover whether there are any patterns of concentration. You may discover patterns of distribution that will be helpful in your marketing work. What patterns emerge?

Alternative Approach

Let's assume your donor records go back about 15 years.

> How many donors have been giving for 15 consecutive years? _____

How many have been giving for 14 of 15 years? _____

13 of 15 years? _____

And so on, down to about 6 of 15 years? _____

The numbers of donors in each category will provide the information that you need to decide how much you should invest in this work, or what size of donor prospect pool you want to start your work with.

Create a chart with the numbers and study it for patterns. Consider showing the chart to board members and volunteers and asking for their insight into the patterns and what opportunities they might see in this information.

Examples of Observations as a Result of Doing This Exercise

"We found someone who had fallen off our screen and reconnected. I don't know why he dropped away from us. There's still plenty of goodwill though. I am going to go see him."

"We discovered we have a good base of loyal supporters at the right stage in life."

"We found many that are in the midst of making their estate plans and are already working with professional advisors."

"We went through a lot of records. As a result, we created a targeted list and will be calling this list about where they see our group going. We are now planning for the next decade. There's a lot of opportunity out there."

"We have a large enough pool of donors to make this work very worthwhile."

2. DOCUMENT AND REPORT YOUR PAST EXPERIENCE WITH LEGACY GIFTS

Has your nonprofit received bequests before? Many groups have. Many have not. For groups that have received gifts, Exercise 7.2 will help you document and describe that history. Creating a chart showing past gifts can be very powerful in helping to create interest and in pursuing future gifts. Too often, bequest gifts are forgotten and your group's potential for legacy gifts will be underestimated

What Is Your History of Getting Gifts?

Purpose: To create a visual presentation showing the support you have received over the years. This presentation can be very helpful when making the case to invest time and effort into building a stream of future bequest gifts.

Using a spreadsheet program (like Excel), create a chart of all the bequests given to your organization for which you have records. (*Note:* Sometimes bequests were never entered into the fundraising history because the checks were sent directly to the bookkeeper or accountant, so don't forget to check those records as well.) In other years bequests might have been applied to fill a hole in the annual fund or special campaign with the result that they "disappeared" from memory. Of those who have made a bequest, what do you know about each? Do you see any patterns of giving or donor types?

Figure 7.1 shows an actual chart created by a mid-size group. Although they occasionally promoted bequests, their efforts over the years were sporadic. The board was surprised to see that they had been regularly getting bequest gifts with almost no promotional effort. It enabled staff and board to discover the value of investing more resources in this area of work.

Based on the number of bequests and the total dollar amount of those gifts, calculate the average bequest (total dollar amount of bequests divided by total number of gifts = average bequest amount).

Our average bequest is $ _____.

When you create your average, include *all* bequests, even the big ones, in your average. Virtually all groups get occasional large gifts and, over the years, you will likely continue to get the occasional larger-than-usual bequest. Thus, it would be misleading not to include such gifts in your long-term averages.

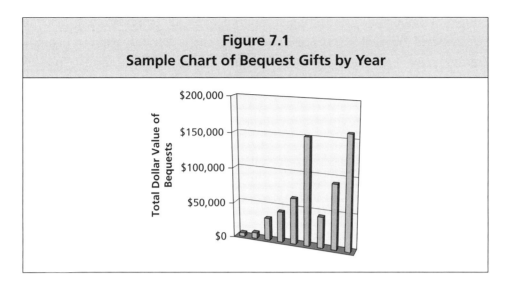

Figure 7.1
Sample Chart of Bequest Gifts by Year

as a result. Visual evidence in the form of a colorful chart helps demonstrate this history in a way words cannot describe. Figure 7.1 is a sample of how one group documented its experience receiving legacy gifts.

If you have not received any gifts, perhaps you have been told you are included in someone's will. You could adapt Exercise 7.2 using information about the size and number of anticipated gifts. If you have no donor history, skip ahead to Section 3, "Assess and Describe Your Potential."

Lessons from the Data

As you study the records of past bequest donors, do you have enough information to determine whether a trend exists for your bequest donors of giving, for example, regularly over 8 to 10 years before the time at which they tell you about their gift? Are there other patterns of giving that might suggest ways you could identify prospective bequest donors who are already in your database?

Do you have donor histories, numbers of gifts, date of first gift, or other information about the donors who have made bequest gifts to your group? If you don't know very much, are friends and family still alive so that you can interview them? Take the opportunity in reviewing their files or visiting people who knew them to discover more about their motivations.

By visiting those friends and family, both to say thank you and to acknowledge that the gift made a difference, you will learn about some of the motivations for the gift. It's all right if much time has passed since the gift was made.

Simply by calling and connecting at any time, you are demonstrating that the gift mattered and that your organization remembers. Not only will you possibly cultivate new donors, but you may also learn critical information that you can put to use in your marketing efforts later.

Visiting family to update your records also communicates to others that you are "family," that you remembered and can be accountable in using the gift when the donor is no longer there to make sure things are done exactly as they wished. This can be a powerful message to current and future donors.

3. ASSESS AND DESCRIBE YOUR POTENTIAL

By now you have a sense of how many people connected with your nonprofit might be prospects for legacy gifts. In mining their databases, some groups discover surprisingly large groups of donors that could be described as loyal and therefore good legacy gift prospects. The following are actual comments from nonprofit staff describing their data-mining exercises:

> "Did you know that we have more than 80 people who have been giving regularly over the last six years?"

> "Did you know we have gotten five bequests over the last five years and that the average was $23,000? We have 125 people in our database who look similar to these donors. What if we had 20, maybe 40, even 50 of those who had included us in their will? That's future income of over a million dollars! Think about what that would change for us!"

When considering legacy gift potential, you may discover specific situations that can also play a role in defining prospective donors. In one case, an organization was nearing its 10th anniversary, and it was also a time when many of its founding members were transitioning off the board. Encouraging legacy gifts from founding board members was an ideal way to send a message to both long-term and new donors that the founders strongly believed in the future of this group. In this case, there were about a dozen early members; this inner circle was the first place bequests were talked about.

In other situations, the nature of your work may embody a larger, existing value system held by donors and society in general. For example, a "friends of the library" support group started up in a rural community not long ago. Most people would not think of a newly formed group as a destination for a bequest. However, in this case, several people immediately considered it as an appropriate place for a bequest because of the large role libraries play in society. In the words of one of their donors, "an informed public constitutes the foundation of democracy." The support group's mission focus neatly coincided with donor perceptions regarding the much larger role libraries play in their communities. As a result of tapping into larger values already part of donor thinking, the group was able to credibly ask for legacy gifts.

The following are examples of how three small and mid-sized nonprofit leaders initially described their potential for legacy gifts. After you read them, how will you describe your opportunities?

Regional Group

"We have a loyal base of support. When we researched our donors we found over 40 percent of our members from our founding years are still giving today. Many of our major donors have given consistently for more than five years in a row— consistent giving being a key indicator of bequest gift potential. Many of these major and loyal donors also volunteer and help us achieve our goals at a variety of levels. Our board president recently challenged the entire board to include our group in their individual wills. We just added development staff and with expanded staff capacity we want to make legacy gifts a focus this year. In short, we have a large number of people who have strong connections with us and our work and now have the staff time to pursue this work."

Statewide Group

"I believe we have incredible untapped potential for legacy gifts. We have a large base of loyal member/donors (3,800) including a large number of donors aged 60, 70, some older. Unfortunately, our membership is literally dying off and we are not bringing on new younger members fast enough. Last year, we lost three of the original founders of our organization when they passed away. While it is too late for legacy gifts for those founders, it's an opportune time to develop this facet of fundraising within our organization. In terms of our mission, we have an exciting message right now—much of that work will leave a lasting impact for generations to come, so the tie-in to pursuing legacy gifts is timely and connected."

Rural State Activist Group

"We have gotten a few bequests but don't get them regularly. The last one we got was almost $200,000. When we get bequest gifts, they tend to be large. The potential for legacy giving for our group is large since the average age of our members is in their early 60s. We have a base of loyal and generous members who have not been 'systematically approached.' While most of us have been trained to ask donors for gifts, we have not been trained to ask for bequests. We want to learn how to inspire and engage our donors so that the number of bequests we receive grows over time. The last bequest really made a huge, positive difference."

It's time to write your own concise description of opportunity. How will you succinctly describe the opportunity presented to your nonprofit?

4. BUILD A CASE STATEMENT WITH THE HELP OF LOYAL DONORS

The moment you bring up the topic of bequests, many board members, as well as some loyal donors, may ask: Why us? Will people actually do this? Will they put our group in their will? How will you make the case and provide not only the reasons, but also powerful motivations, to complete a bequest gift?

Often nonprofits have well-honed documents designed to educate and persuade, sometimes referred to in fundraising jargon as a "case statement." Quite simply, the purpose of the case statement is to lay out the reasons why someone should make a significant gift to your organization. Most are prepared and written from the point of view of a current gift. For example, a current case statement may focus on the threats and dangers that only an immediate gift could possibly correct. (*Note:* I will use "case statement," "case," and "case for support" interchangeably. All are intended to refer to your explanation of how gifts will be used, what impact gifts will have, and why it is important to give.)

The things that make up an effective case for a gift today often may not motivate bequest donors. Often, the things a nonprofit is proud of, or known for, may not share the same qualities that inspire a legacy gift. Research demonstrates that donors think differently when making decisions about bequests than when they think about short-term gifts. Recent research[2] also suggests that fundraisers should use different kinds of language when marketing bequests to donors.

Developing Your Case

Although one or two staff people could write a case statement for support on their own and label it complete, I have observed that such efforts usually fail to produce a document that is actually meaningful to donors. With something labeled "final" and ready to present, donors will react with the mindset of a consumer and consider it much like they would review another product. If you involve prospective donors in its creation, they become invested in helping you and a larger legacy gift effort succeed. Which experience will help your organization the most?

If you write it quickly and declare it "final," you will miss out on one of the most powerful opportunities you have to start a successful legacy gift effort. Keep your case in "draft" form as long as possible. As long as it is a draft, you can continue to invite input and advice and include even more prospective donors. Once it's final, the donor's perception and experience of being included quickly fades.

A process for creating your case is described in Exercise 7.3. Exhibits 7.1 and 7.2 include suggestions about case elements and format.

Exercise 7.3

Crafting Your Case for Legacy Gifts: A Checklist

1. Assign one person to create a rough first draft. Usually this task will fall to the director of development, the executive director, and, in some cases, a board volunteer. Note that this is a draft. Spelling, grammar, and pictures count at this stage. Worry less about fine-tuning phrases, because that's what will occur throughout your upcoming interviews with loyal donors. Use a PowerPoint (or similar presentation software) format because that helps you focus on key points rather than on narrative paragraphs. Use pictures to communicate key points and messages; link text with pictures. (See Exhibit 7.1.)

2. Test your draft with a small number of key donors. Send a copy of the draft accompanied by a letter of invitation to talk about it. Make sure the donors know that it's not a fundraising effort. Advise them to keep their checkbook in a drawer at home. Meet with them at a place of their choice.

(Continued)

---

3. Periodically revise the case based on comments you get from your interviews. You may be pleasantly surprised at the turns and twists that occur as a result of insightful donor suggestions.

4. Visit and interview a number of key donors *before* you share the draft case with your board members. You want the credibility generated by actual donors; plus, you want to use the opportunity to educate the board. Using comments from actual donors will be viewed as very credible by board members.

5. Continue to revise your draft case. Some groups have conducted more than 50 donor meetings during this stage. (*Note:* Those groups often experienced increased annual gifts from these same donors and a large number of bequest commitments later on.) The more interviews you conduct at this stage, the better. If you persevere, you may also stretch this period out as long as you continue interviews persistently.

6. Start using small group gatherings to review the case. Remember, you are using the review process as a way to introduce the concept of legacy gifts to as many people as possible. Recognizing that bequest decisions take time, it is important to plant the seeds early. *Note:* Small-group gatherings are not focus groups in which you observe and judge donors. Rather, they are conversations among friends. The difference in perspective will mean success or failure for your sessions.

7. Report back to all of those you have interviewed by sending them the current version of your case statement.

8. Consider a mail survey to test the current draft of the case statement in order to reach loyal donors you were unable to include, or who live away from your main office. (In one case, a mailing to 2,000 loyal donors turned up 124 people who said, "Yes, you are or will be in my estate plans.") Asking for advice can be powerful.

Exhibit 7.1 Elements to Consider when Writing the First Draft of Your Case

Your case for making a bequest will contain many of the elements listed below. Donor comments and reactions will inform you as to which of these elements need to be emphasized, expanded, or played down.

- What/who makes up your organization (staff, scope, structure, board)?
- What is your long-term mission?
- How was the work important in the past, and how will it be important in the years to come?
- Are you a good steward of gifts?
- How do you manage your money?
- Who is on the board, and what do they add?
- Are the right people on the board?
- Who are the staff, and why are they uniquely qualified for this work?
- What will happen if the group ceases to exist?
- What do the annual budget and the balance sheet look like now?
- Are there any hidden or forgotten issues that need to be addressed?
- Who else is considering such a gift?
- Are there visible leaders or volunteers who must be quoted, pictured, or involved?
- Is there a gift policy?
- Is there an endowment plan?
- How will we know if this effort is on track?
- How will you keep track of this information?
- Why should we tell you about our plans today?
- How does a bequest fit into your long-range plans, and what difference will bequest gifts make?
- How will you address donor concerns such as, "I don't have much; ask others who have more"?

Exhibit 7.2 Tips about the Format of the Case

I urge groups to use PowerPoint, or another kind of presentation software, to create their case for support. Although you will rarely use a projector or a laptop to show it, the format lends itself to pithy, meaningful statements combined with images and charts, and using a large font means that everyone will be able to read it. Ask donors for their help in matching visuals with powerful statements to help make your case.

- Print in color.
- Even though it saves paper (and I am very much in favor of that), please don't print on two sides. This will result in a confusing shuffling of paper, awkward page turning, and distractions in your meetings. Remember that age affects coordination and vision; keeping it simple and in large type will help. (If you wish, make a point of reducing paper use throughout your office in other ways to make up for single-sided presentations. For even more meaningful impact, you could also shift your office purchasing policies to using recycled and sustainable certified paper sources.)
- Some groups have inexpensive binding machines and use those to assemble the statements used for personal interviews. Others use a three-hole punch and put it in a small binder with plastic sleeves.
- Print in full-size pages (one slide per page don't use the two or four screens/slides to a page printing option). Older eyes need the large font for optimal reading comprehension.
- Use dark print on a light background. Don't use reverse type (for instance white type on a black or blue background), since eye research shows older eyes have difficulty reading reverse type. The same goes for type on colored background or printed over pictures. These tips are based on eye and reading cognition research. They apply to anything you want donors over age 50 to read and understand.

Starting Your Interviews

On your list, are there the names of people you or others would describe as "someone likely to make a bequest"? Our objective at this stage is to identify a list of people who, if they were to announce a legacy gift, would be considered leaders or examples for others to follow. Consider showing the list to several longtime donors and board members and asking them to look at your list with those objectives in mind.

How many interviews can you conduct? Invite more people than you think you will be able to see, since a number will have other commitments, be traveling, or be unable to see you for reasons not related to your organization. Set a goal as to how many will you see and over what period. Every meeting will yield useful information and be valued by donors. It's been my experience that the more interviews you conduct, the more satisfied everyone will be with the overall results.

Who will conduct the interviews? The executive director should certainly be involved in some of the first conversations. They stand to learn a great deal about how donors perceive the work of the group. They will also have a chance to test different ways of talking about the vision and value of the work. I have repeatedly heard executive directors say that the interviews were useful from the point of view of donor cultivation, testing ideas, and enlisting help on other projects.

Some groups also involve volunteers and board members to conduct interviews because volunteers may expand their impact. If you have volunteers ready and able to do that, I recommend you schedule several joint interviews to ensure consistent observations.

The purpose of each interview is to discover what about the case does and does not work. Listening is important. Refrain from the impulse to respond to questions with long, detailed, or defensive answers. If the donor raises questions, it's your goal to understand what is important about the question to the donor. If you answer their question immediately, you may lose the chance to better understand something that could help you with many more donors. Sample interview questions are included in Exhibit 7.3. Exhibit 7.4 includes several sample exchanges based on actual donor interviews to give you a sense of some of the kinds of questions you may encounter.

Exhibit 7.3 Sample Interview Question Script

Here is a sample set of questions to use as you begin your interviews. The more sessions you conduct, the less you will rely on the questions and the more you will rely on the responses of the donor. The following responses will lead you to discover what is important to each donor and, collectively, your larger pool of prospective bequest donors.

SAMPLE QUESTIONS AND RESPONSES

What has been your involvement with our group? (or, How would you describe your past and current involvement with _____?)

In your opinion, what are our group's strengths?

When you think about other similar organizations you support, how important is our group to you? Why? How would you rate it on a scale of 1 to 10, with 1 meaning Not Important and 10 Very Important? Why did you rate it that way?

When you think about your interest in all other nonprofits (including those in such fields as education, conservation, health, and religion) that you support, how important is our group to you on that same 1-to-10 scale? (1 = Not Important and 10 = Very Important).

Based on your review of the case for support, what was important to you in it?

What did you learn about our group?

What questions were raised but unanswered? What is important to you about that?

Many people include one or more charitable organizations in their will or estate plan. Have you ever considered including a charity in your will or estate plan? (Please note that we are not asking you for a commitment at this time.)

What advice would you give us to make this a successful effort?

I print these questions in two columns in big fat type to make it easy to follow and read while in the interview. You may choose to use that format or create another that works well for you.

Exhibit 7.4 Responding to Questions

Here are several short sample exchanges between a loyal donor and an executive director. (There are several question-and-answer sets to consider.) Each question is followed by several different responses, one or more of which could be used to draw out larger or deeper donor concerns. I am sure you will have more questions of your own—some will feel more natural to you than others. The more interviews you do, the better listener you will become. You will be better equipped to ask engaging questions and will gain insight into what is important to your donors, as well as what they need in order to complete a bequest.

Question from Loyal Donor: I was involved with your program when I was a child. How different is the program today? Would I recognize it if I attended?

Response from Executive Director: What stood out for you when you attended then? Why was it important to you?

Question from Loyal Donor: During the 90s, it looked like you were going to go under. Those were tough times. Do you think you will be here for the long term?

Response from Executive Director: What do you think about that? Or, What would you have to know or see in order to have that question answered for you? Does our work have lasting value? Should we be here for the long haul?

Question from Loyal Donor: How will you use bequests? You know I don't have much.

Response from Executive Director: Every gift is welcome. Every gift counts. Let me ask for your advice here: What kind of a plan to use bequests do we need to have? How would you like to see bequests used?

Question from Loyal Donor: What is that program doing these days? I wonder about it.

(Continued)

Response from Executive Director: There's a lot going on. What is it important for you to know about it? What is it you want to make sure to know? When you were involved, what stood out as most important about it?

Question from Loyal Donor: I heard they spent the endowment. That was disappointing; what happened?

Response from Executive Director: That happened before I was hired. I've heard and wondered about the details too. I will find out more and report back to you. Is that okay?

AND/OR:

Could you please tell me a little more about what you thought or felt when you heard that? What was disappointing? Why? What would you have preferred the organization had done at the time? How should we handle this in the future? Do you think our group should have an endowment?

MORE SHORT QUESTIONS/RESPONSES

- Wow! Tell me more!
- What happened?
- What was/is important about that?
- Can you say more about that?
- What's missing?
- What would you do? What would you do differently? Why?
- What would your advice to the board be about that?

There will be many opportunities for your work on the annual fund, or major gift campaign, to overlap. For example, if you planned to visit an annual fund prospect, why not use your draft case statement of support for a legacy gift as the agenda for the conversation? Not only will you receive good feedback, you may inspire the annual fund donor with your forward-thinking approach.

5. DESCRIBE YOUR INITIAL INTERNAL OBJECTIVES

Start with simple, short-term items that you think can be achieved in a number of months. Some objectives you describe may be specific while others may be quite general. You can start anywhere you wish. As your work progresses, you will discover how to track or measure progress using metrics that best fit your situation. Sometimes an objective will sound vague, yet the person who wrote it knows precisely what it would take to accomplish that objective. To help others understand, you may also want to use the form of a logic model to develop the details. Here is a collection of objectives, both general and specific, generated by leaders working at a range of small and mid-sized groups:

- During the next 12 months we wish to position our organization as a worthy and appropriate organization to receive a legacy gift.

- We want to use this work as a way to start transforming our organization into one that I would describe as "embracing a culture of philanthropy." That would include a greater emphasis on legacy gifts on the part of the executive director and making both fundraising and legacy gifts a part of everyone's job—including program staff.

- Success would be to orient the executive director to our membership and major donors with the result that he or she feels comfortable talking about legacy gifts.

- Use the conversation about legacy gifts as a way to start talking about our base plans for our organization for the next 5 to 10 years.

- We would like to build a pipeline of bequest income. Some of the gifts would be used for special projects, others would be used to build up our long-term reserve fund, and some would be used to bolster our working capital. Combined, all those things will make us stronger fiscally and to help us to be effective for years to come. We want to get this started.

- We want to create an outline, including attainable goals, for what our work around legacy gifts will look like.

- We want to lay the groundwork to launch a legacy gift campaign.

- We want to figure out how to put the spotlight on legacy gifts while making sure that legacy giving efforts add to our annual gift fundraising at the same time.

- We will determine how we will use bequests and adopt a board policy with regard to that.

6. IDENTIFY HIDDEN QUESTIONS

I have conducted hundreds of interviews with donors over the years. I asked many about why they had hesitated to include their favorite group in their will. Most often it was because they had lingering questions about some aspect of the work or organization. Sometimes they were aware of these concerns; often the concerns were less conscious and needed a follow-up question or two before they were revealed. About half the time it seemed that donors had not consciously articulated their hidden question—they knew only that there was a reason for hesitation.

Some reasons will be unique to the individual. However, while some reasons expressed might seem unique, they are often shared by many donors to the same organization. In Chapter 8, Building Trust and Credibility, we will discuss what to do to address those questions. The most important work you can do at this stage is to identify and describe as many of these hidden reasons as possible. You will respond to them later, *not* during the interviews.

Exhibit 7.5 shows just a few of the kinds of responses you might get during interviews. Listen, take good notes, promise to report back, and say thank you. Keep a list of the larger, hidden questions. As you conduct more interviews, begin including more pointed questions to help you discover more detail and a better description of the core motivations behind such questions.

Exhibit 7.5 What the Donor Said and What It Might Mean

The following are several examples of questions or statements that (may) contain hidden reasons, followed by what the question or statements might also include or suggest.

What the Donor Said: Whatever happened after that embezzlement? (Referring to a small embezzlement five years earlier.)

Possible Hidden Questions: Do you have financial controls in place? Can I trust you to handle a big gift? If you don't have financial controls in place, how can I trust you to handle a bequest when I am gone and not here to make sure it works out? What did you learn

---

and put into place to make sure something like that won't happen again? How can I validate that and do my due diligence?

What the Donor Said: I heard they spent the endowment.

Possible Hidden Questions: Can I trust the board? Do you have an endowment? Is not an endowment a permanent fund and, if so, how could you have possibly spent it? Can't you keep your word? Did the board get lazy and dip into a fund donors thought would be there forever? If that's the kind of board you have, well, you can forget a gift from me. How can I trust you to handle a bequest if this is what you do?

What the Donor Said: I don't think they are around for the long run. They just don't seem to operate like a business.

Possible Hidden Questions: If they intend to be around for the long term, they certainly are not acting like it. What kind of financial planning do they have in place to make sure that they will be around for the long term?

What the Donor Said: I just don't know how my gift would make a difference.

Possible Hidden Questions: It's just me. I have lived and budgeted frugally over the years; I own my downtown house free and clear, but I have a hard time imagining that my gift will actually make a difference. Perhaps there is the fear that their gift alone might not make a "big" difference. What if many gifts were combined and together, those large and small, to achieve the goal? He will not be alone; his gift will make a difference.

What the Donor Said: They are always focused on what they are doing this fall or legislative session; do they have a plan for the long term?

Possible Hidden Questions: All this direct mail refers to emergencies and threats. Are you even going to be around in a couple of years? It always seems like things are so bad, and I prefer to give to

(Continued)

something that will create a positive future. What's your plan there? How can I trust that you have a coherent plan or principles for operating in the years to come?

What the Donor Said: I never even thought of them like that (a bequest). Is there a plan?

Possible Hidden Question: I don't really see the long-term principles or values you use in your work. How will I know what you will be doing in the years to come?

What the Donor Said: Is Bob still on the board? Who is involved now?

Possible Hidden Questions: I don't really know who is running the show. I knew and trusted Bob, but now that he is gone, whom can I trust? How do I know I can trust the board? Who are they, anyway, and what motivates them to volunteer their time? Do they give money too?

What the Donor Said: I don't have much. Most of the people I know don't have much either. Who else will give?

Possible Hidden Questions: If I say I will make a gift, my word is my bond. Some friends had really big medical bills in the last days of their life. That ate up a lot of their money. I just can't promise you a gift because I just don't know how much will be left. My friends and I have been frugal—but after all, it's the wealthy who make gifts. Not people like me; I am just average. Your case might have to demonstrate that your donors who are perceived as "wealthy" participate in a visible way to provide assurance and build confidence among other groups of donors.

7. DESCRIBE HOW LEGACY GIFTS FIT INTO YOUR FUTURE

The decade from 2010 to 2020 may be a difficult time for many nonprofits. During this decade, many longtime, loyal donors will pass away, the economy may continue to sputter along, and the contributions of new, younger donors may not replace the gifts of older donors who pass away.

If this scenario comes to pass, what could the value of legacy gifts be to your organization? Will a small number of bequests enable your organization to survive, perhaps even thrive? Could a larger-than-expected bequest help build your operating reserve to give you financial strength to weather difficult times or unexpected changes in your community? Could legacy gifts be directed to build a modest endowment fund providing ongoing operations support for years to come? Or will bequests be used for special projects that leverage your current work? It's time to describe how your nonprofit will use them. The more clearly you describe the role that legacy gifts could play to enable your nonprofit to accomplish its mission in the years to come, the more likely it is that loyal donors will include you in their estate plans.

Legacy Gifts Are Connected to Your Vision for the Future

"What do the next 10 years look like?" was one of the questions that emerged in board conversations as the organization's 10th anniversary approached. At the suggestion of one of their longtime, more senior board members, a small group came together to talk about what that future might look like.

At the end of the first of several meetings to strategize about the plans for the next decade, one of the founding board members stood up in the back corner of the small meeting room and said, "I've been waiting for years for you to start making plans for the future. Now that you have, I have decided to include you in my own will."

Mark, the man who stood up and surprised the group, was a retired teacher. Several years later he passed away and left $150,000 to this group. His gift will be used exactly as he wished: to make sure that the group he helped found has the financial strength to carry on in good years and in difficult economic times.

It was a surprise to many that a retired teacher would publicly announce he included a nonprofit in his estate plans. His announcement inspired a new level of confidence about the future viability of the group. Although Mark did not seek out recognition, telling others about his gift became a powerful story to encourage others to make like gifts.

8. EDUCATE, INFORM, AND ENGAGE YOUR BOARD

There are a number of ways to approach a conversation about legacy gifts. The process described here succeeds more often than not. There are also some sure-fire ways to stall or even stop your process.

What should you avoid? If you put the topic of bequests and legacy gifts on the board agenda without solid advance preparation and coaching, be prepared to be sidetracked at the board meeting. Well-meaning questions will probably come out of nowhere, causing hesitation, doubt, or confusion. This can be avoided.

How you involve the board will vary based on factors that reflect the maturity of your board, the nature of your work and mission, the age and relative wealth of individual board members, and the ability of your board president and executive director to carry out a strategic plan with a clearly stated (and inspiring) long-term vision.

By now, you have some basic information about the number of donors and gifts you already have. You can use this basic information to open a conversation about bequest fundraising.

One of the first questions that you and volunteers will have to answer is, "Why would someone make an estate gift to us?" Sounds simple. Start with yourself. Have you included a charity as part of your plans? Why or why not? Asking this question and really exploring the responses should give you tremendous insight into what you need to do to build a program. First, engage a few key board members one-on-one. Do *not* bring the topic up at a board meeting without substantial preparation.

Take the time to talk with board members individually. This will give them time to reflect on the topic and how it relates to your organization and to their own situation. During this process, you will have to debunk stereotypes about who makes planned gifts, why people make gifts, and what type of organizations are a good fit for planned gifts. You might suggest they read this book.

Keep in mind age and social status differences. A 55-year-old businessman who is socially prominent looks at the fundraising world in a very different way from that of a loyal donor who happens to be an 85-year-old WWII veteran who owns several apartment buildings. Members of your board may have different age, cultural, and economic perspectives from your most loyal donors. It will be important to be aware of the differences as you prepare board members to discuss legacy gifts and how they will fit into your organization's future plans.

You may also find that although people love the work you do, few think of you as important enough to, as one donor put it, "make it into the golden circle (of giving as symbolized by an estate gift)." You are going to have to spend some time to systematically build your case here. Or there may be strong potential for legacy gifts if you choose to undertake a strategic initiative for a specific "big picture" purpose.

A systematic campaign may be called for here. There may be a timely market opportunity with a large group of very loyal donors who are advanced in age.

Regardless of what direction emerges, the good news is that all those resources large nonprofits spent over the years educating their donors (read "your" donors) about planned and bequest gifts did their job. As a result, your efforts can focus primarily on why your specific nonprofit's work is important for today and tomorrow. Now, the challenge for your board is to make the case to themselves, then to your loyal donors that your organization is, and will continue to be, a solid long-term investment. Exhibit 7.6 reports on the experiences of staff and board in introducing legacy gift work.

Hazards of Not Preparing the Board

It's hard to say "yes" if you have already said "no." Take the time to prepare the board before you introduce any discussion on this topic at a formal board meeting. Often well-intended board members may hold dated and inaccurate assumptions about bequests, planned giving, and estate planning. As a result, questions coming from those perspectives can quickly derail a positive conversation. The next section addresses how to successfully work with your board. Take time to read Exhibit 7.6 which describes the experience some nonprofit leaders had in working with their boards around the subject of legacy gifts.

Exhibit 7.6 In Their Own Words: Lessons Learned

"We got bogged down. One of the things I did to get us unstuck was to have individual conversations that are focused on values. At the next board meeting things went much better."

Development Director

"We tried to move too fast, too quick. 'I am too young to have a will' and things like that came up at the

(Continued)

board meeting. The board member who had agreed to champion this pulled me aside and we were able to flush out some issues later in a working committee. Our mistake was to focus a lot on our own fundraising goals and not as much on the impact of the gifts and the emotion of giving. And that's more valuable in the long term—making the experience of giving valuable."

Development Director

"The conversation in our development committee on this topic really bogged down. We got bogged down when the board champion pushed for 100 percent inclusion—he said it should be mandatory for every board member to include our group in their will."

Executive Director

"I am going to start with a couple of people on my board and start talking. Anything I can do on this is progress because so little has been done. We are 50 years old and have never gotten a bequest."

Development Director of statewide group

"We put a line at the bottom of every board meeting agenda: '___ percent of the board has included our organization in their will or estate plan.' This simple reminder focuses attention on the role of the board and the importance of leading by example."

Executive Director

"We planted the seed several months ago. We are sharing our gift policy with donors. At the next meeting of the board, I am going to report back to the board about what we want to do if we got a substantial gift. We are trying to find the right path for each of the stakeholders to be involved in a meaningful way to them."

Director of Development

"I may be trying to rush everything. I am seeing that's not the right way to do it. Being able to have the conversations with board members and key volunteers and do it in more steps is really the way."

Director of Development

Recruit Champions

Start by recruiting one, preferably two, board members to act as your champions for representing the vision of positive impact a stream of bequest gifts will have on your mission and financial sustainability. They can be people who would be expected to have a will, such as a retired business owner. Choose your representative carefully. One of the most effective ways to discover your team is to ask other board members whom they would suggest. Their answers will tell you who will be the most credible representative able to influence or guide their decisions on this matter.

With very rare exceptions, attorneys and other planning professionals do not fare well in this role. Some board members may perceive a conflict of interest. Whether or not that concern is valid, the possibility can be a powerful negative at this stage. It's easy to avoid.

Consider choosing your second or third champion to provide a balance with the others. If your first champion, for example, is retired, he might be partnered with someone who is much younger and has a family; the duo will powerfully make your case that bequests can be for everyone. They will be able to say things peer to peer that no staff member will be able to say with equal credibility or power of persuasion.

In the process of recruiting your champions, take time for conversations with them about how bequests will fit into your long-term financial strategies. What role will they play for loyal donors? What types of needs can they fulfill? What difference will the gifts make in your work? Take the time to help build a case for legacy gifts in their own words.

Plan for the Board Introduction

Before the topic comes up for a board discussion, have a strategy conversation to outline what you want to have happen during that first board conversation about legacy gifts. Some examples of how you might introduce the topic are included in Exhibit 7.7.

Exhibit 7.7 Sample Board Discussion Questions

WHAT WOULD YOU DO WITH A GIFT OF $100,000?

One of the reasons I have heard from donors as to why they don't make big bequests to small and mid-size groups is that the groups don't have a plan to use a big gift. The theme of this discussion is to start the thinking on how you might use a gift of $100,000 or perhaps even $1 million.

You can do this as one large group or break into smaller groups. I have seen the best discussion come from asking groups of three and four board members to answer that question, then report back to the entire board along with the other groups.

Here are some sample questions from which you could pick and choose to help drive a larger group discussion:

- Since this will be the last gift we receive from this donor, how will we make sure it has lasting impact and/or builds our organizational strength and resilience?

- If you were to meet a family member at a community event, how would you like to be able to describe the impact of the bequest? What would make you proud or pleased to describe?

- How will we use the gift in a way that also sends a powerful, positive message to our loyal donors, organization, and the community at large? (Or how might our choice detract from our credibility or raise questions?)

- How does bequest fundraising fit into our current and long-term plans? How will we budget for them over time? How will we assure donors that their gifts will be used wisely and with impact?

- What themes or principles emerge from this discussion about how you would use a gift?

- How will our decision inspire trust and confidence among other donors?

- Will bequests be used in day-to-day expenses, or will they be used to build a stronger foundation for future work? If it is placed into the annual fund, how will it be recorded and tracked so that it does not distort fundraising records and trend data?

- What else will you need in order to have a successful board discussion?

My suggestion is that the first conversation be very brief and introductory. Give board members a quick peek, and plant seeds for future discussions. Many will need time to reflect on the topic and strategy. By limiting discussion at the first meeting, you give the board champions time to work their one-on-one magic with other board members. All will have some questions or concerns that need to be addressed. That can happen in between the first time the board discusses it and a later, more detailed conversation.

For any board discussion, coach your board chair about the possible outcomes and directions. The chair should not be afraid to table the discussion if concerns about estate planning law or other diversions occur. Use the time between that meeting and the next to address those and other hidden concerns.

Ask for Help

You may also wish to invite some board members to participate in the loyal donor interviews. This will give them real experience with the topic. (*Note:* If you do include board members, make sure they conduct multiple interviews; I recommend at least three. By the third conversation, they will have arrived at a new level of comfort with the topic and be more effective listeners.)

Say "No" to a Traditional Planned Giving Committee

"Start a planned giving committee" is a command that appears on virtually every "how to start a planned giving program" checklist. But it's time to review the reasons it was on the checklist in the first place. Are the reasons valid for *your* situation?

There is some historical background to consider. In the 1950s through the 1990s, charitable organizations were *the* planned giving experts. Planned giving committees were wonderful tools used by the leading nonprofit groups to disseminate the how-to and technical nature of this work to the professional communities of attorneys, accountants, and financial planners. By creating and maintaining a planned giving committee, the charity could demonstrate its technical prowess and ability to manage trusts and other complex arrangements. Dramatic changes in the nature of this relationship occurred in the 1990s and early 2000s.

Of course, there are exceptions and you must factor in the unique characteristics of your organization, community, and location. Table 7.1 charts out some of the activities you may encounter.

Just say "no" to a planned giving committee stocked with lawyers, accountants, insurance brokers, or financial advisors. It won't get you where you want to go. In a later chapter, we will talk about ways to effectively engage professional advisors and build a community of allies who can help you and your donors forward your mission work.

IMPORTANT POINTS TO CONSIDER

- A legacy gift is an ideal expression of important lifetime values combined with a positive message for the future. The close connection many small and mid-size nonprofits share with their loyal donors suggests that there is great potential for future legacy gifts.

TABLE 7.1
Sample Activity Chart for Setting the Stage

At the end of the first step, Setting the Stage, you now have in hand:

Activity Description	Metrics or Measurable Outcome
Database research to create a list of prospective legacy gift donors.	One or more lists of people you have identified as potential prospects either by suggestion or database analysis.
A growing awareness among staff, volunteers, and board of the value and importance of legacy gifts.	You will start to hear comments that demonstrate a realistic understanding of who makes bequests and the role such gifts might play in your financial future. Keep track of comments! You might be pleasantly surprised.
A growing interest among a group of the most loyal donors about the potential of legacy gifts.	An increasing number of loyal donors tell you and others of their interest; you notice that some change their minds and publicly talk about this positive shift.
A working draft of the case that will drive interest in making legacy gifts.	You will have in hand a draft that has evolved with the input and advice from a number of interviews with donors and volunteers.
A list of hidden questions you must address in order for your efforts to create a stream of income from future bequests.	During interviews, you noted questions; afterward, in debriefing, you recorded and made a list of hidden questions that you will address in coming weeks and months.
A growing number of board members and volunteers making suggestions about what should be done next.	You will start to hear specific suggestions prefaced by "We should . . ." or "We need to. . . ." (Keep track of comments!)
A growing sense of the role bequests could play in your intermediate and long-term financial model. A growing sense among a core group of loyal donors that you are on the right track and that this is the right thing to do and the time is right to do it.	You will start to hear comments that express the beginnings of a positive vision of the future. They might start with "It would be wonderful if . . ." Or, "I could see this working." (Keep track of comments!)

- Setting the stage is not just a series of activities. Instead, it is a process to enable you to start, rekindle, or deepen relationships your organization has with its most passionate and loyal donors.

- Take the time to identify your most loyal donors using records, database reports, and interviews with past board members. Many groups discover they have far more longtime donors than they realized.

- Document your experience receiving bequests. Many groups forget their past success and as a result fail to invest resources to encourage future gifts.

- Ask your loyal donors to help you build a case for support for legacy gifts. Make sure it stays in draft form as long as possible. As long as it is a draft, you can include someone's opinion or insight. The moment it becomes "final," donors are usually transformed from interested advisors and allies to passive observers.

- Test this draft case with loyal supporters, and use the interviews and small group conversations as opportunities to collect the hidden questions that might later stop donors from completing legacy gifts.

- As you gather insight from donors, keep your board informed of the results. Often the questions arising in the interviews will raise larger policy and vision questions that it will be useful for the board to address.

Step 2: Building Trust and Credibility

When you start asking donors for advice about how best to make the link between legacy gifts and your nonprofit, you may begin to observe themes among their comments. Often at least three themes emerge, which could be described by the headings *trust, credibility,* and *vision.* You will also hear many questions mixed among comments and suggestions.

Often lurking behind seemingly straightforward questions will be another kind of question: hidden questions. These hidden questions are often key to understanding the real motivations that will drive decisions about completing legacy gifts. Many "hidden questions" that surface in the interviews or conversations you conduct are more accurately described as a request for help to understand why someone should make a gift (trust), or to help validate a choice (credibility), or to boost confidence that their decision will ultimately be a wise one (vision).

Answers to hidden questions generate confidence; and with confidence in the organization and its vision, donors complete legacy gifts.

$$\text{Trust} + \text{Answers to Hidden Questions}$$
$$+ \text{Vision} + \text{Plans} = \text{Donor Confidence}$$
Donor Confidence = Gifts

This chapter focuses on how to address both stated and hidden donor questions. It will also describe how your nonprofit can begin to create a clear path for donors to learn about, understand, and ultimately invest in their dreams and the future of your nonprofit group using a legacy gift. In terms of tasks, there are two tracks to follow. Most groups pursue parallel tracks, using feedback back and forth to fine tune the efforts of staff and volunteers in each track.

One activity track is to create a task force or temporary work group with the charge of creating (or updating) a gift acceptance policy. Creating a policy in a thoughtful manner can help build trust and credibility with key donors. This is also an opportunity to continue testing how your donors feel about legacy gifts and your organization.

The second activity track represents a way to help simplify the conversation around legacy gifts by talking about gifts in terms of *how* they will be used and *when* they will be used. These two aspects of directing a gift are often mixed, resulting in needless confusion. They can be easily sorted out with just a little attentiveness.

The series of exercises included in this chapter are intended to give you insight into how best to respond to themes raised by prospective donors in ways that respond to the deeper interests of your donors. To give you an idea of some of the variety of approaches you could implement, a series of short case studies describes a range of responses of small and medium-size groups.

Of course, no conversation about legacy gifts and bequests would be complete without a conversation about the uses of endowment funds. Although large institutions often encourage bequests be directed to an endowment fund, donors to small and mid-size groups have a wide range of interests as to how and when their legacy gifts will be used. It's been my experience that donors to small and mid-size groups often select many uses of their gifts other than an endowment fund.

Although there will be a number of suggestions in this chapter about possible next steps, much of what you will do next depends on what you hear from your own donors. The key to success at this step is to focus on the activities and work with donors that address hidden (now visible) questions in a way that inspires and encourages trust and builds the credibility of your nonprofit as an appropriate destination for a legacy gift (see Figure 8.1).

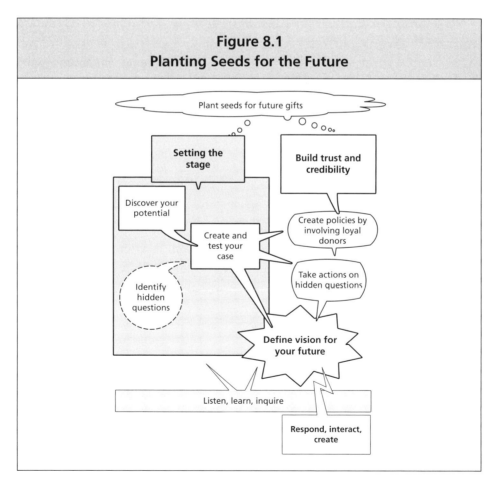

Figure 8.1
Planting Seeds for the Future

Plant seeds for future gifts

Setting the stage

Build trust and credibility

Discover your potential

Create and test your case

Create policies by involving loyal donors

Identify hidden questions

Take actions on hidden questions

Define vision for your future

Listen, learn, inquire

Respond, interact, create

CREATE A GIFT POLICY: BOTH STRATEGIC AND PRACTICAL AT ONCE

It's time to create (or revisit) your gift acceptance policy. This policy will describe how you accept and handle gifts. Your goal is to educate donors, answer questions about the acceptance and use of gifts. It build confidence among donors, ultimately resulting in future gifts. It will be to your advantage to include mostly prospective donors in this process. In addition, the more people you involve in this process, the more you increase your overall chances for later success in securing legacy gifts.

Crafting your policy is not a race to complete a document; rather, it is a process to help loyal donors and volunteers understand how your organization will approach the management of gifts. In the process, more hidden questions will emerge.

I recommend you create (or consciously review) your policy by creating a temporary work group or task force charged with this project. The task force you create to focus on the policy will be an ideal forum to bring up and discuss many such questions. While the task force will effectively wrestle with a number of key questions, some of these questions may require board responses and should be forwarded to the board.

The tendency for most nonprofits will be to copy a policy from another group or something downloaded from the Web, relabel it, and call it done. If you do this, you will save time; you will also lose a unique opportunity with donors. Instead, consider this gift policy task force a useful tool to introduce the concepts of planning for gifts and the roles your organization intends to play in stewarding that money. It is also a time for donors to tell you what is important to them and what they need from your nonprofit in order to feel confident in completing a legacy gift.

The task force will produce a draft policy that will later be submitted to the board for formal ratification. Before that board meeting, an attorney familiar with nonprofit law should be asked to review it for compliance with state and local laws.

How you introduce the work of creating a gift acceptance policy is important. Staff and volunteer leaders will need to understand the reason or strategy behind the gift policy task force. Your explanations will help them see that the process of creating a gift policy is part of a larger effort to build trust and confidence in your organization with regard to bequest gifts.

You will also want to talk with staff and board members about the differences between a traditional planned giving program approach based on large institutional techniques and your donor centered approach. Exhibit 8.1 is a sample script describing one way you might introduce this process. Figure 8.2 shows the process in the form of a diagram and may help some of your more visually oriented board members see the process better.

Unlike large institutions that can rely on techniques that get very low response rates, such as direct mail or planned giving committees, you must make every loyal donor count. As a result, your approaches must involve and connect with your donors. Involving volunteers in a gift policy task force is consistent with the needs of a small or mid-size nonprofit.

Exhibit 8.1 Sample Script for Introducing Your Next Steps

After your initial interviews, you might say something like this to leaders of your organization:

We have talked with a number of our most loyal supporters. They are very interested in making gifts in the future. But they insist we have a plan as to how we will use these gifts. They also want to know we will handle their gifts well.

As a result, we are going to ask some of our key volunteers to help us draft a gift acceptance policy to describe the kinds of gifts we will accept and what we will do when offered the many kinds of gifts that might come through wills and estates.

I am going to ask a small number of volunteers to work with me to create a draft of a gift acceptance policy for the board to review and consider. Since this policy is to help donors understand how we will accept and use gifts, it's smart to have donors themselves create the draft of this policy.

Once we have a policy ready for the board, we are going to begin talking about how we should use bequest gifts as an organization.

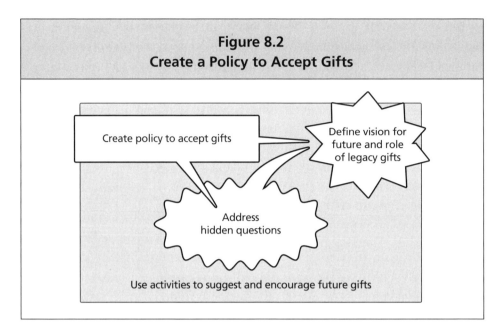

Figure 8.2
Create a Policy to Accept Gifts

Create policy to accept gifts

Define vision for future and role of legacy gifts

Address hidden questions

Use activities to suggest and encourage future gifts

Build Trust and Credibility

The process of creating (or updating) your gift acceptance policy is intended to help build trust and credibility among a core group of donors. If you take the time to involve donors in creating your policy, you will also later increase the chances of success in building your stream of future legacy gifts. It can be an important signal to donors that you are serious about being a responsible financial steward, not only for today but for the years to come. In turn, this can play an important role in influencing how many loyal donors make the choice to include your group in their estate plans.

There are practical reasons to have a policy, too. A well-crafted policy provides a map to guide you, especially when unusual gifts are offered. The definition of *unusual* will vary from group to group. What will you do if you are offered a gift of real estate, mortgaged real estate, mutual funds, or a collection of Eskimo ivory carvings and Chinese snuff bottles? Would everyone agree on what to do with one of these gifts? A policy provides a shared road map. It will help you say "yes" to gifts that forward your work and "no" to gifts that have high hidden costs and divert attention.

But even with a policy, sometimes a gift looks too good to be true. A stumped development officer called me to ask for advice. She described a proposed gift of

40 acres of industrial land directly in the path of urban expansion. Nearby land was selling for several hundred thousand dollars an acre. I did the math: 40 acres x $200,000/acre = $8,000,000. It sounded like a very valuable gift.

She had already visited the property, gotten staff leaders involved (even a bit excited), and staged multiple meetings, but it seems everything was stalled. The landowner insisted the charity meet several demands before he would actually donate anything. We quickly concluded that the deal just couldn't be done that way and that it would not be in the best interests of the charity. She hung up the phone and promptly called the donor to say "thanks, but no thanks."

I later learned that this "donor"/landowner shopped around his proposal to more than half a dozen other charities, big and small. Another organization, one with an up-to-date gift policy, got the same offer from the same landowner. Upon hearing the prospective donor's proposal, they politely assessed and declined that very same gift offer in the space of two phone calls. Two years later, the landowner had yet to find a taker. Perhaps he never intended a "gift" at all. It was unfortunate that the first group spent several dozen hours and precious staff time to come to the same conclusion another did in the space of two relatively short phone calls. The first group has since updated its gift acceptance policy. Exhibit 8.2 provides more examples of pitfalls you can avoid with the right policies in place in advance.

Exhibit 8.2 Creating Your Policy: Political Pitfalls Dead Ahead

Here are some examples of common pitfalls in planning legacy gifts and getting started.

MY GIFT WILL COST YOU

"Of course, you'll pay those costs," the prospective donor told the development officer when talking about a proposed donation of real estate. "That's what the other charity said they would do."

Should you pay? How will you determine that? In this case, the donor was tactfully informed that it was policy to not pay for the costs

(Continued)

in question. The donor's response: "That's fine. I didn't really think it was your policy to pay. I thought I would ask, though. I still want to do the gift."

And he did. A year later, satisfied, he completed a second gift using one of his rental properties. Recently, he started the paperwork to complete a third gift.

THE WELL-MEANING ATTORNEY

The executive director asked the attorney, "What's the most common planned gift?" Without pause, the well-known estate planning attorney replied, "It's the charitable trust." What followed was a 14-minute discourse on the tax advantages of using appreciated assets to fund such a trust. If you had been in the boardroom, you would have observed a number of glazed expressions. Has the same happened to you?

The fact is, most of the money from planned gifts comes in the form of simple bequests and retirement plan designations. Doesn't it make sense to simply focus on such bequests first? Fortunately, the director had been involved in the recent gift acceptance policy process. He had learned from observation that the future for his organization was in bequests.

The perspective of the well-known estate planning attorney was based on a narrow slice of the community represented by his own clients. (How many of his clients were donors was an unanswered question.) What would happen if your organization focused primarily on charitable trusts? In this instance, without the frank discussions that had taken place earlier as part of creating a gift policy, the board might have been diverted and taken a different and less effective path in building their estate gifts effort.

THE RELUCTANT CFO

For more than five years, the CFO had issued dire predictions about "getting involved with planned gifts." With no budget for any such effort, there was only a trickle of gifts. But when invited to help plan a strategy for planned gifts, the CFO's reticence melted away after he discovered that there was a way to promote bequest gifts and be fiscally responsible. He's now an ally.

THE SKEPTICAL DONOR

The 25th anniversary was fast approaching. The executive director asked what we could do to begin securing legacy gifts. Behind the scenes, Robert, a retired businessman and respected board member, said, "I don't think this is the kind of group that gets bequests. My wife and I will not include this organization in our plans."

The executive director persevered. One decision implemented to encourage and create a pipeline of future estate gifts was to assemble a task force of longtime donors with the assignment to develop a gift acceptance policy. The skeptical board member consented to be part of the task force.

After three substantive work group conversations about what kind of gifts to accept or reject, the skeptic announced to the full committee that he and his wife had included the organization in their estate plans. He has since become an active champion for legacy gifts.

WHEN VOLUNTEERS GET INVOLVED

As an unpaid volunteer coordinator, she worked with more than 100 others like herself. Anne was invited to be part of a task force to review what should go into a gift acceptance policy. She worked diligently and contributed many valuable comments and insights to the process. Such topics were new to her, but she clearly understood the concept and power of leaving a legacy.

Not long after the policies were forwarded to the board for approval, Anne dropped by the office of the development director to inform him she had decided to make a charitable bequest. Anne has since enrolled a number of the volunteers to consider and complete bequests.

Crafting a policy that fits the needs of your organization can help you save time as well as inform board members and staff about what kinds of gifts to encourage or discourage.

Ask for Help from Volunteers

It's time to create a task force to build your gift policy. This is an ideal way to involve a group of core volunteers and opinion leaders in thinking about your group and the role bequests could play in its financial future as well as their personal financial future. In the words of one volunteer board member, "Everyone has limited time, but if you give them [board members] specific assignments, such as 'Here is the draft gift acceptance policy. Would you test it and run it by a few people,' they can do that." Not only will they help you create a policy that fits, but also the experience will enable some (perhaps all) of the group to become effective advocates to encourage others to complete bequest gifts.

Who should be on this task force and what are you going to ask them to do? Start with your best, most visible prospects for legacy gifts. Here's how one group approached the invitation list for the task force, using a set of questions to drive their selection of task force members:

- Who will people look to as opinion leaders or respected volunteers with respect to this kind of gift?
- Are there people who have already said they have completed or are considering a legacy gift?
- Is there a board member who could be an effective champion and who could help best represent this work to other board members?
- Is there someone considering a gift who needs help to think it through?
- Are there some retired business executives or their spouses who might lend a level of credibility and consideration to your work?
- Is there someone whose participation would add extra credibility or validation to the process?

Do *not* ask lawyers, trust officers, or financial professionals to serve on your volunteer policy task force. Though they may be well meaning, they often bring a narrow legalistic or financial perspective to the conversation. If an attorney is on the committee and "knows all the answers," you will likely lose the value of task force members having to creatively wrestle with the implications of the policy for the average donor (and their own situation as well). The result is that volunteers other than the lawyer participate less, and that defeats the purpose of getting the group together.

Do check in with the attorney on your board or attorneys who might be among your respected volunteers. As a financial and legal professional, he or she may be an expert in this area, or others may call on him or her for an expert opinion. Inform this person early on in the process so that when the topics come up for discussion, he or she can look smart and add to your momentum in building a stream of bequest income.

The typical task force might meet three times: the first session will be an overview and general discussion; the second will focus on comments and drafting progress; the last session will focus on the final draft to be recommended to the board. Occasionally, some groups meet for a fourth session to enable them to expand discussion or get the answers to new questions.

Between meetings, volunteers or staff or both will need to put the ideas, requests, and solutions into words and distribute drafts to board members to give them time to study proposals before upcoming sessions.

For most groups, the resulting policy will be both an internal guide and something that can be shown to donors as part of gift cultivation, so don't let a well-meaning attorney turn it into legal mumbo jumbo. Your policy should state your intent in clear language and spell out what donors can expect from you. One board member described his hopes for a new policy this way: "I want our policy to be more conversational and more donor-friendly. We have one that seems very internally focused right now—too much legalese. Nobody pays attention to it in that form."

The value of a gift acceptance policy is almost nonexistent if it is forgotten on a shelf or in a file drawer. The same is true when you have a policy that doesn't fit your organization. There have been times when I was shown a copy of a gift acceptance policy and could identify the group from which it was copied. If that's your case, it probably means it won't fit your organization when you need it. Could an ill-fitting policy also send the message to the board and volunteers that you don't consider your larger fiduciary duties all that important?

A sample gift acceptance policy to use as a starting point is in the Resources section. Remember, laws and regulations vary from state to state so, at the end of your process, be sure to have an attorney familiar with nonprofit law in your state review the policy you create. (*Note:* Attorneys will always find an issue with something, that's their job; so be prepared for a few changes when comments return.)

In the Resources and sample forms section are a number of documents that may help as you organize and start up your gift policy task force. Additional resources are available on the Web. These include a:

- Sample invitation letter
- Sample agenda for your first meeting
- Sample first meeting agenda
- Sample policy
- Sample summary of policy

HIDDEN QUESTIONS: IT'S TIME TO RESPOND

As you test your draft case for legacy gifts, you will hear many clues as to what might give pause to donors as they consider your organization for a legacy gift, or even stop them from donating. It's been my experience that many of their questions don't have simple answers. Some will require new policies, such as an endowment policy or clarification of bylaws about conflict-of-interest policies. Others will require discussion followed by policy choices on the part of the board.

Several of the following exercises and exhibits are intended to give you a better understanding of how best to proceed with your unique group of donors and volunteers. The exercises (Exercises 8.1 and 8.2 in particular) include many examples of donor questions and comments. I invite you to study these questions, combined with the responses you get in your own interviews. Look for the patterns and concerns behind the questions. Often nonprofit staff will try to answer the immediate, specific questions. It's natural to want to respond. But questions in the territory of legacy gifts and bequests may not always be adequately answered at face value. Perhaps you provided the "right answer" but notice that the donor is still not satisfied, leaving everyone with a vague feeling of dissatisfaction. Here's an example:

Donor: Whatever happened after that embezzlement anyway?

Nonprofit Staff Leader: We fired that person, pressed charges, and she was convicted. It turned out her boyfriend was her accomplice, passing along the checks she stole. We ended up recovering some of it but not all. The good news was that it was not a very large amount. We have good staff in there now. We have new fiscal controls including regular audits.

The staff person gave a factual answer, downplayed the impact, and talked about what was going on now. If you look at the question at face value, it seems as though it was answered.

If this question was asked during a legacy interview, what other meanings might it have contained? Is this a question about your nonprofit's ability to handle money? Is the donor concerned about your ability to manage large gifts? Is it a question to learn how the nonprofit approaches its entire financial operations? None of those questions are truly addressed in the initial answer.

Following such questions with simple probing questions such as, "What did you think when you first heard the news about that embezzlement?" Or, "What was important about that to you?" Or, "When you think about your gifts and gifts of others in the future, what must you know to have confidence in our ability to manage money?" All of these questions get closer to the larger concerns behind the words in the initial question.

How Will You Respond?

In Exercise 8.1, the question, "What is this agency all about?" was voiced by a donor with more than 20 years of giving history to that same group. If you were in the conversation, how might you have responded? It turned out that he wanted to see articulated a larger or more holistic vision connecting the collection of programs operated by this social services group. Each program was good in and of itself, but his real question concerned what he perceived as a lack of a set of operating principles that would guide the board and staff as they made choices in the future. He didn't want a list of programs or a list of reasons why each was valuable. Rather, he was asking for what was then an intuitive process of decision making to be documented in a way that both guided staff decisions, and provided clarity and inspiration to donors. If a set of written or articulated principles to guide future decision making was in place, it was clear that he would make a legacy gift.

How Will You Respond?

If you heard the following comments, what questions would you ask to probe for and discover hidden questions? All of the following are actual comments recorded in interviews with longtime donors. I have included many of these comments because I suspect you will hear quite a number of them along the way. If you are prepared to listen instead of react to them, you will more likely stay on course toward success.

1. My background is in numbers. I had no idea of the volume of activity of your organization's work. The operation is much bigger than I thought.

2. How does your group differ from other groups, such as the Salvation Army and others that do similar work?

3. You need clear indicators of success; show me what you have done. How do you measure your work?

4. What is this agency all about? What are you going to be doing in the long term?

5. You need principles that will stand the test of time.

6. You have to give investors confidence for the future.

7. When I look at the names of the people on the board, there are not a lot of people who have a lot of connections. I do not want to discourage this board from trying. On paper it looks good, but how will you make this plan work?

8. Most of the people that I would think of might feel there are other organizations that need help more.

9. I'll work. I don't like to raise money. I'll call people. Using our house is fine, as we like to entertain.

10. No idea exactly how I can help, but I'm used to being very busy and now I'm retiring so I have time. Just ask, I'll try.

11. People will probably say that the last campaign really fixed us up. I thought the future was set. Do we really need this?

12. Project descriptions are clear enough. But are they are important enough?

13. I don't think they are ready. They need a year or two of cultivating.

14. The slides were too wordy.

15. My daughter was affected. If your group would have been there then, she could have been helped.

16. Put more emphasis on the root causes of these problems.

17. I am a huge supporter, but there are a lot of basic human quality-of-life problems on the planet right now that seem more needy than this.

18. There are too many details in your case statement. We have to face the fact that most people don't like to read.

19. Keep trying to get as many small donations from the public as possible. You have a lot of well wishers in the community.

20. I have complete faith in this group and the ability of the executive director and the board.

21. We need to see how your work will really make a difference and make things better.

22. The (pages at the) end mentioned endowment but I never really got a clear idea of the structure of that, how it would be invested, and so on.

23. In the statement of the _____ (endowment) Fund, it says that it is a permanent fund and that principal will not be touched ever. Is that written up so that there are no loopholes?

24. What public monies are received?

25. Include more details on the budget to show how it is self-sustaining.

26. We are huge believers in what the executive director can accomplish. I see it as achievable.

(Continued)

27. I am working on it (a will) right now. I think many should consider it. I prefer a direct approach. Consider asking, "Are you in the middle of making estate plans?" Or "Are you making an estate plan?" If you are honest about your approach, people respect that.

28. Due diligence is really important to my giving. It's true the more involved you are, the more you will give. Boards need to understand that.

29. (Your group) is in our will.

30. I am a strong believer a good source of endowment money is planned giving.

31. No, we have not made a planned gift. Excuse me, I didn't understand the phrase "planned gift." Your group is in our will for a bequest. It's in for 50 percent of her estate.

32. I won't be a major donor to this. I live modestly.

33. This is really Mark's and Roberta's project (referring to two well-known volunteers). What have they done?

34. I just don't know enough yet to say yes.

35. I understand what you are doing and think it is duplicating services already available in the community.

36. I love this type of case statement. Short, easy to read, much better than a narrative-style report.

37. This is an emotional campaign in my judgment. You've got to find people that have a strong emotional tie.

Among the comments in Exercise 8.1 are several suggesting that donors did not know your work was of such scale or had as much impact. Because the people making these comments are longtime, loyal donors, in some cases former board members, the answer is not, "You should read the newsletter better." Rather, these comments suggest that your nonprofit needs to do a better job connecting the specific activities or parts of your work today with a more encompassing or strategic framework. It also suggests your newsletter might not be working, or perhaps because of small type, older donors stopped reading it.

Group Exercise: Hidden Motivations

Purpose: Explore hidden motivations and concerns of loyal donors that might get in their way when it comes to considering and completing bequest gifts; discover how to better talk about your work to address the different kinds of concerns and questions loyal donors have regarding your work and how bequests will fit into "your plans." This exercise can also build internal support for this work and enroll other staff in helping you execute your plans.

Format: A small group of staff, volunteers, or board members

Preparation: Print out comments from your interviews (or you could use the above examples listed in Exercise 8.1) on 3-by-5 or 4-by-6 index cards (you could also use large type on standard paper and cut it into sections). Print one comment for each card or piece of paper.

Group Introduction (sample):

Thanks for taking the time to help us take a look at and think through some of the feedback we got from our donor interviews. As you know, our plan is to create a stream of future bequest gifts that over the years will help us _____ (add to our reserve fund, build an endowment, provide a savings account for the future, build a fund for stewardship, create a fund that will make sure our facilities are always maintained, etc.).

We started by identifying a core group of loyal donors—in fact we found ___ donors who have been giving for more than __ years. We put together a rough draft of a case for why someone might consider including us in his or her will.

We asked a number of these loyal donors to give us some feedback about that. Is it on track? Does it make sense? For those of you who already have a will, you know that it takes time to think through your plans and a bit more time to actually get the paperwork done. That's the way it is for almost everyone. So, by asking for feedback now, and not asking for a gift,

(*Continued*)

we are giving everyone a chance to think about how a gift like this might fit into their plans.

What we are doing today is asking for *your* help in sorting through some of the comments, what they might mean, and how we might address the concerns and questions that these donors have sincerely brought up.

I am going to start by handing out a copy of the case that each of the donors received. I printed it out a little smaller than what the donors saw. As you know, older eyes are not able to see as well, thus the big type, full-page presentation, and big pictures are critical if we are serious about communicating. We will use this case later today.

Exercise Group Instructions:

1. "I've printed out a number of the comments we got back from donors on these cards. I am going to lay them out (use large tables or the floor or tape to a large blank wall in advance). The first thing we are going to do is to group them in categories—putting ones that seem related together. You can move them around as much as you want. I realize that this will be a little disorganized. At the end of 5 minutes, I will call time and we will see what we have in terms of categories. How you define the categories is up to you. If you want to create a card and label a category, you could do that too." Time: About 5 to 8 minutes; if there is a lot of interest and emotion, let it go a little longer.

2. "Time. Stop moving the cards. I know that some definitely could fit in different places. Let's take a look at the different groups. How many do we have? How would you label this group of cards? This one? Could someone write up a label for each?" Time: About 3 to 5 minutes.

3. "We are going to divide into __ small groups (varies with the size of your group). Each group will take _____ (one or more) categories of cards. The assignment for each group will be to review the comments and look at the case statement. Start marking it up, making suggestions, adding or subtracting sections or bullet points. Do whatever you think is useful to create something that reflects these donor

comments. I am writing a couple of questions on a flipchart for you to consider while you sort through the comments:

- What must be demonstrated to foster greater trust among donors?
- What experience or quality is missing for donors when it comes to considering our group credible or a place worthy of a bequest?"

Time: About 8 to 15 minutes based on quality/intensity of group interaction.

4. "Let's come back together as a single group. What did you see? What stood out in your discussion? What changes should we make and why?" Time: About 10 to 15 minutes.

Another group of comments suggests that donors need to develop more confidence in the plan you are creating. It's important, too, to distinguish between questioning your plan with the intent to understand and questions that are more accurately assertions that the plan won't work. These are quite different. I have seen nonprofit staff often confuse the two perspectives and draw inaccurate conclusions. Often, comments like these reveal that donors don't yet have the complete picture they need to feel comfortable moving forward with a bequest plan. When soliciting current gifts, current projects with deadlines or urgency work well as a focus. When suggesting bequests, vision, values, and principles are most important.

One set of comments may reflect a generational dynamic. Many older volunteers and donors came of age during World War II and the 1950s, times in which there were leaders and followers. Many are also veterans and appreciate or see value in structure and hierarchy. Some of these donors may not perceive themselves as leaders and therefore they may not initially want to "lead" by making early legacy gift commitments. Often when donors like this learn of the number of loyal donors you have already identified, they can be inspired by the promise that such a number represents. You can also describe your plans in a way that assures them that others are involved, there is a plan, and you are committed to making this work successful. People want to participate in successful efforts. Yours will be exactly that.

As you complete Exercise 8.2, you could also include your own list of hidden questions you have compiled from your conversations with donors. I also suggest that you spend some time reflecting upon what your donors have told you in the conversations regarding your case statement. Replay them in your mind, recalling the words in the voices of donors. What did their facial expressions or tone of voice tell you in addition to the words they used? What themes or trends emerge as you reflect upon their comments, ideas, and advice?

WHAT THEMES DO YOU SEE?

Questions donors ask at this stage can be often be grouped around three general themes: (1) Trust, (2) Credibility, and (3) Vision.

1. **Trust:** Can you be trusted to handle money well, to keep your word "when I am not here to check," to keep doing the work well, to keep doing this good work, to have the financial resilience necessary, to do the fundraising it will take to survive, to have a good board, or to retain an executive director of whom we can be proud?

2. **Credibility:** Do you have the plan that can succeed, the number of donors needed to make this new endeavor work, the right kind of donors or the right mix of funding, the infrastructure to handle bigger gifts, the staff to carry this out, the volunteers who will help you, the financial controls in place, the right people on the board, or the right kind of business plan to survive over time?

   As previously discussed, one of the most important first steps to help foster trust and credibility is to create (or update) your gift acceptance policy. I have found that the process of creating a policy by involving volunteers gives them a chance to think about all of these questions. As they consider them, often they will discover their own answers. Many will also share their conclusions or thoughts, with the result that others are inspired with greater trust and confidence with regard to completing a bequest gift.

   Creating and formally adopting a gift policy will take time. Along the way, a number of questions will emerge that raise larger issues, often related to your long-term plans (or lack of them). If you approach these questions with the perspective of arriving at solutions and intent to expand and bolster donor trust and confidence, you will find the journey much more satisfying. Such a perspective will also enable you to generate even greater feelings of trust and confidence among donors. As donor confidence and trust increase, gifts will increase too. In response to donor comments one nonprofit group created and passed a board conflict-of-interest policy, another created a multiyear plan to reduce the debt it had incurred in response to an emergency repair project, and another began to shift its communications approach to donors. All were intentional acts undertaken in direct response to uncovered donor questions. As a result of their actions, donor confidence was bolstered, later resulting in new legacy gifts.

3. **Vision:** In one case, donors had high confidence about the nonprofit's day-to-day work, but had low confidence about long-range plans that group created a business plan that described how it would grow. They followed that plan with new fundraising to put it to work. Those concrete actions spurred several longtime donors, without being asked, to make legacy gifts.

HOW AND WHEN WILL YOU SPEND THE MONEY?

There are two important aspects to the bequest decision-making process: How will the gift be used? and When will it be used? You will have to address both questions to the satisfaction of donors. Using the distinctions or filters of "how" and "when" in a gift conversation can quickly simplify a discussion and help you and your donor focus on what is most important about the gift. Figures 8.3 and 8.4 graphically show some of the relationships and uses of how gifts are used and when they are used.

There are many purposes for which bequest gifts can be used. Often I hear nonprofit board members say: "When we get a bequest, that's when we will decide how to use it." I am familiar with several groups whose boards operated with that perspective. Over the years, as far as I know, they have yet to get a single bequest. Donors want to know how their gift will be used before they commit to making it. After all, it's their money, and asking for a degree of control over the

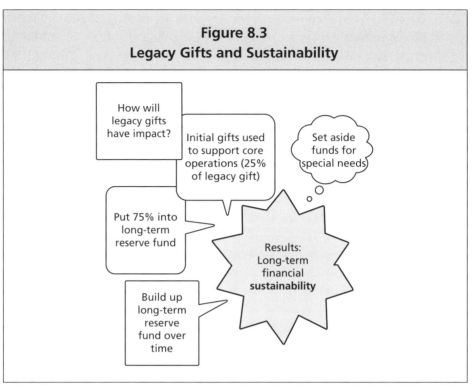

Figure 8.3
Legacy Gifts and Sustainability

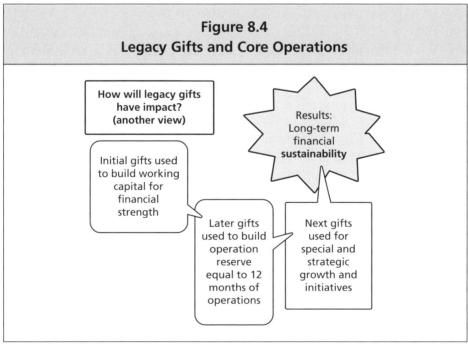

Figure 8.4
Legacy Gifts and Core Operations

use of their gift is quite reasonable. In fact, for many, knowing where the money will go is a critical part of their decision to complete a bequest gift.

What have your donors told you in your initial conversations about how they would like to see their gifts used? Would they like gifts used today, for the most important things? Perhaps they would like to see money put in a savings account for the future. Or perhaps they would like to see you create a permanent fund, most often labeled an "endowment," and use only a percentage of the fund's value each year. Or would they prefer their bequests held in anticipation of special projects still to come, or for specific activities or places?

How Will the Money Be Used?

One of the motivating reasons for writing this book comes from repeatedly seeing donors complete bequest gifts to big organizations, neglecting the many small and mid-size groups that are so important to them. Although I was not privy to every factor involved in these decisions, it was clear that a primary factor in their choice was the notable *lack* of any sort of financial plan on the part of the small or mid-sized nonprofits to use large gifts, either as gifts today or as bequests.

What would your group do if it got $1 million? What if you received a gift of $145,000? A gift of $475,000? Now is the time to start imagining how you would best put to work this gift of a lifetime. When an unanticipated large gift arrives, immediate or urgent situations often grab everyone's attention and the result can be a poor decision. If you have planned in advance, you can put the gift to work for maximum impact. There are also hazards to not planning.

Here are two examples of how a lack of planning played out (as with all the examples in this book, both of these are real situations). Both are examples of failing to plan both how and when to wisely use legacy gifts.

We Can Live Out Our Dreams!

One group received a very large bequest and the board immediately responded with celebration and adopted big plans: "We don't have to fundraise and we can hire more staff to get a lot done." Two years later, it became clear that the money was going to run out soon. They had spent the entire bequest gift.

In the meantime, almost no fundraising had been done; major donors had moved on to other groups that needed their support. Now, in just a few weeks, it appeared that this group might not have enough cash to meet payroll; its reserves were all spent. Bankruptcy appeared likely. Staff layoffs started. Many projects that had been started were abandoned or being cut back. Did the decision about how to use the bequest help or hinder the mission of their nonprofit?

Gift Masks Failure

Another group occasionally received bequests. Last year, they received the proceeds of a bequest about two-thirds of the way through their fiscal year. They had no plan in place to use bequests in a strategic manner. Since the annual fund was behind goal, they plugged the $61,000 bequest gift into that account. At the end of the fiscal year, they proudly announced that, in a difficult fundraising year, they had managed to make their annual fund goal.

A year later, the annual fund was even further behind than the year before. The bequest had been forgotten; there were no new surprise gifts to fill the hole this year. The decision to use a one-time gift to plug a budget and fundraising performance hole allowed the group to avoid facing the message that its annual fund techniques and performance were faltering and needed fixing. Instead of recognizing this gap in performance, they persisted in repeating things that were proven not to work for one more year. Now they were further behind and in more trouble than ever before. If they had had a plan to use bequests, they might have put the gift to use in a way that moved them forward instead of contributing to digging a deeper budget hole.

THERE CAN BE HAPPY ENDINGS

Although there are examples of bequest gifts being used poorly, there are also many more examples of these kinds of gifts being used strategically and positively. In the examples that follow, each group approached how they used bequests, or the tools of bequest fundraising, in strategic but different ways. These examples combine answers to both questions of *how* and *when* a gift will be put to work.

Statewide Group Builds Resiliency

Background   A statewide group had more than 25 years of history; its annual budget was about $1.2 million.

Challenge   It was heavily dependent upon foundation grants. Its leaders acknowledged that this tilted funding model would not serve them well in future years, and as a result decided to boost their work to significantly increase the number of individual donors.

What Happened   Recognizing that increased fundraising work and needed program expansion would place a strain on their resources, the board decided to implement a short, 6-month campaign to raise about $600,000 for working capital to enable growth to occur. As part of that plan for growth, all board members were urged to include the group in their estate plans in some way; in addition, the group pledged to donors that they would continue to encourage and seek bequests from their many loyal donors as a way to continually build long-term reserves. Donors were impressed and inspired as several board members stepped forward to report that they had included the group in their wills or estate plans.

How Used   New funds were first used to build an operating reserve up to a target amount. Once the target was achieved, funds would be directed to a revolving fund to be used for special projects and expansion.

When Used   Immediately placed in operating reserve up to target amount; later, the revolving loan fund for special projects used when needed and only upon approval of two-thirds of the board.

Making Big Dreams Real

Background   It was a young organization but its founding board had big dreams. Their funding model was skewed toward several sources of funds that they knew they would not be able to sustain over the years. The group had many volunteers engaged in its day-to-day work.

Challenge   How to start the process of diversifying income sources and reducing reliance on a small number of individuals and businesses that were major sponsors. How could this group communicate to major donors that there was wider support for the work and a source of gifts in the years to come?

What Happened   Board members started by explaining to their many donors and volunteers exactly where their current revenue came from and what a more diversified funding model might look like. Using simple pie charts labeled "today," "interim," and "future," they showed donors their plans to shift to a more stable and sustainable path.

How Used   The board asked that donors direct their bequests toward supporting core operating expenses.

When Used   When the size of the endowment fund reached a certain size, the board would begin using a percentage of the fund each year.

As part of the "future" pie, there was a slice labeled "endowment." The group planned to place all bequests in an endowment. Funds would not be used until the endowment reached a certain dollar amount. At that time, they would begin spending 4–5 percent of the amount and use the funds for core operating support. Every gift of any size would be important and would be counted.

We Don't Trust You

Background   Over the years, the small school had allocated some of the gifts it received to replace what some teachers thought were low-priority items. Despite disagreement, many teachers and volunteers still felt passionately about the students, community, and work of the school and its role in the larger community.

Challenge   Prospective donors did not have full confidence in the decision makers; thus, they hesitated to make gifts or, if they did consider a gift, it came tied up with many restrictions. Yet many donors were passionately connected with the mission.

What Happened   Recognizing that one of the first things cut by schools is teacher continuing education, a group of retired teachers suggested that bequests from teachers be directed into a fund that would be used primarily for this purpose. Naming and defining the teacher education fund gave teachers the experience of having control over their gifts. It will provide support for excellence in teaching, something all agree on.

How Used   For specific purposes, in this case teacher continuing education.

When Used   A portion of the fund would be used each year.

Our First Real Bequest

Background   Although the group had been around for some years, it had only recently hired its first staff. It had quickly grown to a staff of five with a budget of several hundred thousand dollars. One of its founding board members, a local dentist, passed away unexpectedly early in life, leaving an unrestricted bequest of almost $100,000.

Challenge   The donor did not direct her gift. At first, the board was overjoyed: we don't have to do any fundraising this year! Others on the board were more levelheaded, saying that this is a one-time gift and asking, "How will we use it in a way that can forward our work and build our organization?"

What Happened   After much discussion about the future of the group, the board decided to use part of the bequest today to grow the organization and to invest part in a way that communicated to current and future donors their intent to be around for many years to come. A portion of the bequest was used to fund a complete revamping of the group's website, making it more useful as a communication and volunteer-coordination tool—very much advancing an integral part of their mission. Another part was used to open an endowment account with a local community foundation as a way to declare to the community that this group had "come of age" and was making plans for the future.

How Used   Part was used for immediate one-time projects that helped move the entire organization forward; another part was placed with a community foundation to be used for core operations.

When Used   Part was used immediately; another portion was placed in a permanent endowment with a local community foundation.

Wealthy Donors Make Gifts Someplace Else

Background   The group had been around for quite a number of years. Several groups of loyal volunteers put on a series of fundraising events each year. But over the years, these volunteers were getting older and less able to put the time and effort into these events. Some of the donors had significant means and resources.

Challenge   Several past board members questioned how funds would be used if estate gifts were received. Some of the younger businessmen on the board suggested that they wait and make decisions when the gifts actually arrived. That way, they argued, the board could make the best decision.

What Happened   After one of their longtime donors passed away and left a gift of more than a million dollars to a local community foundation instead of to their group, they decided they needed a plan that prospective donors would understand. They adopted a policy to place 25 percent of all bequests into a long-term endowment; the balance would be used for current work.

How Used   Generally core operating support; wherever the need is greatest.

When Used   Part now, part later.

Another group in a similar situation did this:

What Happened   Recognizing the value of honoring small bequests, the board adopted a policy that the first $25,000 of any bequest would be placed in an endowment fund—a permanent account. For gift amounts over $25,000, the remainder would be used where the current needs were greatest. Of course, if a donor directs his or her gift to other purposes, these wishes would be honored.

How Used   Core operating support both today and in the future.

When Used   A combination of today and for years to come.

Another group created a menu that mixed how the gift would be used, combining flexibility and permanence.

What Happened   A local land trust relied upon a group of donors, many of whom were, in the words of one of the group of loyal donors, "not getting any younger." There was no single clear direction when it came to using bequests. There were many good ideas and purposes. As the conversation continued, the concept of having three pots of money evolved. The first was called a "permanent revolving fund." This fund would be used as a loan fund to pay for special projects. Fundraising would repay and replenish the fund. The second was an endowment fund; revenue from this fund would be used each year to finance the core work of the land trust. The third fund was an operating reserve fund that could be used at any time to launch new programs or to cover budget shortfalls. This combination of "when" and "how" demonstrated that a well-thought-out menu of how gifts could be used addressed many donor needs and interests.

How Used   A combination of uses, including general and specific purposes.

When Used   A combination of today, in the future, and in times of special opportunities.

When Will You Use the Gift?

Now or later? A number of the plans created by this collection of diverse groups included a combination of *how* the gift would be used and some degree of *when* the gift would be used. Most often, gifts are either used immediately or they are directed by the donor to be placed in an endowment. There are no hard-and-fast rules as to the how or when to allocate gifts unless a donor directs the use of the gift in writing.

Some donors ask that their gift be spent over a short period of years; some place no restrictions at all as to when the gift should be used. Some wish it to be used for special projects at some point in the future.

You will have to determine the mix of options that best fits the interests of your donors. The most effective way to do this will be to create a menu of gifts based on your donor interviews. Then, as your interviews with the draft case continue, begin to include this draft menu in the discussion. What is of interest? What appeals to them? What combination of how and when most effectively supports your work and the financial sustainability of your organization? (A sample gift menu is included in Exhibit 10.1.)

ENDOWMENT = PERMANENT

Offering donors the option of making a gift to an endowment fund is a powerful tool that can enable wonderful things to happen today and far into the future. Endowment building is not just another fundraising or gift option: it is about the entire fabric of your organization. Your donors consciously or unconsciously realize this and will direct their dollars accordingly. Please be very clear about how you label the giving opportunities: donors really are paying attention.

An endowment is defined by state law, and the details vary from state to state. It will have a specific legal definition in your state. (Exhibit 8.3 describes some of the definitions in more detail.) Often your organization will be able to choose a number of key aspects as to how your group may use its endowment funds. However, if you don't make specific choices, often state law will dictate the rules you must follow by default. In general, only a donor, not a board of directors, can actually place an endowment restriction on a gift.

I have observed that nonprofits, board members, accountants, CPAs, and lawyers use the word *endowment* differently—despite state law definitions and some basic common sense definitions. When you hear the word *endowment*, what's the first word that comes to mind? I hope it is *permanent,* because that's what most donors believe (or insist upon). Ignore this simple, honest definition at your own peril.

Sometimes accountants insist upon using the phrase "quasi-endowment" to describe a fund that the board has voted to label this way. Since the board can also vote at its very next meeting to spend this board-designated endowment, is this really a meaningful definition of the word *endowment?* Although the phrase is technically correct and consistent with accounting regulations, it misleads donors.[1]

Unfortunately, I have witnessed the use of many "correct" but contradictory definitions of the phrase "quasi-endowment." I have had to answer questions from perplexed donors as they struggle with mismatched concepts of "permanent" endowment or "true" endowment and hearing a report from a trusted friend that "the board spent the endowment at the last meeting." What does it matter if one is technically correct within a narrow, professional context but confuses or misleads donors? Please consider not using the phrase "quasi-endowment." It suggests permanency where absolutely none exists. If donors are confused, they don't complete gifts. It's time for simple words that tell the truth.

Plain, simple words are powerful. Nonprofits are under increasing scrutiny today, and we not only have to live up to the letter of the laws, we must go beyond that and live up to the spirit of our donors' interests and intentions. This also means it is important to use clear, simple language when talking about your finances and how you manage your assets.

Exhibit 8.3 Useful Endowment and Operating Reserve Definitions

Erik Dryburgh, a principal in the law firm of Adler & Colvin, a San Francisco firm specializing in representing nonprofit organizations, answers the question of what is an endowment with four definitions:

a. To a donor, an endowment is a sum of money given to a charity for charitable purposes, with only the "income" being spent and "principal" being preserved.

b. To an accountant, it is a fund that is "permanently restricted."

c. To a lawyer, it is an institutional fund that is not wholly expendable on a current basis under the terms of the gift instrument.

d. Thus, a "true" endowment is one established or created by the donor.

MORE DEFINITIONS

QUASI-ENDOWMENT: a fund the board of directors has decided to retain; it may vote to spend the fund at any time. Practically speaking it has nothing to do with the concept of "permanent." I strongly suggest you ban this term from your vocabulary because it confuses donors. When donors are confused, they do not complete gifts.

WORKING CAPITAL: Positive working capital means the organization can pay off its short-term liabilities. With private businesses, investors look at working capital as a measure of efficiency:

Working capital = current assets − current liabilities.

OPERATING RESERVE. A fund set aside to stabilize a nonprofit's finances—a savings account. Operating reserve or unrestricted fund balances are similar to retained earnings or equity in a business. Reserves can provide the flexibility and financial cushion to survive

(Continued)

lean periods and unexpected events. Nonprofit revenue can be quite fickle and cyclical. An operating reserve can enable an organization to survive, if not thrive, and also have the financial flexibility to take on new opportunities. How much is enough of a reserve? This will vary by type and size of group. Some groups use a rule of thumb of 3 to 6 months of operating expenses; recently, in the face of changes in the economy, some are considering increases of up to a year's worth of reserve.

Is an Endowment for Us?

While staff or board members may not be interested in starting an endowment, there may be donors with dreams to make a gift to a fund that will live on for many years after they are gone. It may be a way for them to "continue the good fight." Remember, an endowment fund is a tool to use: it may fit some situations; however, it is not a solution in and of itself. So start by talking with your donors. (*Hint:* If you assume you already know what donors will say, this is an indicator that you don't know and should make this an immediate priority.) Comments from your prospective endowment donors may just write the copy for you for your next ad, article, or mail invitation.

Donor comments can also be a guide as you craft the purpose and structure of your endowment plans. Many nonprofits have been successful energizing supporters by linking plans and dreams for the future that resonate with donors to a specific tool (endowment). You can start now to integrate questions into your donor interviews to help you discover what is most important to donors about the future of your nonprofit's work. What might a prospective donor think about an endowment fund at your organization? Here are some examples of possible perspectives:

- "I get lots of mailings about endowment from my college. I can see how it works. I was really impressed that the university got 23.4 percent return on its endowment last year. They all seem to do well—but if you don't have to pay taxes on the gains and trades, it's still impressive, though less so." (Actual comment and percentage return for a large university endowment fund for 2007; later years were not as inspiring for this school.)

- "Do all these nonprofits actually need endowments? It used to be that only big universities or medical research facilities did that sort of thing."

- "An endowment fund is a tool; one of many different philanthropic products in the charitable marketplace. Like any investment (product), I want to choose the right one."

- "Why an endowment? So they don't have to fundraise? That's not a good reason—I want them to be responsive to donors and the public, and the only way to do that is make sure they must fundraise every year."

- "All these groups I give to each year, well, their work is focused on immediate needs—after all, those appeals tell me how urgent and dire things are right now. How does an endowment fit into that?"

- "I have been waiting for them to set one up. I know our work is going to be something we have to keep at year after year. We are going to need something like an endowment to keep going. I want my gift to keep giving for a long time."

- "I think endowments are a thing of the past. I want my gift used soon—perhaps in equal amounts over the next 5 years."

If you talk about the tool (an endowment fund) like a product—a common nonprofit approach—you invite consumer-oriented comparisons about performance, fund management, and other legitimate due diligence questions. Although these are relevant comparisons, if you are a small to mid-size nonprofit, you will consistently lose out when donors "shop" and compare you with the biggest, most publicized endowment funds. Instead, focus on the impact of your work and how donors can use an endowment gift as a tool to accomplish their own goals.

How Much Control?

The less donors trust an organization, its board, or its long-term performance, the more control they insist upon when it comes time to make a bequest gift. Of course, often nonprofit leaders resist control, believing it will tie their hands. The result: an impasse resulting in a token gift or no gift being completed by the donor. In the meantime, the passionate donor is faced with settling for making his gift to another group. I would describe this as a lose–lose scenario, and one that is entirely avoidable.

Trust can be quickly created even among donors with high numbers of hidden questions. It is important to acknowledge that they support the work of the organization; they want to help; they want you to succeed. You have immediate evidence of their interest because they took the time to talk with you about the case or gift policy. By answering their hidden questions, you will rapidly build or rebuild trust among loyal donors.

What if We Close Our Doors?

The question of dissolution is one often fretted about but rarely voiced out loud by many donors to small and mid-size groups. It has a simple answer. Start by checking out your existing bylaws. Often, at the end of the bylaws, you will find a section that actually specifies what would happen to the assets or money left over if you had to close your doors. Occasionally, the bylaws will specify that another group of "like purpose" get the funds. Is this an acceptable answer to you or the board? Did you like what you read?

Often when board members review the dissolution clause, they want to update it and make it more relevant. That is good for all concerned—donors and the organization. Several solutions present themselves. One of the most simple involves your local community foundation.

A local or regional community foundation can be especially helpful in this type of discussion. These foundations are specifically chartered by law to hold funds either temporarily or on a permanent basis to be used for charitable purposes.

For example, one scrappy advocacy group rewrote its bylaws to state that if it were to dissolve, any remaining assets would be transferred to the community foundation with specific directions that the foundation use the money to fund exactly the same kind of advocacy work. In the case of several longtime donors who were considering making a gift but were unsure about the long-term future of their group, this new policy was enough give them the extra confidence to complete their bequest gifts and include the group in their will.

In another instance, a development director wrote me describing one of their strategies to respond to comments donors made in their case statement interviews: "We have a board meeting coming up in the next few weeks and we'll discuss working with a community foundation. We want to address the question of what would happen if our organization were ever to cease to exist. We want to answer donors that there is something compatible that their money will go towards."

IMPORTANT POINTS TO CONSIDER

Trust and credibility are critical elements in the decision-making process of prospective donors; without trust or credibility, donors will not complete a legacy gift to benefit your nonprofit.

As Stephen Covey writes in his book, *The Speed of Trust:*

> Low trust causes friction. . . . Low trust is the greatest cost in life and organizations, including families. Low trust creates hidden agendas, politics, interpersonal conflict, interdepartmental rivalries, win-lose thinking, defensive and protective communication—all of which reduce the speed of trust. Low trust slows everything—every decision, every communication, and every relationship. On the other hand, trust produces speed . . . one of the greatest trust building keys is results. Results build brand loyalty. Results inspire and fire up a winning culture.[2]

By taking the time to listen to their concerns and understand their questions, you will enable your donors to see the matches between your mission and their lifetime values, enabling them to move forward with confidence and work with their professional advisors to complete plans for a bequest.

During this stage of activity you will have:

- Continued to refine your draft case to describe why your group is worthy of a legacy gift. The case links your work and mission with many lifetime values of your donors.

- Addressed many of the "hidden questions" that emerged in your donor interviews and policy discussion.

- Based on an analysis of responses and comments, you will be able to describe one or more themes regarding actions your nonprofit must undertake or address in order to be perceived as credible and trustworthy and deserving a legacy gift.

- Created (or updated) your gift acceptance policies.

- Begun to identify and describe your vision for the role of bequests in the future of your nonprofit.

Step 3: The Tipping Point

*Well if I'm going to be involved in this committee,
I'll just have to make my own gift.*

Donor and gift policy task force volunteer

As a gathering of past board members was breaking up, one of the men who had been a board chairman some 20 years earlier remarked, "You know, this always was a good group." His warm, strong, clear tone of voice, and the people to whom he addressed his remark suggested to me that the work of this group had reached a kind of tipping point in its bequest work.

A "tipping point" is described as the level at which the concept or idea catches fire and the numbers of people accepting or embracing it start to take off. The term was popularized by the book titled *The Tipping Point*, by Malcolm Gladwell.[1] The phrase quite accurately describes what your organization could experience with regard to building a stream of future bequest gifts.

It will take a concerted effort to arrive at a point at which loyal donors begin to shift and embrace the concept, when staff start thinking "there is something to this," and when board members start talking regularly about the role of legacy gifts in your future. Arriving at this point should be celebrated and acknowledged. However, this is also a fragile point in the process of starting or building a legacy gift effort.

This is a moment at which doubts or questions can result in choices that take you off on a tangent or lead to slow progress. The most important things you can do at this stage are to establish activities that reinforce the legacy gift message and describe and validate the importance of these gifts to the organization. It's now also time to put in place expectations of performance and activity that will keep you on track.

Once you start getting gifts, messages and performance measures will be strongly self-reinforced by the positive results and the attention they attract. Until then, leaders will have to be consciously aware and vigilant. Choosing the right metrics to measure can have a long-term positive impact. Key elements in this third step include:

1. Understanding your progress and potential

2. Telling your story

3. Selecting the tools and activities to expand your work. Options include report-back sessions, staff education opportunities, targeted work with professional advisors, website changes, and putting storytelling skills to wider use with donors.

4. Measuring and tracking your success. What metrics are meaningful and relevant for your organization?

1. UNDERSTANDING YOUR PROGRESS AND POTENTIAL

How will you know whether your nonprofit has reached such a tipping point with regard to legacy gifts? It's been my experience that the number and content of donor comments can guide and help you recognize when your organization reaches its own tipping point. You will notice a difference in the volume, quality, and passion in comments among board, staff, and volunteers. There will be a difficult-to-describe—but palpable—shift that might be exemplified by the words of one board member who excitedly blurted out at a gift acceptance policy task force meeting: "We need to include more people—I know they will want to do this!"

This stage I describe as a tipping point could correspond to movement along the stages of the adoption process well documented in sociological and business marketing research. This research focuses on understanding how individuals and groups discover, adopt, and use new ideas, products, or innovations. Understanding how individuals and groups adopt new concepts or innovations can be very instructive in your efforts to create and build a base of support for bequest gifts.

In adopting an innovation, individuals pass through a decision-making process called the "stages of adoption."[2] Adoption of a product or concept begins first with exposure to the concept, followed by seeking information, then deciding to accept or reject the innovation. If accepted, implementation follows as the individual puts the innovation to work, ultimately using the innovation to its fullest extent.

Individuals also pass through similar stages of adoption. You are likely familiar with the phrase "early adopter." This is one of the categories described in research documenting how people adopt and respond to new ideas. The categories describing adopter classifications include, in order (also see Figure 9.1):

Innovators: Willing to take risks; venturesome; financial flexibility

Early adopters: Opinion leaders, more socially forward than late adopters

Early majority: Adopt an innovation after a varying period of time

Late majority: Adopt innovation after the average member; approach innovation with skepticism

Laggards: Show little opinion leadership; show an aversion to leadership

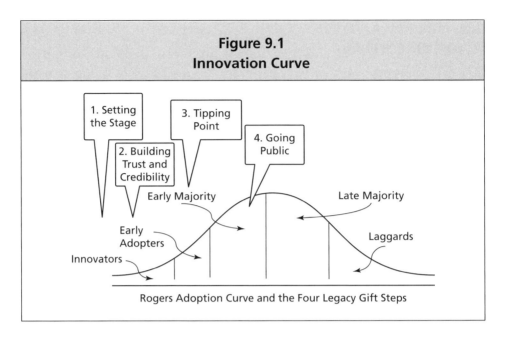

Figure 9.1
Innovation Curve

Rogers Adoption Curve and the Four Legacy Gift Steps

The stages of innovation, looked at through the lens of legacy gifts, might be defined this way:

- **Exposure:** Introduce concept of legacy gifts through draft case assistance and interviews. Figure out hidden questions.

- **Seek Information:** Address questions such as: Is a legacy gift for me? Is this the right group to receive my legacy gift? Address hidden questions. How do legacy gifts fit into the big picture? Use a gift acceptance task force to create a policy and answer the questions of how gifts fit into longer-term plans.

- **Decision to Accept or Reject:** Define vision for the future and the role of legacy gifts. Donors might see where their gifts could fit. They can see that this group does important work—they have long-term guiding principles, and the nature of their work will be important for many years to come.

- **Put the Innovation to Work:** Donors think: "I can see how this could work in my situation." "I have a will, and I can see that it would be easy to put this group in my plans." "I can see where I fit." "I can see how my gift could make a difference."

- **Confirmation**: Donors think, "This is the right place for a gift. This always was a good group. I am pleased to be able to make a difference—it's a story

I can be proud, pleased, and enlivened in telling it to my friends and family. Can I afford to increase my annual gift this year?"

When to Ask for a Gift

Your activities building a case for legacy gifts and a gift acceptance policy were designed reflecting the adaption and innovation curve. A small number of people will adopt a concept; their involvement in turn triggers greater interest among a larger group. Building a case and policy helped you engage supporters who correspond to the "innovators" and "early adopters" stages.

Consistent with the stages of adoption, focusing on the process of creating a case and policy gave prospective legacy gift donors the opportunity to be exposed to the concept, followed by a chance to seek information, then an opportunity to decide whether the idea fit their circumstances, and ultimately to confirm that they wished to complete a legacy gift. The adoption process also provides a structural explanation of why it won't work if you ask for a legacy gift in your first meeting: You can't move from the first step of exposing someone to the concept, then skip to the end and ask them to confirm a decision.

There's another aspect to impatience about asking for a gift. Implicit in the question of "Why not ask today?" could be an embedded belief that might be described as "It's all about me and my organization—we *need* the money today." Of course, your group is well-deserving. But there are thousands of other groups that are equally, if not more, deserving.

Rather than focusing on *your* need, how will you help donors fulfill *their* needs and desires to have an impact on the world? This shift could represent a shift in thinking and communicating for many. Recognizing your perspective will help you become much more effective in your interactions with donors, as you shift from how to get a gift to helping donors realize their dreams.

One executive director asked with some impatience, "We've been talking to donors about our case for several months, when do we get to ask for a bequest?" Estate gifts are connected with a host of life-planning issues, expectations, and hopes. These decisions take more time to process than smaller gifts and often involve more people, places, and things. As a result, the decision-making process will take some time.

Early gifts may require more attention to drawing out and expanding your relationship with prospective donors. Much like an early stage on the innovation curve, this period will draw in a relatively small number of legacy gifts. Even if you have known the donor for quite some time, the conversation about bequests, legacy gifts, and estate planning will probably be new emotional territory. However, what you learn, the examples set by early donors, and the experience gained in introducing the concept will prove invaluable moving forward.

2. TELLING YOUR STORY

It was just a tree stump. But it was alone in the middle of a nature preserve high in the mountain meadows. One of the donors along on the field trip hike I had organized asked the obvious question, "What happened here?"

"Well, there's a story about that," said Mark, the nature preserve manager who was accompanying us. He began telling what happened one August afternoon two years earlier. It began with the sound of a chain saw. The nearest house in the direction of the whining was more than a mile. The sound was much closer.

Getting on a mountain bike, he pedaled furiously toward the sound. Two men had just cut down an ancient tree well inside the preserve boundary. They were now cutting it up for firewood and loading it into their pickup.

Mark colorfully described how he put an end to that wood-cutting escapade. It probably didn't hurt that Mark was an ex-Marine and came visibly prepared for any kind of backwoods encounter, with a Colt .45 tucked in his jeans.

The moral of the story was abundantly clear to all on that hike: without active protection, places like this won't last long. Preserving these kind of places is exactly what these donors had in mind for their legacy.

That evening at dinner every one of the donors commented colorfully about the story. In its own way, it showed the charity's commitment to its mission and core values, highlighted the passion of its staff, and demonstrated the case for short- and long-term financial support. It was a bit of entertainment, too.

From the point of view of a legacy gift fundraiser, I privately thanked the preserve manager for the telling the story—it accomplished more than any brochure or presentation could have. To coin a phrase, "My work was (almost) done."

Fine Tuning Your Stories

Stories can be more than "just" stories. What stories are in your repertoire? Do you have at least one story about each of your program areas? If you don't, what can you do to gather or create some? When working for a national conservation organization, one of the first things I did as a new planned giving officer was visit key staff and a number of beloved nature preserves with the intention of leaving after each visit with a colorful story.

I used the stories to connect and reconnect donors with the mission, people, and places. Vivid stories always worked better than charts and graphs. They provided wonderful opportunities to slip in the latest news about a donor's favorite place, too. The listeners responded by telling stories of their own that told me much about their passions and needs as a donor. The conversations always seemed to expand and grow more interesting for everyone.

There is much to storytelling. Storyteller Andy Goodman says that there are specific aspects to a well-told story:

- Stories are about people.
- The people have to want something.
- The stories are fixed in time and place.
- The stories are used to show (not tell).
- There's a moment of truth.
- The stories have clear meaning.

The best stories begin with your own experiences. Painting a vivid picture in words is powerful. Take the time to harvest your own stories and you (and your organization) will be amply rewarded.

What Did You Do?

One of the most effective ways to introduce or expand the conversation about legacy gifts is to tell the story of what prompted you to make your own charitable bequest plans. Imagine telling a story including some of the emotions, questions, and challenges faced while making your plans. You don't have to reveal personal details like names or dollar amounts. Rather, it is the emotional experience that is most valuable. Telling a personal story can also give permission to your prospective donor/friend to tell or imagine they could tell a similar story about their own philanthropy.

Storytelling Tips

Storytelling is an art. Andy Goodman, storyteller extraordinaire, says stories are about showing and not telling. Here's an example[3]:

> *Telling:* "When the nurse visited the family at home she was met with hostility."
>
> *Showing:* "When they all sat down for the first time in the living room, the family members wouldn't look her in the eye."

A useful resource written specifically for nonprofit organizations is *Storytelling as a Best Practice*, written by Andy Goodman and available at http://www.agoodmanonline.com.[4]

3. SELECTING THE RIGHT TOOLS

As you prepare to take action to involve a larger number of your supporters, there are a variety of techniques you might consider using. The combination of tools you choose to use will depend on the needs and interests of your donors. Often you will hear a range of clues as to what tools will work best for your organization from donors in your continuing interviews or work on the gift acceptance task force.

Here is a small collection of suggestions and examples of how different groups moved through the tipping point stage toward expanding the number and size of legacy gifts. All focus on deepening your ability to make a powerful case for a legacy gift to donors using personalized connections. As you reach out to further involve your loyal donors, you might choose to use tools such as a mail survey, small group conversations, updated marketing materials, and a website. No one tool is right for every group. Take time to look for what your donors need, not what tool you like the most.

Using a Mail Survey to Expand Your Reach

Opportunity/Challenge   The group had conducted more than 40 interviews of loyal and longtime donors. The case for a legacy gift had evolved and been refined. "How do we reach the other 4,000 loyal donors?" the staff at this mid-sized nonprofit asked. Initial interviews had been very positive and constructive. The case was revised dramatically based on donor suggestions. It was a departure from how the organization had traditionally talked about its work, putting much more focus on the value to the community rather than on specific services. How would this play to other loyal members?

Activity Details A packet was prepared, including a letter of invitation, a full-size copy of the legacy gift case (it had a color cover but was otherwise printed economically), a one-page questionnaire, and a return envelope with a colorful commemorative stamp. The survey was sent out in waves to make the mailing easier logistically. The letter of invitation requested advice and counsel. No mention was made about making a gift or asking for anything other than advice.

What Happened Over a period of several months, more than 400 people responded. Of that group, 168 said that they had already included, were planning to include, or would consider including this group in their estate plans. Based on earlier research of past bequests that determined that the average bequest to this group was about $44,000, this number represented a stream of future gifts of more than $7 million. In this example, a well-honed case for legacy gifts showed many loyal donors that their gift could make a difference, fit into a plan, and would be well used. They responded by telling of their interest and plans they had.

Reporting Back/Small Group Meetings

Opportunity/Challenge In interviews, many donors expressed strong interest in hearing what others said about the case for legacy gifts. This group decided to use a series of small group gatherings to systematically report on the revised case for legacy gifts, to report on the range of questions and comments they had gathered, and to ask for feedback on their recently update gift policy. It provided prospective donors a chance to meet with each other and confirm that they were not alone in considering this group for a legacy gift, to ask questions in a comfortable environment, and to meet staff and board members.

Activity Details Three small group gatherings were held at different locations and different times of day. At each, the executive director presented the case for legacy gifts and described what donors had said, their concerns, their questions, and their hopes. Each session presentation ended on time, but donors often lingered for up to 45 minutes talking with the director and staff who attended.

What Happened The meetings were moderately attended. But every person who attended left excited and more passionate about the work of this group. A number who were unable to attend and expressed regrets asked that staff or board call them personally to follow up with them. Others who got the invitation and declined recalled the initial interviews and expressed verbally and in writing their appreciation for the invitation. The events were successful in helping build trust—we said we would keep you up to date and we are keeping our word. They helped build donor confidence: donors heard what other donors were thinking and feeling and were able to validate their choices.

Educate and Engage Staff with a Will Seminar

Opportunity/Challenge   A number of staff had young children, some still newborns. They had a hard time imagining why someone would make a legacy gift. They had difficulty bringing up the topic with prospective legacy donors. It was also hard for them to imagine that their groups "rated" or deserved bequest gifts. In the words of one staff member, "After all, those gifts are such a long way off, aren't they?" Because many program staff regularly interacted with volunteers and loyal donors, it was important for them to understand legacy gifts and be able to encourage and support donors considering these gifts.

Activity Details   A local estate planning attorney was asked to make an educational presentation to staff about how to make a will and on the basics of estate planning. The group paid her a small honorarium, less than what the attorney's hourly fee would have been. The session included a question-and-answer period. Some of the questions that were submitted were written on cards so that questions that might be perceived as personal could be asked anonymously. Of course, the session was labeled as an educational event—not legal advice.

What Happened   Staff members got a valuable education on planning and tips on what they could or should do in their own situations. They got to experience working with a lawyer so that they now have a better sense of what donors might also experience as they plan and make legacy gift decisions. They also understand more about the role of attorneys in legacy planning and will be able to more effectively include and work with them. With expanded confidence, they began introducing questions about bequests into conversations with donors and actively listening for clues about interest in legacy gifts.

Storytelling Workshop

Opportunity/Challenge   A very committed and well-connected board was stymied about how to talk about legacy gifts. As part of their annual retreat, a day-long event, they hired a consultant versed in facilitation to help coach board members.

Activity Details   The exercise started by asking board members to describe how they first got involved with the group. Then they practiced their story with a small group (one person told her story, another played the role of prospective donor, the third was an observer/coach). Roles were rotated so everyone got a chance to play each role. Then each person had the chance to tell the story of how they got involved to the whole group. Along the way, board members got to know each other much better, they practiced their stories, and they left the meeting with much greater confidence in talking about the emotional value of giving.

What Happened   Board members left feeling invigorated, ready to listen and comfortable telling their stories to donors. Hearing board members tell of their passion for the mission can inspire legacy donors: they know their gift will be in good hands even though they may not be present to monitor how it is used.

Start Talking to More Professional Advisors

Opportunity/Challenge   There are a number of "go-to" estate planning attorneys and financial planners in this small city, a regional hub in a rural state. Recognizing that only a small number of professional advisors handled a large proportion of the will and estate planning for the community, this group decided to formally introduce themselves to each advisor. The intent of each visit was to demonstrate that this 10-year-old group was worthy of a legacy gift.

Activity Details   Seeking introductions, at the next board meeting, board members were asked to bring the cards of their professional advisors or their names written on pieces of paper. As an incentive, a drawing for a great bottle of champagne was held in which each board member was entered once for each name he or she provided. They collected almost 30 professional references linked to board members. Next, they began to contact those advisors using the board member's name (mentioning that the board member was a client of the advisor) to open the door.

What Happened   Over the next several months, staff and board members held face-to-face meetings with most of the prominent practitioners in their community. A number of advisors had questions that focused on the organization's business and management practices—something that is rarely addressed well in nonprofit materials or newsletters. One said that several of his clients had talked about the possibility of including this group in their plans. "Now that I have had a chance to ask you these questions, I am comfortable about their choice to include you in their will," he told us. Not only did they end up with a list of advisors they could use if donors needed information, but they also introduced their work and established their credibility with an important group of gatekeepers. (*Note:* Although this example described took place in a city, it can be particularly effective in small towns and rural regions.)

Website Update

Opportunity/Challenge   "Our website just grew; we added things from time to time. Today, it's a mess. We don't look competitive. Our donors might even question our professionalism," is the way the associate director described the situation facing his organization.

Activity Details   When a longtime volunteer passed away, she left the group a bequest. Since she knew many of the board and staff of this small group, she had confidence that they would use it wisely—she did not restrict or direct the gift. Recognizing that the website work would be a one-time cost, was strategic in nature, and, if done well, would increase their ability to involve volunteers, the board decided to use part of the bequest for this work.

What Happened   Making the discussion about how the gift was to be used, a board-level conversation helped elevate the strategy involved in the choice. The website was professionally updated. The discussion about how to use the gift spurred several other board members to make their own legacy gift plans. Their choice also sent a message to members that this group had already received its first bequest; in a sense, getting and publicizing this gift was like a seal of approval or validation.

4. MEASURING AND TRACKING YOUR SUCCESS: METRICS AND LOGIC MODEL

The processes described in this book are designed to be respectful approaches to enable donors to discover how personal lifetime values match or connect with the core values of your nonprofit work. In the realm of legacy gifts, there are a number of indicators based on activities and attitude shifts you could choose to track. What might be most important in your effort may be different from that of other groups. Start by thinking more broadly about what will most accurately measure things that contribute to your short- and long-term success.

Type A managers will have some initial difficulty in figuring out how to fit this legacy gift fundraising into their management styles. Asking for gifts is important. Timing is equally important. If donors are not ready to be asked, if they have important unanswered questions, they will hesitate and say "No." While a "no" can often present later opportunities for follow-up, the decision about estate planning, designation of a retirement plan, or other larger life decision is much harder to reverse. You want a "yes" or "that's interesting" as a first response.

There are a number of ways you can count and keep track of progress. For example, in one annual fund campaign, board members counted up the number of "no's" their board members got, with a prize going to the person who got the most "no's." They recognized that they had not spent much time with many of their donors nor had they much experience in asking for gifts. Recording and celebrating a "no" meant that they had asked. It turned what could have been a discouraging statistic into a more accurate affirmation that, by asking for gifts, they were on the right track to doing all the right things.

About Measuring Your Results

There are a variety of levels of measuring[5] results. John Sawhill and David Williamson assert that nonprofits need a "family of metrics" to measure: (1) success in mobilizing resources, (2) staff effectiveness, and (3) progress toward fulfilling their missions.[6] In the context of legacy gift fundraising, how will you measure results? What will be the larger "contribution toward fulfilling the mission," utilization of resources, and leveraging staff investment?

Mobilizing resources might be measured by levels of donor involvement and connection, the performance of the annual fund or membership programs, donor retention rates (since donor loyalty is one of the best predictors of future legacy giving), and growth in the annual fund (since annual members may be the future legacy givers).

Staff effectiveness measured with regard to legacy gifts could initially be weighted toward successful completion of activities; later it might tilt more toward specific fundraising results. Many types of activities could be tracked. In addition, simple electronic donor surveys could help document shifts in perception, or interest, in a number of areas that help you track qualities, or attributes, related to the trust and confidence of donors in your organization.

Approaching legacy gifts as a method to build a stream of income to help your nonprofit become more financially sustainable may require a shift in perspective of how you communicate about your work and how you allocate staff resources. This shift might also be defined as a shift in the culture of the organization, from using donors as ATMs to engaging with them as part of an extended family; the implications of such a shift for current and future fundraising could be profound for some groups. It might also be described as a part of larger move toward creating a culture of fundraising throughout the organization, a shift in attitudes, level of engagement, and awareness of staff at all levels and in all roles.

Important Motivations for Legacy Giving

As you choose what you want to measure, it might be worth reflecting on two sets of data about the motivations for donors and legacy gifts. Table 9.1 lists motivations; Table 9.2 cites factors that would prompt gifts.[7] How will your activities and the results of those activities match what donors need to be motivated to complete legacy gifts?

TABLE 9.1 Motivations for Making Charitable Bequests	
Motivation	**Percentage**
Meet critical needs	86.3
Giving back to society	82.6
Reciprocity	81.5
Bring about a desired impact	68.5
Believe nonprofits should provide services government cannot provide	64.4
Being asked	62.4
Set an example	62.1
Identification with causes	62.1
Religious beliefs	57

TABLE 9.2
Factors That Would Prompt Additional Gifts

Factor	Percentage
If donors:	
Saw charities spending less money on administration	74.8
Were able to determine the impact of their gifts	58.3
Felt more financially secure	52.7
Received a better return on investments	46.6
Were not already financially committed	40.2
Knew of more nonprofits	36.3
Were able to use skills in nonprofits	36.1
Had more access to research	34.7
Understood goals of nonprofits	31.1

Sources: Miree, Kathryn. "Asking the Right Questions: The Mysteries and Metrics of Planned Giving Programs." Paper presented at the National Conference on Planned Giving, October 11, 2007 p. 9; and "Bank of America Study of High Net-Worth Philanthropy Portraits of Donors." Researched and written by The Center on Philanthropy at Indiana University, December 2007. p. 16.

Creating Your Own Metrics

Here are several points to consider as you define how to best measure your success:

1. In the beginning, evaluate activities, not dollars.

2. Evaluate and track activities that contribute to both short- and long-term success.

3. Identify the purpose of your metrics and how they will evolve as your needs evolve.

4. Involve your donors' feedback in measuring your success.

5. Create a baseline report using data available and use the same format over time, adding categories as needed.

Too often, the single-minded pursuit of dollars for the annual fund forces staff and volunteers to miss or ignore many clues that might lead to a legacy gift.

Although current dollars are important, work that contributes to the long-term financial viability of your organization is important too. For example, research by Target Analytics draws a direct connection between annual fund donor retention rates and future legacy gifts. In other words, the success (or failure) of the annual fund will have a significant impact on whether you are successful securing legacy gifts. Thus, donor retention rates will be a key metric in measuring whether you are on track to successfully building a stream of future legacy gift income.

At the end of this chapter is a sample activity tracking sheet that includes specific definitions for activities that one mid-sized group developed as it expanded its legacy gift work (Table 9.4). It is an example of tracking activities that will ultimately translate into gifts. Since legacy gifts arrive over a long period of time, tracking the things you to do encourage such gifts is a useful tactic to make sure you keep on track.

For the first step of setting the stage, some of the metrics you might track and report on could include:

number of interviews conducted

total number of people reviewing the draft case for legacy gifts

number of people who reviewed the gift policy

numbers of donors who have given for more than 8 years who participated in interviews

Other kinds of organizational metrics that affect legacy giving, such as donor retention rates, could also be tracked and reported on. You could expand your donor retention tracking to include the number of retained multiyear donors at 5, 8, and 10 (or more) levels or the growth rate of annual giving, number of personal visits, number of personal contacts, number of personalized thank you's, and so on. All are connected to building relationships with donors and positively correlated to legacy gifts by research studies.[8]

Logic Models[9]

A logic model provides a road map of the events and activities that you will undertake in order to move toward accomplishing your long-term mission. "A logic model brings program concepts and dreams to life. It lets stakeholders try an idea on for size and apply theories to a model or picture of how the program would function."[10]

There are a number of forms and approaches. I have found for many small and mid-sized groups that it's better to keep it simple, but put some time and good clear thinking into the process.

Table 9.3 is the beginning of a logic model focusing on legacy gifts. Of course, you will want to include database needs, the role of existing publications and other ongoing activities in the chart you create for yourself so that you can leverage and include legacy gift work into many of your daily activities. For more about measuring success with legacy gift work, see the articles noted in Exhibit 9.1.

TABLE 9.3 Sample Logic Model for Legacy Gifts			
Activities	**Outcomes**	**Short-Term Goals**	**Long-Term Vision**
Draft case statement Donor base research Plan created and executed to contact, interview, and report back to loyal donors revolving around case statement Draft gift acceptance policy Create work group for gift acceptance policy Educate board members about gift acceptance policy.	We connect with all of our loyal donors and ask for their advice about the case for bequest gifts. A gift policy is created, vetted, and approved. It is acknowledged as a useful tool in making our case that we are an appropriate place for a bequest gift. Gift policy is reviewed by more than __ volunteers and donors. Gift policy is adopted by board. __% of the board have included our organization in their estate plans.	During the next 12 months we wish to position our organization as a worthy and appropriate organization to receive a legacy gift.	We will build a stream of bequest income with gifts: first to build an operating reserve equal to 100% of our annual budget; second, to start and build a "founder's fund" for the purpose of providing ongoing annual revenue to fund at least 20% of our core operating expenses.

TABLE 9.4
Sample Legacy Gift Activities Progress Report

Activities	Current Period	Current Period Target	Year to Date	Target for Year
Educational contacts/mailings[a]				
Newsletters mailed to legacy prospects				
Product pieces				
Personal contacts[b]				
Individualized/personal letters sent[c]				
Gift proposals to donors/prospects[d]				
Home/office visits to donors/advisors[e]				
Phone calls to donors[e]				
Prospect "sightings" at events, etc.[f]				
Donor responses[g]				
Responses from newsletters				
Calls received from donors				
Calls received from advisors				
Individuals at group presentations				
Commitments				
New _____ (legacy giving recognition society) members[h]				
Estimated value, new legacy gifts[i]				
Number of gifts without valuation[j]				
Continuing education[k]				
Professional networking				

TABLE 9.4

Sample Legacy Gift Activities Progress Report

[a] Legacy gifts are triggered by events in the donor's life, making it important to educate and inform our nonprofit's constituency on an ongoing basis.

Newsletters/annual reports—Newsletters include an article or information about legacy giving and a reply device to request more information or to inform our nonprofit of a bequest plan. Annual reports acknowledge Legacy Society members and also contain the reply device.

Product pieces—Legacy giving brochures, Legacy Society membership certificates, and small gifts, informational pieces, and articles.

Group presentations—Presentations regarding legacy giving opportunities (seminars and presentations at board, committee, staff, and volunteer meetings).

[b] Personal contact is key in generating legacy gifts. Ongoing contact with donors who have planned bequests maintains the relationship and honors the donor's plans. Generating new commitments requires strengthening relationships with prospects and providing information tailored to individual circumstances. Building a cadre of advisors (attorneys, financial planners, and tax advisors) helps our nonprofit to offer appropriate resources and to generate more gifts.

[c] More and more people say that they read only handwritten materials. Short notes help you keep in touch and build relationships in a highly individualized and personal way. *Individual letters*—Typed, personalized letters that speak to individual circumstances and the donor's/prospect's history with our nonprofit send the message that you value their support.

[d] Donors are often unaware of possibilities available through various gift planning vehicles. Proposals tailored to individual circumstances of major donors are an effective, personalized way to inform and encourage legacy gifts.

[e] Depending on the individual, one or more of these ways of ongoing personal contact are important to build and maintain relationship, keep open lines of communication, and share information.

[f] More than just seeing someone at an event; entails some conversation and relationship building. The contact may not directly mention legacy giving.

[g] *Responses from bounce backs*—Reply devices inserted in annual reports, newsletters, and other mailings allow individuals to request information about gift planning or to inform you that they have named our nonprofit in their plans. *Letters and phone calls*—Tracking calls and letters from donors, prospects, and advisors is another way to demonstrate personal contacts.

[h] New Legacy Society members have informed us that they have named our nonprofit in their estate plans.

[i] This estimate reflects only gifts for which the donor has provided an estimate of the value.

[j] Gifts that have been identified but for which you have no confirmed information about the value.

[k] Ongoing training is important for staff to keep abreast of new developments in the field and to sharpen knowledge and skills. Includes meetings with legacy giving consultant.

Exhibit 9.1 Articles Related to Measuring Performance:

Bull, Joseph. "Measuring performance of gift planning officers, part 1." *Planned Giving Today*, March 2008.

Miree, Kathryn. "Mysteries and metrics of planned giving programs." *Planned Giving Today*, January 2008.

Lagasse, Paul. "Measure for measure: How measuring performance can transform fundraising." *Advancing Philanthropy*, September 2007. Published by the Association of Fundraising Professionals, http://www.afp.org.

Johnson, Kevin. "Measuring success for new and growing planned giving programs." This can be viewed at http://www.retrieverdevelopment.com, in the tab labeled Resources.

A detailed overview of using a logic model approach is included in the presentation at: http://www.exinfm.com/workshop_files/logic_model.ppt.

Sawhill, John, and David Williamson. "Measuring what matters." *The McKinsey Quarterly*, 2001;2:98–107. This article can also be viewed on the McKinsey & Company website at http://www.mckinsey-quarterly.com.

IMPORTANT POINTS TO CONSIDER

- A "tipping point" is a point at which a concept or idea catches fire and the numbers of people accepting or embracing it start to take off. The phrase quite accurately describes what your organization could experience with regard to building a stream of future bequest gifts.

- You will know when you have reached a tipping point in your legacy gift work when staff and volunteers start thinking, "There is something to this," and when board members start talking about the role of legacy gifts in the future.

- Don't rest here, however! Use your next activities to reinforce legacy gift messages and emphasize the value of these gifts to accomplishing your mission and long-range vision. Such activities could include getting better at telling your story and making sure all your staff and volunteers are included.

- It's also time to put in place expectations of performance and activity that will keep you on track. What metrics are meaningful and relevant for your organization? Think about the ones that will keep you focused on the right activities, that with time, will produce the right results: a stream of legacy gifts that contribute to your nonprofit's financial sustainability.

Step 4: Putting It to Work: Going Public

Setting the stage was valuable because it gently introduced the concept of legacy gifts to donors. Often they don't see small and mid-size groups as appropriate places for bequests. By taking the time to build trust and credibility, you made it possible for many donors to look at your nonprofit in a new, more positive light. Your carefully, considered steps gave them a chance to think through the idea.

With time, it became clear to a core group of supporters that they could trust your group with a legacy gift. This tipping point was the beginning of a shift in interest and awareness and corresponds to documented patterns of how ideas are adopted by groups. Following this innovation curve upward, your next step should focus on what you can do to significantly increase interest in legacy gifts and increase the number of gifts.

Your work will continue to be relationship-based. Unlike large institutions with big mailing lists, every donor must count. One director of development described his nonprofit's experience this way: "We get several (bequest) gifts a year and primarily it's based upon a pretty personal relationship the donor has with our organization. It's rarely a pure luck situation." Another executive director describes the importance of relationships, saying, "Nonprofits have to know about legacy giving. They have to talk about it. They need to build it in to their everyday work. I have found that by really focusing on relationship building, truly and authentically, and pushing the legacy giving a little to the background while the relationship is being built, is a great way to go. [In seeking legacy gifts] the most important things I see are to inspire and build trusting relationships."

It's also time to declare that your case is "final." It may also be time to structure what might be best described as a campaign to solicit legacy gifts. In this section we will focus on:

1. finalizing your case for support;

2. defining the role of legacy gifts in the long-term plans for financial sustainability of your nonprofit and how they fit into your plans for accomplishing your vision for the future;

3. tactics you can use much like a targeted major gift campaign or a larger public solicitation; there are a number of options you may have based on your unique situation.

FINALIZE YOUR CASE FOR A LEGACY GIFT

There were distinct advantages to keeping your case labeled and considered a draft. The label helped engage and include donors. By now, some groups may have gone through more than a dozen versions of their case for support, and their case will look and feel quite different from the first one.

You heard a lot from donors in your interviews and small group meetings about what worked and what was missing. Listen to and apply that advice. A final length of 10 to 20 pages seems to provide enough information to answer many questions and make a case, but it is also short enough to still invite new, useful questions. I have seen an effective case presented in under a dozen slides/ pages; the longest was about 48 pages. (*Note:* This 48-pager also included a new, very complex project description.)

You involved a number of people in creating this case and it's time to formally share the final copy by systematically reporting back to everyone who was involved. By way of acknowledging their involvement, a personal visit or small group gathering will have the most value.

Delivering the document in paper form will likely generate more interest with donors than e-mail attachments. The decision to make a legacy gift is more deliberative and considered than dashing off a check in response to an urgent direct-mail appeal or e-alert. As such, a simple attractive paper copy is something that can be considered, referred to, and shared. Having a paper copy to reflect upon when the time is right is also consistent with the nature of a bequest decision. Copies of a case for legacy gifts tend to stay around on a desk or coffee table and can be a reminder to act, or may even serve as conversation starters with friends.

DEFINE THE ROLE FOR LEGACY GIFTS FOR YOUR NONPROFIT

One of the themes that will emerge from your interviews testing the case statement will be an understanding of how donors believe legacy gifts will make the greatest difference. In the case of large institutions, tradition suggests that bequests go to endowments, but there is no rule binding nonprofits to this. In fact, it has been my experience that legacy donors to small and mid-size groups often want their gift put to work immediately. As a result, they place few or no restrictions on how their gift is to be put to work. The short case studies in the next section on tactics include a number of approaches to how legacy gifts were integrated into nonprofit business models and vision statements. An example of how legacy gifts were integrated in the business plan of one nonprofit is described by a sample menu of gift choices prepared by one land trust (Exhibit 10.1). Given the nature of their work, protecting land for many years to come, the emphasis on an endowment is appropriate. Other types of groups, such as advocacy groups, have different needs and interests, and their menu of gift

Exhibit 10.1 How Will Your Bequest Be Invested?

In general, bequests are placed in the permanent Land Preservation Fund. This option, as well as others, is explained below.

Land Preservation Fund

The Land Preservation Fund is a permanent revolving fund with versatile applications for land acquisition and preservation. We may borrow against the principal to buy land of ecological value and pay back the loan through a fundraising campaign. Meanwhile, the interest that the fund earns serves as an endowment for our organization. Bequests that are otherwise unrestricted are normally placed in this permanent fund.

Stewardship Endowment

Your bequest would be used exclusively to care for existing and future properties and protected areas. Should this be your desire, in addition to naming our organization using the language suggested above, add these words: "to be used to endow the management of the properties and protected areas."

Sometimes individuals are especially concerned about the future of a single property. Should this be a concern, please add these words: "to be used to endow the management of the properties and protected areas with first priority given to the _____ property."

Operations Reserve

In addition to endowments, we maintain an operating reserve fund. We will use this fund from time to time, without repayment, to, for example, launch new programs, to take advantages of special opportunities, or to adapt to changing circumstances. Should this be your desire, please add this language to your general bequest designation: "to be allocated to the operations reserve fund to support the general operational needs."

options should suggest different kinds of choices as to how and when a legacy gift might be put to work.

TACTICS YOU CAN USE

During interviews, you may have heard donors suggest or allude to a range of tactics and activities such as:

- "We have a lot of volunteers."
- "All the board should do this."
- "We need to work with all the founding board members. . . ."
- "If we had a group of about 100 legacy gifts. . . ."
- "If we had at least $1 million of identified gifts, some people might give."
- "Matching gifts would drive decisions."
- "Legacy gifts can pave the way for a capital campaign."

Each comment suggests a possible approach to how a nonprofit might move forward to add structure to its legacy gift work. Efforts could range from an insider-focused board campaign to a very public effort focused on generating a combination of cash and legacy gifts for specified purposes such as an endowment. The "right" answer is the approach that matches the interests of your donors. Here are a series of possible tactics you may be able to use or to adapt to your own situation. Each example defines the opportunity or purpose for choosing that tactic, a short description of activities, and a description of possible outcomes.

As you review each tactic, keep in mind that your goal is to leverage what you have learned about the potential role of legacy gifts for your group. Tactics should match needs and interests of your donors *and* the role legacy gifts will play in your nonprofit's vision for the future.

"We have a lot of volunteers. They need to know their gift could be combined with many others to make a real impact"

Opportunity/Purpose   A longtime volunteer noted that more than 50 people regularly volunteered. Most were retired. He added for emphasis, "and we're not getting any younger." His idea was to encourage volunteers to include the organization in their estate plans.

Activities A small campaign was organized around volunteers. They decided to focus their gifts, directing them to support the volunteer program. Because the nature of the volunteer program was critical to the mission of the group, the donor direction was an appropriate one. The group was large enough, and diverse enough in terms of economic status, that a group approach would enable everyone who desired to participate to make a meaningful gift.

Possible Outcomes A campaign to include and involve volunteers encouraged wide participation and avoided barriers of perceived differences in wealth and financial capacity. Volunteers were excited that they were able to direct their gifts toward an area of particular value to them. Using a volunteer-focused approach overcame possible objections such as "I give my time" or "I'm not wealthy like ____." It enabled the entire group to focus on something important to all without singling out people for economic reasons.

"All the board should do this"

Opportunity/Purpose Often the board must lead by example. Imagine if you were told that 100 percent of board members had included the nonprofit in their estate plans. It's a powerful statement, demonstrating confidence and trust in the quality, longevity, and mission focus of an organization. If the organization had a century or half century of history, this would be a welcome endorsement. If a board of a young organization made such a commitment, it could be even more powerful. It would be noticed by donors of all kinds. It would also be very impressive to note on any foundation grant application as well.

Activities Board members should now understand the value of legacy gifts, having been involved in the case interviews, creation of the gift acceptance policy, and discussion of how legacy gifts will fit into future financial plans.

Ideally one or two members will have emerged as board champions—people who will consistently advocate the cause of legacy gifts within the board.

One or two board members could work with other members individually and ask their peers to include the organization in their plans. This work is best done one-on-one.

However, estate planning is a personal matter and requires time, often because it can involve an array of decisions, people, and professional advisors. Rushing this process usually results in nonprofits being excluded or being given a limited, minimal gift.

If individual board members challenge others to do it, that can result in a fizzled effort. Rather than approach it from the perspective of "you need to do it," consider it as a way to help uncover the passion and commitment each board member has for the mission. Announcing it as a goal and challenge at a full board meeting often generates unexpected obstacles. Most successful board efforts need to be conducted behind the scenes, one-on-one, over time.

One group used a portion of their annual board retreat to talk and practice how they talked about why they were volunteers and why the work of this organization was important to them. The result was an excited, passionate group of people. This was a perfect prelude to visits by the board champion to talk about legacy gifts.

Possible Outcomes Large numbers of participating board members can have a powerful impact in terms of inspiring others to give, proving that there is a good case for legacy gifts, and in bolstering support from foundation donors.

"We need to work with all the founding board members"

Opportunity/Purpose Though the group was almost 50 years old, many longtime board members had drifted away over the years. Some were no longer contributors and were prominent donors to other nonprofits.

Activities The first challenge was to reconnect with board members. A board reunion was created to bring together many board alumni. More than 45 attended the first reunion.

These former board members were later invited to join the newly formed legacy society as "founders," and a number did.

The board reunion has since become an annual event. Each year, it grows in size. I expect that an increasing number of former board members will join in coming months and years.

Possible Outcomes   Reaching out to a group of committed people proved valuable in terms of new legacy gift commitments but also in terms of current fundraising and expanded connections. The reunion became a regular (low-cost) event that continues to provide benefits to the organization.

"If we had a group of about 100 legacy gifts. . . ."
Or
"If we had at least $1 million of identified legacy gifts, more people might give"

Opportunity/Purpose   Initial goals can be described in terms of the number of gifts or the estimated value of gifts or both. The value in describing a goal by counting each gift is that every gift counts equally. Counting using dollar estimates may increase gift size. There are advantages and disadvantages to each approach.

It's been my experience that, with rare exceptions, donors of all ages don't have a good sense of their relative economic status in society. They often feel as though they have much less than they actually do, and they often think of themselves as much farther down the economic ladder than they are. As a result, a campaign that counts each gift as "one" regardless of gift size, can be successful in engaging a wide range of people and bypassing the concern that "I don't have anything."

Sometimes, focusing on an estimated dollar goal can serve to increase the amount of individual bequests. I have watched donors reflect on a total dollar goal, then respond saying, "Well, since it's that large a goal, I should give more to help you get there." A combined goal of both numbers and dollar amount can help you include everyone and to encourage those who are more aware of their favored economic status to give greater amounts.

Activities   How will the objective of 100 gifts or million dollars fit into larger, long-term plans? For example, if a million dollars were received over the next few years, where would it be used? What impact would it make? This question will have to be answered before you arrive at a number or dollar amount for your goal. If you have taken the time to set the stage for legacy gifts, campaigns like this can be structured and operated much like a major gifts campaign, though with a slightly longer time line reflecting the nature of how legacy gift decisions are made and carried out.

Possible Outcomes   A target number combined with dollar amount can be effective in leveraging both numbers and size of gifts. Your number should be intimately connected with the purpose for which the money and gifts will be used. One group set a goal of creating an endowment that would later provide 20 percent of the funding for their core operations. Using simple math, they then calculated the ultimate goal figure for the endowment.

"Matching gifts would drive gift decisions"

Opportunity/Purpose   How to jump-start a stream of bequest gifts to an organization focusing on advocacy issues was the question for one group. They had many loyal members, but their work was not the kind that people traditionally supported with estate gifts. Their annual budget was about $1 million. A donor offered to provide a matching gift for each documented bequest.

Activity Details   Mailings, a brochure, and newsletter announcements were used to publicize the cash match. Each bequest commitment would be matched by a $10,000 cash gift from the donor. Each bequest was documented in writing and with details, such as the estimated value of the bequest and the date the bequest was originally planned. To qualify for the match, the value of the new bequest had to be $10,000 or more in current estimated value. A brochure provided a detailed application used for documentation, as well as links to a number of website pages with expanded information about estate planning, how to designate the group, and background about their overall mission. The match was so popular that the period of the match was extended. When extended, the match amount was cut in half but donors continued to respond enthusiastically.

Possible Outcomes   The campaign established a deadline for notifying the group about bequest commitments, which were combined with a match of a cash gift from another donor. The donor and the staff were surprised with the positive response. The match period was extended. Over the period of the match, more than $15 million in future bequests was identified and confirmed for this advocacy group—a stream of future income about 15 times their annual expenditures.

The match proved very effective in motivating people who had not considered this group as the kind that gets bequests and it encouraged people who had already made plans to identify themselves.

"Legacy gifts can pave the Way for a capital campaign"

Opportunity/Purpose   Effective legacy gift fundraising is about establishing relationships revolving around the long-term values of donors. If your organization spends time engaged in values-oriented conversations before a big campaign—which is precisely what a legacy gift conversation is all about—you effectively and powerfully lay the groundwork for a later, successful capital campaign.

Focusing on legacy gifts in advance of a capital campaign is a perfect use of legacy gift concepts, both in terms of timing and tactics. The best time to start legacy giving work is well *before* you start the quiet phase, or lead gift phase, of the campaign.

Activities   Early conversations with current or prospective bequest gift donors can help clarify the case for giving to your institution. They can also uncover organizational issues (another way to say "hidden questions") that might get in the way of future major gifts or the success of a capital campaign effort. These conversations can also save time by serving as a reality test as campaign planning gets underway. Often issues are identified in planning or feasibility studies just before a launch. Imagine if you had already identified most of the issues and had a year of concerted effort to make changes before that study was conducted.

Another important reason for focusing on legacy gifts early is that it can take time for a stream of bequests to become more predictable. Starting an effort a year or two in advance of a campaign means that by the time the campaign is winding down, bequest gifts may be arriving and increasing both in number and value. From the perspective of total funds raised, bequest gifts could add to your organization's bottom line at the close of the campaign at a time when current donors feel tired, staff are worn out, and the board is ready for a breather. Bequest gifts will be quite welcome in this climate.

Possible Outcomes   Systematically pursuing legacy gifts can build a strong foundation for any future major gifts or capital campaign. Talking about legacy gifts, and the barriers and motivations related to those gifts, will help bring to the surface issues that might later slow or stall a larger cash-oriented campaign.

Research demonstrates that donors who have made charitable bequest plans give twice as much annually; for wealthy donors, it is four and a half times as much each year. By focusing on legacy gifts, you will build a group of loyal donors who won't ask, "Should I give to this project?" More likely, they will ask, "How much can I give?" Which question would you rather hear?

IMPORTANT POINTS TO CONSIDER

- Figures 10.1 and 10.2 graphically portray the steps leading up to "going public" and include some of the many choices you may have available as you expand your efforts.

- Use the opportunity of "finalizing" your case to systematically report back the results to the many donors, volunteers, and community allies you initially asked for advice and input.

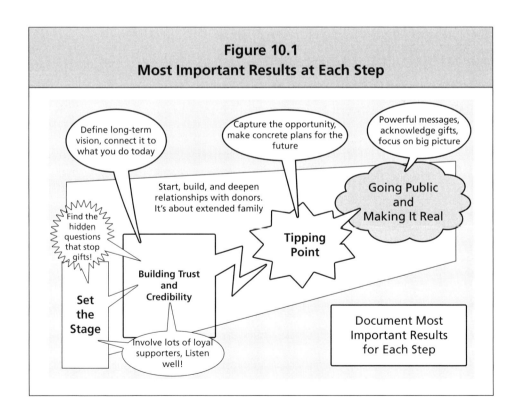

Figure 10.1
Most Important Results at Each Step

Define long-term vision, connect it to what you do today

Capture the opportunity, make concrete plans for the future

Powerful messages, acknowledge gifts, focus on big picture

Start, build, and deepen relationships with donors. It's about extended family

Going Public and Making It Real

Find the hidden questions that stop gifts!

Tipping Point

Building Trust and Credibility

Set the Stage

Document Most Important Results for Each Step

Involve lots of loyal supporters, Listen well!

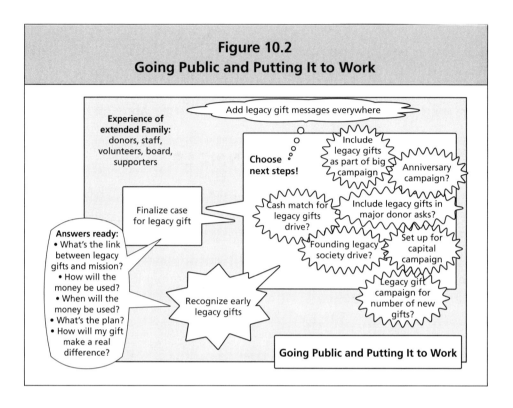

Figure 10.2
Going Public and Putting It to Work

Add legacy gift messages everywhere

Experience of extended Family: donors, staff, volunteers, board, supporters

Choose next steps!

Include legacy gifts as part of big campaign

Anniversary campaign?

Finalize case for legacy gift

Cash match for legacy gifts drive?

Include legacy gifts in major donor asks?

Answers ready:
• What's the link between legacy gifts and mission?
• How will the money be used?
• When will the money be used?
• What's the plan?
• How will my gift make a real difference?

Founding legacy society drive?

Set up for capital campaign

Recognize early legacy gifts

Legacy gift campaign for number of new gifts?

Going Public and Putting It to Work

- Describe how legacy gifts fit into the long-term plans for the financial sustainability of your nonprofit and how they fit into your plans for accomplishing your vision for the future.

- Create a menu of gift options that reflects how legacy gifts fit into your future. This menu should give donors choices and also provides evidence to donors that you have a clear plan they may embrace with confidence.

- Depending on how large a part legacy gifts are expected to play in your future plans for financial sustainability and mission, there are a number of tactics and campaign tools you could now choose from to systematically expand the number of gifts and the size of the future stream of legacy gifts. Which one or combination of tools and tactics will your nonprofit select?

Part
Three

Integrating Legacy Gifts into Daily Work

Too often our urgent work gets in the way of the more informal, but important, kinds of fundraising work. A focus on the current quarter's fundraising numbers inevitably leads to actions that may neglect, or even block, legacy gifts. Once you have invested the time and energy to establish a stream of legacy gifts, you will have to work to maintain that momentum and ensure that the donors who have stepped forward and declared their intentions stay involved and connected.

How will you evaluate your progress and choose the right things to measure to keep you on the right track? Picking the right things to measure can also play an important role in keeping your focus on the right kinds of activities.

To be successful you don't have to add a lot of new activities. Integrating legacy gifts into your day-to-day work might start by simply adding one or two questions to the repertoire of questions you use in donor visits. Paying a little extra attention to the nature of your messages and how you communicate your long-term vision can also help bolster your legacy gift work. The same can be true for the many forms of communication you already prepare and distribute. Don't forget the events and myriad interactions that staff, volunteers, and board members conduct routinely that could double as vehicles for powerful legacy gift messages.

Recognizing and keeping track of those who have already made legacy gifts can also fit into and amplify the impact of your existing recognition plans.

This chapter includes suggestions about how to recognize and communicate with legacy gift donors and prospective donors. Also included are suggestions about simple questions you could include in your next visit with a donor.

RECOGNIZING LEGACY GIFTS

Large institutions often put names on plaques in building lobbies; others publish long lists of names in widely distributed magazines; or staff travel to hand-deliver pretty plaques to each planned gift donor. Larger nonprofits also acknowledge planned gift donors by sending them the regular newsletter (85 percent) supplemented by a special planned gift newsletter (31 percent), by inviting them for personal visits and tours (52 percent), by featuring donors in articles, and by holding special events for this group of donors (33 percent).[1]

Is this recognition effective? Cygnus Applied Research reports in its statistically based research[2] that many recognition methods that charities practice may not be valuable to donors. For example, their research finds that 76 percent of individual donors get plaques or certificates that acknowledge their philanthropy, but 73 percent either throw them out or put them into a cupboard; 12 percent keep some and throw most away; only 5 percent display them.[3]

What is important to your donors? The answer to that question will tell you what will matter most to them—and by extension, to your organization. The most powerful and effective recognition will probably be something unique to your organization. Since legacy gift donors will not be around to be sure their gift is used in the way they direct, it will be valuable to them to have confidence in how your organization will handle their gifts. The experience of recognition may best come in the demonstrated form of good records, accurate and timely acknowledgement, continued updates about the impact of work, and personal calls; all those things that recognize the donor and gift but also serve to reinforce the donor's sense that his gift will be well cared for.

As you consider what forms of recognition you will use (see Exhibit 11.1), rely on suggestions and feedback from donors. What matters to you and your

Exhibit 11.1 Recognition Ideas

- Photographs are appreciated: 76 percent of individual donors report that they appreciate pictures of their gift at work. Personal letters from people who have been helped are also valued highly by donors.[4]

- Recognition events achieve mixed results. Too often, the events stray from recognition to fundraising. This dilutes the value of any recognition.

- A social services group created a beautiful walnut pedestal and on the four sides were inscribed small golden plaques with names of legacy donors. Regardless of what building or location the service organization occupied, this pedestal could travel with them.

- Another social services nonprofit prepared an elegant calligraphic list of founding legacy gift donors, and the picture was prominently displayed in the lobby of their offices.

- One conservation group inscribed names of donors on river rocks. A small group of donors and staff would find a favorite place along the donor's favorite fishing river, and with some degree of ceremony the donor would loft the stone into the river. The rock would disappear in the current; only they knew it was there.

- In the case of a mid-size group anticipating a campaign for a building, a 90-year-old donor in failing health offered to promise a bequest. His gift was intended for an endowment fund to generate revenue to help defray costs of the new building for years to come. Initially, he had no interest in recognition even though his gift was to be $1 million. Once the building started to take shape, the executive

(Continued)

director showed him pictures of the progress. She wondered out loud whether he might want to have his late wife's name on the building. Yes, that was the recognition of value and interest to him: It was now a gift in memory of his late wife. I saw him at the opening ceremony sitting in his wheelchair with a beaming smile.

- Articles featuring legacy gift donors can combine recognition as with encouraging others to give. From the point of recognition, the most useful stories feature a story or lesson from the donor's life. It's hard to predict what that will be; listening will be important here. From the perspective of encouraging new gifts, the most important part of the story will be a description of the emotions and processes related to the decision—not about any specific gift tool. Some stories focus much on the individual and such things as their hobbies but little on the values embodied in the decision to make a legacy gift. Don't waste your precious newsletter pages that way.

- Consistent with helping donors gain confidence in your nonprofit's ability to remember the gift and put it to good use, consider asking the donor to write a letter to include in your permanent files. The letter could describe why the donor made the gift, what was important about it to her, and what her hopes are for the gift in the years to come. Some people don't feel comfortable writing such a letter. In that case, consider interviewing them and writing up a draft of a letter for them to review and approve. (*Note:* Interviews could be conducted by other volunteers, or even by students, who write well.)

organization or what other nonprofits do to recognize gifts may not matter to your donors. Combining meaningful recognition with a plan for how legacy gifts will be used in the future is a powerful, influential combination that will help to persuade others that "this is the right place for a bequest." Remember to always ask donors' permission before publicly recognizing a legacy gift.

KEEP GOOD RECORDS

How will you keep track of your legacy gifts? If you approach documentation from the perspective of offering a service to the donor, requests for more information about a specific gift are often welcomed by donors. If you approach documentation with the intent to seek information to make sure that when the time comes, your organization fulfills the donor's directions exactly as wished, donors will see it as valuable benefit. If you approach a donor from the perspective of wanting to "lock up" or "count" the gift, your actions are likely to be perceived as an unwelcome intrusion and will be met with resistance. (You will find samples of a Legacy Gift Confirmation and File Form and introductory script in the Resources section.)

Here are some tips and suggestions about keeping your legacy gift records.

- Create paper files for each legacy gift donor. Electronic files can be lost too easily; when it comes to paper, someone has to make a conscious decision to discard a paper file, and this increases the chance that these permanent records will be retained and retrievable when needed.

- Put everything into the paper files, even the most mundane of correspondence or thank you card. Years later such notes can be of tremendous value in reconstructing or chronicling relationships. Cumulatively, a collection of correspondence and notes can also be very revealing and helpful.

- Keep the files in a locked cabinet.

- Periodically you might want to scan some of the key documents in each file and store the digital copies with your other off-site back-ups. The point is to make sure you have solid records of these legacy gifts in the event of fire or other catastrophe.

- Keep notes of conversations and put these in the files too. Remember to write in complete sentences. Here's a short horror story to demonstrate the value of notes: One nonprofit was named as the beneficiary of a large estate. The business partner of the single person who had passed away contested it. Looking at files created earlier that consisted of—among other things—scribbled half sentences on torn scraps of paper, while trying to figure out and demonstrate donor intent, was frustrating. Ultimately, the skimpy documentation was not enough to win in court. The business partner got several million dollars that was truly intended for the deceased donor's favorite small and mid-size nonprofits.

- Pictures of the donor, family members, and pets can be quite valuable when honoring and recognizing donors in the future.

START USING LEGACY MESSAGES TODAY

There are a number of communication tools that small and mid-sized groups already use regularly such as newsletters. Be sure to integrate legacy messages into these. It's not only mentioning legacy gifts specifically, it is including the perspective of legacy gifts as a part of what you write. Connecting work today with long-term vision sometimes means changing only a word or two; other times it may mean writing an article with a new, broader perspective.

If you are serious about pursuing legacy gifts, you will likely need to reexamine your existing materials to make sure you draw clear connections between the work you do today with the long-term principles that guide your work. Every time you do that, you help make the case in favor of a legacy gift.

Newsletters

One newsletter I receive regularly is from a small advocacy group. In a recent issue, two pages were devoted to an article about a recent court case. It appeared they were instrumental in the pursuing the case. After reading about half the article, I put the newsletter down; I had no idea what the point of the story was. Several weeks later, I happened to see one of the staff and I asked about the story. "Oh!" she exclaimed. "That was a landmark court case, it will change the whole way this work is done." She continued to tell me why it was important in two more short sentences. I was impressed. As a donor, I immediately felt my gift made a real difference.

Why did it take two pages in the newsletter to fail to make the point? I realized the article dealt with things important to the attorney preparing the article, but completely missed the perspective of why it would matter to a donor. How will you avoid the same mistake when it comes to discussing legacy gifts? Here are some tips and suggestions about newsletters and legacy gifts:

- Articles about donors that focus on the nature of their choices and insight about their deliberations can be very useful. Stories of what they did in their youth are less interesting to legacy donors and of little help in helping provide insight into a values-based decision.

- Older donors also often read advertisements. Using that format in your newsletter to note legacy events will be noticed by the right audience. Don't assume because you may not read ads that no one else reads ads. Since the ads appear in a trusted publication, they have in effect been vetted, and some donors will pay extra attention to them as a result. Sometimes using an ad format can help you focus on bigger type and work around a naive, typeface-oriented newsletter designer.

- Any lists of memorial or tribute gifts should be in a typeface that can be read easily. Research reports that the minimum type size should be 12 points.

- Each and every newsletter should have one or more articles, ads, or sections focused on legacy gifts. Planning decisions are often driven by life events; thus, ads or articles need to appear continuously or you risk missing the moments when the ads will be useful to your donors. Don't worry about repeating ads in consecutive newsletters or venues. Scheduling one ad per year fails to take into account how legacy gifts are actually considered, then completed.

- Offer information in the nature of a service—not with the perspective of pitching a product. For example, in an ad format, copy might read: "Please save for reference: We get inquiries about how to include ABC group in wills and estate plans. Here is the information should you need it (then list the designation information)." Contrast this with a sales approach that might exhort someone to "Give a bequest today!"

- Avoid glossy and metallic papers because the reflection makes reading more difficult. If donors don't read it, they can't respond or take action.

Will Your Donor Read It?

The executive director and I had spent long hours preparing for a meeting with a prospective donor. Finally, the day came and we were all together in the donor's living room. We presented the retired businessman with our carefully crafted proposal outline. He thumbed through it, never settling for long on any single page. He paused, looking intently at the cover, then put the document aside and asked, "Why don't you just tell me about it instead?"

At that moment, we knew he was unable to read the text easily. Rather than struggle to read it and risk embarrassment, he decided to ignore what we had painstakingly written and ask for a verbal explanation. How many of your appeals, letters, newsletter articles, and Web stories will not be read by the very people who have the financial capacity to make the greatest impact with their nonprofit giving? If we had not been in the same room with him, I wonder whether he would ever have had a chance to learn about the project. It's quite possible we would have never gotten his gift.

What's really cool for the eyes of a 20-something designer is generally a visual disaster for older eyes. Exhibit 11.2 illustrates the impact of ignoring this visual reality. "Is the type large enough to read?" should be a question every nonprofit asks about every document and online message it creates.[5]

Studies of how eyes perceive type size and color demonstrate that by age 43, in order to be effective, the type size should be at least 12 points. Type size, color, shading, reverse type all drive reading comprehension; they are not merely design preferences. Rather, how design is used will determine whether your donors will bother to read what you write. If they can't read it, why are you investing staff time and resources to write it and send it out?

Based on research into how eye function and aging affect reading comprehension, here are some more tips for marketing to people over 40: use serif type in print sans serif in e-mail and Web-based communications. Type size should be at least 12 points. Orange, red, and yellow colors are generally more readable. Blues, greens, and purples are the least readable. Avoid reverse type in anything you want older donors to read. You may also want to look at the AARP website for tips about designing for older eyes and readability.

OPPORTUNITIES FOR LEGACY GIFT CONNECTIONS

Acknowledgments and Thank You Letters

Like most good nonprofits, you probably acknowledge each gift with a thank you letter. What if you included in the envelope of each thank you letter "reference card" with information needed to include your group in an estate plan? If it is a "reference guide," it will likely be saved. However, if you create a reference guide from the perspective of a sales pitch, it will be likely pitched into the trash.

Donor Visits

In visits with prospective donors, constantly talk about and vividly paint a picture of the positive, desired future and how legacy gifts will be a vital part of that future: "This is something we can do only if we all work together." The results of focusing on a long-term vision when combined with a couple of simple questions can be powerful. Here's how one development officer described her first attempt at doing exactly that: "The visit went fine. Then when the gift conversation came up, I asked him about what was important to him about his decision (to include our group in his will). When I left that day, he gave me a hug—surprising to me because we had only just met and talked about an hour. That single question had really opened things up." Exhibit 11.3 includes a number of possible conversation starters you could use for legacy gifts.

Imagine the result if every donor visit conducted by your board, staff, and fundraising volunteers included something like the following:

> As you know we are in the process of getting set up to accept estate gifts. The most common are simple gifts in a will. We are creating a formal gift policy and financial plan on how to use the gifts when they are received. There will be a plan in place. Of course, if a donor wants to direct their gift someplace specific, we will be able to do that too.

> The reason I bring this up is I wanted to ask for some advice. I am not asking you to do anything. I am just trying to understand.

> I was wondering whether you have ever considered including any charity in your will or estate plans.

> Would you ever consider including our group? Why, or why not?

> If yes, tell me more.

> If no, what would have to be different or to change in order for you to be willing to consider our group?

Exhibit 11.3 Introducing Gift Planning to Donors: Conversation Starters

Although some of these questions may appear basic, they can often be used to trigger a donor's memories and key emotions about why the organization or its work is so important to them. They may also provide you the chance to gain insight about what values are most important to the prospective donor and, subsequently, gift planning opportunities.

How did you first become a donor to the NONPROFIT? Why did you give what you gave? (Get them back to the emotional point at which they made their first gift.)

How did you choose NONPROFIT? (Stories about their life and how NONPROFIT changed their life could emerge here. This question provides the opportunity reflect on their entire life between then and now.)

What is so important to you (and your spouse or children) about its work? (Is there a desire to make a gift or bigger commitment because of family or community? How does this match their core or lifetime values?)

What do your friends think about it? (Should they be giving more? Do they know people who should be giving as well? Are they proud of it, or do they have reservations that must be addressed before solicitation?)

What other organizations do you support? Why? (Where do we stand in terms of priorities? Is there a partnership possible? Are there advantages to giving to other activities at NONPROFIT?)

Have you ever considered including any charity in your estate plans? (Emphasize the word *charity*, since it applies to any nonprofit, including a local school, church, or hospital. If the answer is "yes," you can help by describing some opportunities that apply to any charity, including NONPROFIT.)

What went through your mind or what did you think about before you made your decision to include NONPROFIT in your estate plans?
What does your spouse think about it? Your children? (If any.) (Opportunities to discover more about assets, values, and family concerns.)

If the opportunity presents itself, ask for their opinions about the kinds of events, information, or even solicitations they would prefer to receive:

If we had an event to tell people about the NONPROFIT and gift planning information or opportunities, what kind of event should it be? Is that something you would come to?

We list all of the Legacy Society members in our publications (include other benefits). What do you think would be most interesting to others considering or in the position to make such a gift?

What do you think of the magazine? Do you read it? What do you find most interesting? What do you never read in it?

If we were to put information about gift planning into the magazine or a newsletter, what would be most useful to you or to those you know?

You probably get a lot of mailings about this sort of thing. Do you find them useful? Do you read them? What advice would you have for us if we were to do any mailings?

Would you mind saving the mailings that you get that you think are particularly good?

As we grow a gift planning effort, what advice would you have for us? What would you like to learn about?

Volunteer Activities and Projects

I spent the day enjoying fantastic scenery and good company on a member hike with a conservation group. During conversations, one couple suggested that they were interested in getting more involved; another person actually brought up the subject of her will and her interest in making a gift through her estate. At the end of the hike, I pulled the staff member aside to check whether he had heard these comments. He had. But he continued, "Fundraising isn't my job. There's no reason for me to get involved." Then he walked away. The couple had already left; I had no way to let the organization know of their interest and gift potential. Did the nonprofit miss a large gift? I suspect the answer is yes.

There are many opportunities at events of all sizes and formats that contain opportunities to draw clear links between the work your nonprofit does today and your vision for the future. In your interviews about the case and gift policy, I suggest that one of the questions you ask is about how to talk at your events about the issues important to legacy gift decisions. For example, in the case of a conservation group, the question might sound something like:

> Mary and Bob, you have been on some of our member hikes. A lot of people come on those. At the end of each one, virtually everyone is excited about what they experienced and got to see. They often have questions about what we do and how they can help. If I were to talk about our work in a way that makes a case for a legacy gift—but is not a sales pitch—how would you advise me to talk about the topic?

Annual and Other Appeals

Appeals for urgent, crisis funding undermine your case for legacy gifts. Legacy gifts are awarded to successful groups, not groups that "need" gifts.

Most large organizations approach planned gift fundraising using techniques that rely on a small percentage of return from large numbers of prospects. For example, a mailing to 100,000 grateful patients might be considered a success if 15 people respond asking for information. If a small nonprofit with a mailing list of 2,000 used the same criteria, the percentage result would not even round up to 1 response. Nor can small and mid-size groups afford many special mailings.

MEASURING RESULTS AND KEEPING ON TRACK

How will you measure your success? Of course, you will keep track of actual gifts received, as well as those anticipated. But what about all the work it will take to secure the gift? Effective groups include metrics and goals related to both securing and documenting legacy gifts in staff work plans at all levels of their organization.

Often the board must play a primary role ensuring that legacy gifts continue to be a priority. One of the most effective ways to accomplish this is to establish the role of "board champion" for legacy gifts. It will be the role of this champion, or team of champions, to make sure legacy gifts are kept front and center in budget, fundraising, and strategic planning conversations.

Among the most important metrics will be your annual fund donor retention rates. Research documents that donor retention rates are one of the most useful predictors of future legacy gift success.

Here is a range of different metrics you might track that could contribute to successfully securing legacy gifts:

- Annual fund donor retention rates for the current period and trend data over time

- The rate of growth of the pool of consistent annual or regular donors by periods (for example, the total number of donors who have given consistently over a five, eight, or ten-year period)

- The actual numbers of donors who are regular givers for five, eight, or more years

- Numbers of members in your heritage or legacy society (or the number of people who have told you and provided documentation that your nonprofit is included in their estate plan)

- The number of your legacy society members who are under age 50

- The percentage of your annual fund donors who are members of your legacy society

- The total estimated value of legacy gifts that make up your pipeline of future gifts

- The percentage of board members who have included your organization in their estate plans

- The percentage of staff who have included your organization in their estate plans

- The number of donor visits or substantive interactions in which a legacy gift was a topic of conversation

- The number of board member and staff combined visits to donors to discuss a legacy gift with a prospective donor

- The number of program staff and fundraising staff combined visits to discuss a legacy gift with a prospective donor
- The number of marketing touches (e.g., articles, fliers, ads, etc.) your donors experienced regarding legacy gifts
- The total number of marketing and fundraising touches donors experienced overall
- The number of downloads of the gift acceptance policy from your website
- The number of page views of your legacy gift pages
- The number and sources of inquiries regarding legacy gifts
- The number of referrals regarding legacy gifts from program and field staff (nondevelopment staff)
- Trends of the relative or average ages of donors in your database or age concentrations
- For bequest gifts received, how many were known about in advance, the trend over time, and current period
- Overall revenue trends of incoming bequests by dollar and number, over time
- Donor survey results that report on whether you are making an effective case (or not) in terms of legacy gift knowledge, the connections with legacy gifts and your long-range vision, and the role legacy gifts play in your long-term plans for financial sustainability

What other activities will contribute to building a stream of legacy gift income to support the long-range vision of your nonprofit?

IMPORTANT POINTS TO CONSIDER

- You have the opportunity to continually set the stage and build trust and credibility with new and prospective donors. Take the opportunities presented daily in how you implement your routine and special communications, recognition, and special events to help continue to build interest in and commitment to legacy gifts.

- Make a point of reporting on and describing the *impact* of gifts that have been received or committed.

- Focus on the values that played a part in the decision of the donor to make the gift.

- Finally, make sure that your donors can actually read what you spend hours or days laboring to craft by using appropriately sized type styles and layout rules that match the physiological needs of older eyes. If they can't read it, your efforts will have been wasted.

Gift Tools

Donors today are faced with an array of philanthropic products. Tools that have received a great deal of attention include donor advised funds, gift annuities, and charitable trusts, among others. Large nonprofits have done an excellent job in educating donors and their financial advisors about gift annuities and charitable trusts. Commercial providers have also done an excellent job marketing the product of donor advised funds, and to a lesser extent charitable trusts of various forms.

When many fundraisers talk about "planned giving," it is this set of tools to which they most often refer. However, most of the money in this category—perhaps more than 90 percent—comes from legacy gifts in the form of bequests. This is where most small and mid-size nonprofits should focus their time and attention. It is also where nonprofits of this size will be most competitive in terms of fulfilling donor interests and needs.

This chapter describes some of the more commonly discussed gift tools. It is included to give you background information about tools you will hear discussed. Considerations and questions to explore if you were to use some of these tools are followed by descriptions. But please don't forget that in terms of charitable gifts, most of the money is in bequests, and that is where almost all of your efforts should be expended.

WHAT GIFT TOOLS ARE FOR YOUR ORGANIZATION?

I would suggest any small or mid-size group today take a very hard, calculating look at whether to offer either charitable trusts or gift annuities. There are many risks in terms of investing, coupled with significant hidden, internal staff and hard costs. If you cannot strongly commit to invest the time and energy to build up a large enough pool of annuity donors, the quick answer is "No, don't start a program today." If you are committing both time and resources, have the internal capacity, and are certain of this long-term drive, it may be a solid choice. The same qualifications are true for charitable trusts.

For some large groups, gift annuities and charitable trusts have proved profitable. However, before a small or mid-size group begins promoting either gift vehicle, it will be important to look at the many hidden costs. The following are some questions to consider before you make your decision about both charitable gift annuities and charitable trusts:

Legal Matters Matter

For annuities: Does your state require registration? What are the costs of registration? What are the costs of continued compliance (such as annual reporting)? Do you have donors in multiple states? For trusts: what are the legal costs and obligations of creating trust documents and interacting with the donor's legal advisors?

Accounting Responsibilities Increase

For both gift annuities and charitable trusts: Do you have the internal capacity to make sure checks go out on time monthly, quarterly, or annually? From the right account? For the right amount? Who's going to do the tax statements each year? Who will be responsible for keeping up to date on the requirements (and costs of that attention)?

Investments Will Be Watched

For annuities: Many states require separate administration and investment of the funds. Can you manage this? Will the amount of the funds invested be large enough to enable you to achieve the diversification that is assumed in the calculation of gift annuity rates? What are the costs of separate investment management and administration? For trusts: Will the trust be large enough to diversify and withstand market fluctuations? Who will manage it? What will external advisors cost and what minimum trust size will apply?

Donor Relationships May Change

For both annuities and trusts: Who will handle the phone calls when a check is late or goes missing in the mail? Will accounting staff, usually not trained in dealing with donors and the public, now be the ones dealing with your donors? Will the problems in gift administration be visible to you, or will you be surprised by donor comments at your next visit?

Investment Returns Will Vary

For annuities: Suggested charitable gift annuity rates developed by the American Council on Gift Annuities (ACGA) are based on an assumed set of investment returns. If you start out with a small investment pool, will you be able to diversify enough to meet these investment return assumptions? For both annuities and trusts: Did you know that if your investments lose value in the first year, this has significant, long-term negative effects? Imagine if you had started an annuity program (or created a trust) in 2008 and then lost 30 percent of the core amount. At that rate, you are now at risk of breaking even or more likely losing money on the "gift" annuity. In the case of a charitable trust, it may also fall short of expectations. What risks are you willing to assume?

For more about gift annuity rates, assumptions that go into the rate calculations, and a compendium of state regulations, see the ACGA website at http://www.acga-web.org.

Politics Count Too

For annuities: Sometimes a key donor wants a gift annuity. For what may be best described as a political decision, you say "yes." In some cases, this can be a smart, donor-relations move. Depending on state regulations you may have the option of "reinsuring" the gift—in other words, paying an insurance company to take the risk. You still get a gift, but it will cost you. In the cases of charitable trusts, a number of bank trust departments offer services described as "trustee of a trustee"—in other words, while your name is up front, they do all the work. There are administrative costs, of course, but if your primary concern is to take good care of a donor, this arrangement might work. Note that there will be minimum amounts that will be needed to make such arrangements work. For charitable trusts, minimum amounts may be in the $250,000 range. Lower amounts might be agreeable or accepted if your organization does a lot of other business with the bank.

Are You Credible?

For gift annuities: Remember, the gift annuity is a contract and backed by the assets of your organization. Will a donor risk placing a large sum with you based on your size and financial history? (Litmus test: would you put part of your personal retirement assets into a gift annuity with your organization? Your personal answer may be all the advice you need on this matter.) The advantages in marketing gift annuities are heavily weighted toward large institutions with significant assets. Will you be competitive? Is it worth your time and money trying to compete in this specific niche market?

How Can You Hedge Risk?

For annuities: Some groups starting a program set the age and gift minimums high until they reach a predetermined amount for the gift annuity pool. They may also decline gifts from higher ages associated with the highest suggested rates. Others may intentionally offer lower rates to hedge risks. Plus, they plan on and execute a multiyear marketing effort designed to build demand. There are a variety of insurance products that can sometimes be used to hedge your risk. Is reinsurance worth your cost?

Opportunity Costs Incurred

For both trusts and annuities: How much time will it really take to set up these gift vehicles? How much time will be spent in accounting and making sure the rules are being followed? (*Hint:* It will take a lot more than you expect.) Development officers tend to prefer dealing with people, not insurance department bureaucrats and obscurely worded IRS regulations. Are you prepared for this change in job description? Will staff have time for this potential additional work? What is the opportunity cost when staff spends time mired in IRS regulations instead of spending time face-to-face with donors?

What about Your Mission and Fundraising?

I hear more and more development and gift planning officers lamenting the cost and the time consumed by the details of gift administration. There is a growing threat in that time spent in administration is time not spent with donors. In most cases, time spent with donors yields far greater fundraising and total dollar return as compared with almost any other activity. How will you choose to spend your time?

Should you promote charitable gift annuities and charitable trusts? For most small and mid-size groups, my recommendation is "no."

COMMON PLANNED GIFT TOOLS

Bargain Sale

Imagine if someone wanted to use a piece of real estate to make a gift but did not want to give 100 percent of the value of the property. A bargain sale is the purchase of real estate by a nonprofit from a seller for less than its fair market value. The donor receives an immediate payment for the sale amount and a charitable tax deduction for the difference between the cash payment and the fair market value. The donor avoids the capital gains tax on a portion of the capital gain—the same proportion as the gift divided by the fair market value. A large amount of wealth is held in real estate. As real estate values fluctuate, this tool may become more widely used to complete charitable gifts.

Charitable Remainder Trust

This trust makes payments, either a fixed amount (annuity trust) or a percentage of trust principal (unitrust), to whomever the donor chooses to receive income. The donor may claim a charitable income tax deduction and may not have to pay any capital gains tax if the gift is of appreciated property. At the end of the trust term, the charity receives whatever amount is left in the trust. Charitable remainder unitrusts provide some flexibility in the distribution of income, and thus can be helpful in retirement planning. Many donors find the trusts useful in preparing for retirement (especially if they have highly appreciated assets to sell, for example).

Charitable Lead Trust

This trust makes payments, either a fixed amount (annuity trust) or a percentage of trust principal (unitrust), to a charity during its term. At the end of the trust term, the principal can return either to the donor or to heirs named by the donor. The donor may claim a charitable tax deduction for making a lead trust gift. A lead trust can reduce gift and estate taxes or provide a charitable deduction for the donor. Charitable lead trusts are most appealing to wealthy donors who want to pass appreciated assets to their heirs without paying a substantial amount in taxes.

Donor Advised Fund

Community foundations pioneered the concept of donor advised funds. If you make a gift to the foundation, it will administer the fund, distributing annual payouts as you direct. For example, one might designate a community foundation as the beneficiary of your estate and direct it to set up a fund for underprivileged children. When you pass away, assets will be transferred to the foundation, it will set up the fund, and in years to come earnings from your gift will be used to help such children. In recent years, a number of commercial funds have entered the market and become among the largest product providers of this service. Commercial funds usually offer the donor more control over how the fund is invested and how much of the fund can be given to charity at any one time.

Gift Annuity

A gift annuity is a contract between a charity and a donor. In return for a donation of cash or other assets, the charity agrees to pay the donor, or a friend or family member the donor chooses, a fixed payment for life. The donor can also claim a charitable tax deduction. Income from a gift annuity can be deferred for a period of years. Gift annuities are attractive to donors who want to receive a fixed income from assets that have risen sharply in value, such as long-held stocks. In return for gifts of such assets, the charity guarantees the donors a fixed annual income for the rest of their lives and helps the donor avoid capital gains tax on the transfer of such assets. The donor also gets an income tax break on a portion of the earnings from an annuity.

Pooled Income Fund

A charity accepts gifts from many donors into a fund and distributes the income of the fund to each donor or recipient of the donor's choosing. Each recipient receives income in proportion to his or her share of the fund. For making a gift to a pooled fund, a donor receives a charitable income tax deduction and will not have to pay capital gains tax if the gift is of appreciated property. When an income beneficiary dies, the charity receives the donor's portion of the fund. Donors can earn income on stock and other assets and bypass capital gains taxes. Unlike an annuity, a donor's income from a pooled income fund is tied to fluctuating interest rates.

Retained Life Estate

A donor may make a gift of his or her house to charity and retain the right to live in the house for the remainder of his or her life. The donor receives an immediate income tax deduction for the gift. As defined in federal tax law, donors irrevocably deed their home to a nonprofit but retain the right to live in it or use it for the rest of their lives or a term of years or both. In return, the donor receives an immediate tax deduction.

IMPORTANT POINTS TO CONSIDER

- "What would you like to accomplish with your gift?" may be one of the most powerful questions you can ask in discovering the purpose behind interest in a gift vehicle such as a charitable gift annuity or trust.

- Gifts of real estate can be important if structured correctly. Small and mid-size groups don't have to shy away from such gifts.

- In many cases today, it will not be worth the time, effort, hazard, or opportunity costs to establish a gift annuity program.

- With rare exceptions, small and mid-size groups will not want to take on the responsibility and burden of managing charitable trusts. However, donors can still be encouraged to designate small and mid-size groups as the beneficiary of any charitable trust.

- Most of the gifts in the category of planned gifts—perhaps more than 90 percent—comes from legacy gifts in the form of bequests. This is where most small and mid-size nonprofits should focus their time and attention. It is also where nonprofits of this size will be most competitive in terms of donor interests and needs.

- You may get calls asking for gift annuities or inquiries about setting up a charitable trust. There is a reason the prospective donor is calling you: they are interested in your work. Instead of saying, "That is not something we do," why not ask the question, "What would you like to accomplish with your gift?" This can lead you to a meaningful conversation about values and the impact of your work. Help them make the connections between a bequest, a legacy gift, and the impact their gift could have if you were to receive it.

Advisors Moving
to Center Stage

For decades, large nonprofit organizations were a primary source of information about charitable gift planning tools. In the past decade, all of that has changed. Charitable giving advice has now become a common product offering of professional advisors.

This shift was driven by a combination of changes in population demographics, wealth distribution, information distribution, and law. These changes, combined with the arrival of an array of new philanthropic partners and structural changes in the financial services industry, make the current world of professional advisors quite different from only a few years ago.

Today, when seeking detailed information about estate planning and the more complex forms of charitable gifts, donors increasingly turn to an array of professional advisors. This is good news for small and mid-size nonprofits. It means your donors won't expect you to provide them with detailed gift planning expertise or estate planning advice. Instead, you can focus on the most important thing: the intended use of the gift. With respect to the charitable decision as to

215

how and where the gift will be used, the nonprofit's staff or board member is *the* expert.

Although donors should be, and are, consulting professional advisors as they make their legal or financial plans, they still favor consulting nonprofit staff about their charitable decisions.[1] Table 13.1 lists sources of charitable advice based on 2006 and 2008 research reports.[2,3] The shift in expectations of prospective donors is clear.

This section is divided into two parts: the first for nonprofits; the second addressed to professional advisors and the importance of their role.

FOR NONPROFITS: WORKING WITH ADVISORS

The Good: Mary,[2] the executive director of a client organization, met with longtime donor Mr. Robinson. The 91-year-old donor told her he would like to make a bequest for $1,000,000. The next day she received a phone call from Mr. Robinson's attorney. He said, "I understand that you met with Mr. Robinson yesterday and that you did some paperwork with him about a $1 million gift. I have a problem with the paperwork, I don't think it's enough. Can we make this agreement for a million dollars a little more iron-clad?" The answer was, YES!

TABLE 13.1 Sources of Charitable Advice		
	2006 Report	**2008 Report**
Fundraisers/nonprofit staff	40.2%	26.0%
Peers or peer networks	35.9%	16.1%
Accountant	26.6%	44.3%
Financial/wealth advisor	16.6%	27.8%
Attorney	16.4%	44.9%
Foundation staff	15.1%	14.8%
Bank or trust co. staff	8.7%	16.5%
Broker	7.1%	9.9%

At the lawyer's insistence, a written agreement was created that promised a gift through the donor's estate when he passed. The ultimate result was an irrevocable bequest commitment for $1 million for the organization. Several donors later attributed this commitment as one of the main reasons that they made a larger current gift to the nonprofit.

The Bad: Several years ago, Roy, a retired doctor, and his wife planned to make a gift to an organization they both felt passionately about. After discussing the opportunity to diversity their portfolio, they made the decision to take a small portion of their assets to create a charitable trust. They called the planned giving officer with an invitation: "Let's get together with our trust officer and take care of the paperwork."

The nonprofit gift officer, along with Roy and his wife, met with the trust officer. After a brief introductory greeting the trust officer blurted out, "Why would you want to do this?" Roy and his wife were stunned. They expected a more deliberated response. They left the meeting disappointed and confused, with no gift on the horizon.

The nonprofit gift officer reflected on the meeting and noted that the trust officer, who was early in his career, didn't have a strong personal relationship with the donors and didn't understand what they dreamed to accomplish. As time passed and additional information surfaced, the "real" reason for the trust officer's exclamation that day became clear: The trust officer's first priority that day was his fee and the prospect of losing funds under his management.

Both stories suggest the power of professional advisors. The role an advisor plays in a donor's philanthropy decisions depends on trust. It's important to understand motivations and expectations as well. The actual role of an advisor or member of a team of advisors can be looked at in two ways: the point of view of the prospective donor or client and the point of view of the advisor.

From the perspective of your donor, the role of an advisor could be determined by the type of profession, the longevity of the relationship, the level of community involvement, or the ability of the advisor to understand and represent the prospective donor's desires and objectives. It may also be determined by positions in the community or by the fact there is interrelated business.

From the perspective of the advisor, drivers for them may be the nature of the business model for their practice; the volume of business they get or would like to get from this client (or the client's network); prospects for other business; professionalism (or perceived lack of it) on the part of the donor's charity; the form of compensation (fee only, hourly billing, commission, or fees based on assets under management); or their past experience working with a team of advisors or a charitable organization.

What Doesn't Work?

Over the past several years I surveyed more than 200 legal and financial professionals about what they see nonprofits do that influences donors (their clients). I asked, "What are nonprofits doing that hurts their connections with donors?" Here are the top two according to planning professionals:

- *Selfish or singular focus on only one charitable beneficiary.* Multiple research studies document that donors rarely make estate gifts benefiting only a single charity. Often a variety of charities are included, reflecting the lifetime values of the donor. Charities must recognize that simple fact. Consistently, reactions are negative to a singular focus: "Let's talk about MY organization, MY gift, THIS project." The reality is that professional planners urge clients to look at a larger philanthropy portfolio reflecting a range of donor interests. In my practice, when I preface a conversation about estate gifts by telling the donor/prospect that these approaches can be applied to any charity they wish to support, there is greater interest on their part throughout the entire process.

- *Lack of relationship coordination.* This comment is most often made with regard to larger organizations, but can be equally applicable to small to mid-size groups. The development officer doesn't talk to the activist e-alert coordinator, who doesn't talk to the project coordinator, who never mentioned it to the executive director. There are numerous reports of offended donors and cancelled gifts. The donor often views an organization as a whole, not the many different departments or arbitrary categories we create. In one case, a field worker was told by a major donor that the donor intended to make a bequest of his house and ranch to the nonprofit. It was a full two years before the field worker mentioned it to anyone else at the nonprofit. Imagine if you had informed your favorite nonprofit about intentions to make a meaningful gift and then were ignored for two years. Is the gift still in place? Were the donor's best interests served?

Professionals also were concerned about other things as well:

- *"Donors think you just care about their money."* This is just a reminder that no one is fooled. More than one donor has used the phrase "I sometimes feel like they think I am an ATM." A legacy gift will not result from this kind of relationship.

- *"Nonprofit staff forget that advisors need to be neutral as to the charity but versed in the tools of charitable giving."* It's easy to think that advisors control charitable gifts, but in several surveys advisors repeatedly stressed that they were not going to "steer" donors toward any one charity. However this sentiment on the part of professional advisors may be true less often than expressed, based on the actual experience of many development professionals. There are many examples of conduct representing both neutral advisors as well as those who advocate for specific charities.

- *Not enough long-term cultivation.* "But I hardly know you" might be the unvoiced thought of the donor when asked for a major or estate gift. The pressure to close gifts within some arbitrary fiscal or calendar year hinders larger success. Buck Smith, the creator of Moves Management, asks himself the question, "What is it that I can do each month that will penetrate the consciousness of the individual about my work or our organization?" He offers good advice. How do you connect with your top prospects? How would they like you to connect with them?

- *Nonprofit business practices are not what they should be.* Too often nonprofits don't operate with the financial planning, internal controls, gift recording, and financial processing procedures that demonstrate they intend to be in business for the long haul. How will you demonstrate that your nonprofit could responsibly accept, account for, and use a large gift?

What Works?

Many testimonials report that the marketing done by the nonprofit community is working and that donors are becoming aware of charitable estate gift opportunities. Here are some of the professional advisors' responses to the survey question, "What are nonprofits doing right?" based on interactions with their clients (your donors):

- *"Focusing on their mission."* Many compliments were directed toward nonprofit staff that focused on the careful matching of mission and donor interests. These comments suggest that advisors and donors place greater value on understanding how their gifts will be put to work, rather than on the details of specific charitable gift techniques.

- *"As boomers retire, they'll need something to do."* Many will eventually become volunteers and the best source of legacy gifts to organizations to which they donate their time. Volunteer development is now key.

- *"Focusing on the passion of the donor for the work of the nonprofit."* With increased awareness and knowledge, advisors rely less on any individual charity for their technical information.

- *"Everyone appreciates a time to connect without the pressure."* Professional planners report that such "no-strings-attached" stewardship does work and *is of value to their clients.*

Involve Advisors in Program Work, Not Legal Advice

One of the clear themes in comments from advisors surveyed is that they would like to get more involved with nonprofits—but more on the service and program side, and less on the legal or technical side.

Nonprofit organizations have a wonderful opportunity to involve professional planners in new ways. From the nonprofit perspective, getting advisors involved in the more emotion-oriented side of your work can help advisors feel more comfortable expanding a discussion of values with their clients. Providing substantive volunteer opportunities enables advisors to connect with and better understand your guiding mission. Through such volunteer work, they will see firsthand the impact of your work. It also allows them to garner experiences they can turn into stories to share with their clients, and this strengthens the advisor's relationship with clients.

When You Need Advice

There will be times when you need to talk to a well-versed legal or financial professional, or a loyal donor will ask you for a referral. If you have taken the time to invite local planners into your organization as volunteers, many will volunteer time to answer a question from time to time. In more complex situations, it would be appropriate to retain their professional services. You may be tempted to ask for a donation of time and professional services. If the matter involves a large bequest or prospective gift, it will be worth it to pay for services. In fact, I strongly recommend you immediately offer to pay their going rates because you will get focused attention and better service. Later, you may get a discounted bill, or perhaps gift referrals.

Professional advisors are compensated in a variety of ways, including fee only, hourly billing, commission, or fees based on assets under management. If you demonstrate that you respect their professional skills and commonly accepted billing practices, you will create allies and the possibility of future referrals. If you demonstrate ignorance, you will lose potential friends.

Here's an example of how one nonprofit not only lost an ally but soured an entire office of brokers on nonprofit gifts. Securities brokers are often compensated by commission on sales. When a prominent broker brought up the idea of making a $4 million gift to a nonprofit, his client quickly agreed. Immediately the nonprofit whisked the stock away to another firm and sold it using another broker. From the nonprofit's perspective, the move was efficient in that they only had to maintain one stock account. From the broker's perspective the quick transfer was both a business and a personal insult. Privately, this socially prominent broker was later heard to describe this nonprofit in negative terms. He also publicly pledged never to suggest to his clients that they make any large gift to this nonprofit; his other brokers adopted the same perspective. Was being efficient by not taking the time to open a local securities account worth the cost to the nonprofit? Did ignorance of the compensation structure send the wrong message to the broker? If your purpose was to build a relationship, an ally, and a source of future gift referrals, what might you have done differently in this situation?

Build a Reference List

It's important that the donor freely choose their own professional advisor. Occasionally, a donor may ask you for a referral for an attorney or estate planner. It's not appropriate for you to give them a single, specific referral. Instead, create a list of possible advisors to present to donors. Suggest they contact one or more of the professionals on the list and interview each to discover the best fit for their personal situation. The choice of professional is an important one and must be made by the donor, not the nonprofit. A sample questionnaire to help you document and build your advisor list is in the Resources section (see Advisors Referral Form).

For many organizations, particularly those involved in advocacy work, it will be important to identify and create a list of advisors sympathetic to your cause. Although rare, I have observed instances in which attorneys who are political opposites stall large gifts and in the process provide prospective donors with questionable advice.

Having the sympathetic ear of an advisor will help when a donor explains how they would like their charitable gift used, say, for immediate political activism, which is not a "traditional" use for a bequest. Even in these instances, it will still be important for the donor—not the nonprofit—to choose her own advisor.

Do You Need a Planned Giving Committee?

"Start a planned giving committee" is a command that appears on virtually every nonprofit's checklist. But it's time to review the reasons it was placed on the checklist. Are those reasons still valid for *your* situation? Today, most often the answer will be "no."

There is some historical background to consider. From the 1950s through the 1990s charitable organizations were *the* deferred gift, planned gift, or gift planning experts. Planned giving committees were wonderful tools used to disseminate the how-to and technical nature of this work to the professional community. At the same time the charity could demonstrate its technical prowess and ability to manage trusts and other complex arrangements. It was good business networking for both charities and the professionals involved. Dramatic changes in the nature of this relationship occurred in the 1990s and 2000s.

Today, planned giving is a frequent and common topic at legal and financial planning conferences and continuing education events. In addition, the array of philanthropic financial products and providers is staggering and was unimagined only 10 years ago. Legal and financial advisors have aggressively expanded and now often include the phrase "charitable gift planning" in their list of services offered.

There is much less incentive for a planning professional to participate in a planned giving committee, because in many communities there are many such committees diluting their individual value. More often, today's committees are used by professionals looking for clients. Of course, there are exceptions, and you must factor in the unique characteristics of your organization, community, and location.

With this background in mind, here are some questions to help focus on what your organization needs. Explore these questions with your board members, planned gift donors, and prospective committee members.

- Why do you want a planned giving committee? What specific outcomes will you accomplish by creating, staffing, and maintaining one?

- Do you need a committee? What role or need in your organization will this fulfill?

- What purposes will this committee serve? How will your members know it is accomplishing its goals?

- How will it make a positive difference in your work raising money today and in the future?

- Will this group be primarily used to help market planned gifts? (Remember, many professional advisors will publicly and emphatically assert that they must be "charity-neutral" when working with their own clients.)

- Will the committee members accompany you on donor visits and help make your relationship-building and, ultimately, your solicitation more credible?

- Or will its role be primarily to provide "free" technical advice to you or to a planned or major gift officer in your organization? Do you really just need permission to call a few trusted, friendly advisors occasionally for a quick "reality check" about a gift or donor interaction?

- How will it benefit local or regional professionals to participate?

- Do you need a committee to help with policies and recommendations to the board? Would several task force groups focused on, for example, investment policy, gift policy, or endowment spending policy, fulfill your short-term objectives?

- Do you need advocates for planned giving? Do you need help to address organizational politics?

- Do you need assistance with board members and help encouraging them to make their own gifts?

- Do you need help with communicating or explaining some of the legal and financial requirements and responsibilities of managing planned gifts of all shapes and sizes?

- Are you looking for ways to bolster internal support for expanded planned gift marketing?

FOR ADVISORS: ADVISORS ARE IMPORTANT

"For advisors who wish to be their clients' primary advisor, it is essential to engage the client's charitable side. When this subject (of charitable planning) is raised, the advisory role changes, almost always for the better. Clients seldom expect to be engaged about their dreams, ideals, hopes, and concepts of worth and significance," writes King McGlaughon, executive vice president and chief academic officer at The American College.

"When an advisor is able to do so, she or he is perceived as much as a confidant and colleague as a service provider. Advisors generally find this kind of engagement very satisfying once they understand the longer-term benefits to their own business that can follow—not to mention the 'intangible' lift in the advisor's sense of personal and professional accomplishment that inevitably results from such conversations."[3]

Many financial- or legal planning opportunities can also be an excellent time to begin discussing charitable strategies that could have useful planning or tax implications. (See Exhibit 13.1 for a list of examples.)

Exhibit 13.1 Clues to Trigger Opportunities to Talk about Charitable Plans

Here is a short list of opportunities for gift planning that may combine tax, timing, and charitable advantages. Each concept is followed by several possible charitable gift options. A detailed discussion of each is beyond the focus of this book. Rather, briefly noting these situations or trigger points may stimulate useful discussions about charitable gifts.

- Selling appreciated property (gifts of assets for tax deductions)
- Taking a closely held business public (various trust and gift options for donations, establishing valuation, easing transfer, buyback of shares, and more)
- Selling appreciated stock (it can be a very cost-effective gift when compared to cash)
- "It's time to talk about a family foundation or plans for the next generation."
- A colleague or family friend has passed away and the estate was not handled as well as it could have been. "How can I avoid that?" the client asks.

- A wish to make a gift to a housekeeper or other such persons (A charitable trust or a gift annuity could give a housekeeper or trusted friend lifetime income.)

- Receiving a large bonus, several payments, lottery winnings, or other one-time payments (Gifts or vehicles such as a charitable trust could be used to soften the tax impact, set aside for retirement, or provide a one-time special gift for charity.)

- The client has low-yielding securities but is grumbling about capital gains taxes (Charitable gift vehicle examples may be just the thing to trigger a good discussion.)

- Large IRA or retirement account balances (Recent legislation allows special transfers; gifts of IRA funds can be tax-advantaged ways to give compared with other assets.)

- Desire to transfer the business to heirs (various trust and gift options for donations, establishing valuation, easing transfer, buyback of shares, and more)

- Unmarried family or partners who wish to financially benefit others in their estate planning (a charitable trust or gift annuity can provide income, professional fund management, and economic support for loved ones)

- International travel to unique, unstable, or very isolated locations ("If something were to occur, what would you like to make sure happens?")

One of the most useful things an estate planning attorney might do for an organization he supports is to provide will preparation assistance to staff members. Rather than spend time in meetings that don't go anywhere, help staff understand how a will is constructed, what goes into the thinking in making up a will, and help them with their personal situation. Too many nonprofit staff do not have wills. How can you realistically ask someone else to make estate plans including a charitable bequest if you have not done so yourself? And, without the experience of having made a will, the staff person will likely not have the empathy or shared experience necessary to make the conversation meaningful to the prospective donor.

The Usual Questions: Do They Get the Usual Answers?

"Do you have any philanthropic intent?" or "Do you want to leave anything to charity in your estate?" are common questions advisors pose to clients. Such questions technically address the topic but may not truly enable a fruitful discussion of the larger questions and values that drive charitable bequest choices. One retired doctor with whom I worked wanted to "die broke";[4] he managed his affairs to provide himself with a stable lifetime income and made liberal use of large charitable gift annuities with his favorite charities. His financial advisors were aghast. So he sought help and established business relationships elsewhere. Would the result have been different if the financial advisor had sought to understand and perhaps begun a new conversation with an open-ended question like "How do you view your circumstances today?"

Open-ended questions are valuable opportunities to begin conversations about the future, as well as explore dreams and values. Here's an excellent one to further a conversation about philanthropy:

"If you had unlimited resources, what would you do _____ (to help, make the world a better place, etc.)?"

More questions to expand a positive conversation might include:

"What excites you most about the future?"

"In which of your traits and characteristics do you take the most pride?"

"Where have you achieved your greatest successes?"[5]

"For what do you want to be known?"

IMPORTANT POINTS TO CONSIDER

- The shift toward donor use of advisors continues to grow rapidly. This is good news for small and mid-size nonprofits because that means you can focus on what is most important to donors: the ultimate use of any estate gift. You don't have to be an expert on the technical aspects of estate planning, nor will your donors expect such advice from you.

- The advice most often proffered to nonprofits regarding professional advisors is to "form a planned giving committee." This is another tired habit that will not likely serve small and mid-size groups or the advisors who support those groups. There is value in identifying local professionals you could call on for advice when needed—but you don't need to create, staff, and maintain a committee.

- From the perspective of fundraising and real impact, involve estate planning professionals as volunteers in your program work, but not legal projects. If you enable them to discover the real value of your work, they could become passionate advocates for your mission in the larger community. They will benefit from the experiences as well.

- Don't be afraid to pay for professional advice. There will be times when friendly, pro-bono advice just won't be enough. Remember that professionals are appropriately compensated in many different ways, ranging from hourly rates to fixed fees to commissions. Honor their professional services and fee structures. Focus on relationships with them, because their future goodwill and referrals have far greater value and fundraising potential than any minor cost savings you might accrue today as a result of pushing for discounted fees, pro bono services, or donated projects.

Transparency and Ethics

Any discussion of ethics and transparency seems fraught with difficulties about definitions. There is a difference between compliance with the law, compliance with the spirit of the law, convenience, ethical behavior, and the interests of donors. Certainly, they overlap, but they may not always be a perfect match—and therein lies the rub.

Of course, there is a rather complex set of IRS and Treasury Department regulations defining charitable giving and prescribing nonprofit behaviors. Many laws and regulations were written in reaction to real and perceived abuses. Even the creation of the legal category of nonprofit in the 1950s was a reaction to a growing trend of activities that were "not quite for profit" in nature. The drafters of the legislation never imagined the size that the nonprofit community would become, and as such, much of that structure could stand to be reexamined in light of the value, consequence, and role nonprofits now have in our society.

Faced with a complex assembly of laws and regulations crafted primarily in reaction to abuses, my personal rule of thumb is that "a gift is a gift." That is, you freely present something of use or value to another without the expectation of something in return, save perhaps gratitude or an acknowledgment. A gift cannot be described as a "real deal" (except when you get to brag about the impact the gift made). If it sounds like a real deal, it's worth questioning—or perhaps rejecting.

Transparency is another concept with an evolving, expanding definition. In a time in which transparency is increasingly valued, nonprofits have a long way to go to live up to expectations donors already hold about disclosure and making information available. It is not enough to be willing to disclose something; rather the information must be accessible. Today, the definition of "accessible" is that it can be readily discovered on your website.

TRANSPARENCY

Trust in a nonprofit, its mission, and its leaders is a critical component of the donor's decision to complete a legacy gift. In turn, transparency and ethics are key themes in how donors experience or assess how much trust to place in your nonprofit. If defined in a formula, it might look like this:

Trust = transparency + accomplishments + leadership.

In the political realm, transparency is described as clarity about a range of areas, including who gives money to candidates, access to the voting records of public officials, and information about who gets government contracts and whether the contractors produce the results promised. Said differently, it is the ability of citizens and voters to see the trail of money, taxes as well as contributions and money spent to influence lawmakers, coupled with the ability to link to the results. There is continuing and growing public interest in greater transparency from a range of political interests of many persuasions.

How will your donors be able to track how their gift is used and the impact it makes? Their interest in greater transparency will only increase. Accountability and ethical issues will also continue to become more important to nonprofit board

Exhibit 14.1 Website Transparency Checklist

- Your 990 in PDF format
- Annual budget
- Balance sheet
- Income and expense statement
- Annual report
- Profiles of key staff (pictures help personalize this)
- Profiles of board members, including their affiliations for background or identification purposes
- Description of board conflict-of-interest policy
- What are the key metrics that measure your success?
- How did you choose these metrics?
- Using these metrics, how are you doing?
- What are the standards for your work, or a report card, that can demonstrate you are doing the right work and producing the right results?
- A short description of how your organization views transparency and what you do to foster sharing information
- Consider posting the salaries of all employees. The top salaries must already be disclosed by law on the IRS form 990. Such forms are already accessible over the Internet by anyone with a yen to search for it. If anything, it might embolden donors to suggest that wages must be higher! (And in the cases of many rank-and-file nonprofit staff, this is quite accurate.)

members, foundations, and other responsible observers such as states' attorneys general. How will you respond? Exhibit 14.1 contains a basic starting list against which you can compare your current efforts with regard to transparency.

Additional resources: The Minnesota Council of Nonprofits has assembled a webpage with several dozen links to resources related to ethics, accountability, and transparency. It can be found at http://www.mncn.org/

info_paccountability.htm. While this resource is focused on a single state, many of the articles and links have wider applicability. Additionally, the Ethics Resource Center's website (http://www.ethics.org) provides guidance for those in the professional world.

TAKE THE HIGH ROAD

"I want to write you a check for $3,000," he said. That got my attention. He was a longtime donor, and I was new in my position with the nonprofit. "But," he continued, "can we do the same thing we did last year for credit at the auction?" He explained that in the past years he had made a donation for several thousand dollars, gotten a receipt documenting his gift for tax purposes, and later was given a credit to use to bid on items at the annual auction.

As a reader, you already know what's going on here. If you get a benefit in return for the check you write to a charity, you can't also deduct the amount of that benefit from your taxes. Tax law is quite clear on this matter. But in day-to-day activities, it sometimes gets a little blurry.

In this case, I had an advantage as a new employee with no history to bind me. I explained that if we accepted his gift and later gave him credit at the auction to buy things for himself, the nonprofit would have to notify him (and the IRS) of the benefit he received, effectively canceling out any tax deduction. By the tone of his voice, it was apparent he already knew this. He said thank you and hung up. It felt like I had not only lost a gift I had also lost a donor. To my surprise a check for $3,000 showed up soon after—with no strings attached. He also attended the auction and was a solid bidder that year. Take the high road and those around you will follow your example.

EASY MONEY AND HOW TO LIE WITH STATISTICS

In recent years a very resourceful insurance salesman created a plan to insure board members and older donors of nonprofits. This pool of insurance would pay death benefits to the charity. The plan called for an investment in insurance policies that would eventually result in an endowment fund of millions of dollars for a cost of only pennies on the dollar. Variations of these insurance plans would insure pools of donors, board members, and staff, among others.

Armed with a positive-sounding opinion from a law firm, this scheme was introduced in many places around the United States. The first time I heard it described I thought it was interesting but a little too good to be true. Many groups rejected the concept outright, saying it did not quite pass the smell test. They were right.

At the same time, many groups diligently invested time and effort to explore the option in search of easy money. They used board and staff time that could have had greater impact by building relationships in the community or focusing on the core work of the organization.

It later turned out that huge commissions were paid up front to the originators of the policies, and the IRS ultimately raised questions. Soon the IRS ruled against the plans. Legal entanglements and court cases promptly followed.

USING THE RIGHT QUESTIONS

Sometimes an arrangement acceptable between business owners is inappropriate between a business owner and a nonprofit executive because of the different standards of trust and public accountability. In the case of two business owners, there is a clear exchange of value by willing participants. In the case of the nonprofit, it has received its tax-exempt status and donors their tax deductions in return for the good they contribute to our society. Also, specific tax advantages are granted to nonprofit donors to encourage and stimulate gifts for the public good. The ground rules are different, and as a donor and nonprofit leader, I invite you to bring that larger perspective to your giving and interactions with nonprofits.

Over the years, I have found that considering the spirit in which the law was created is a useful rule of thumb and can quickly provide a useful answer or clue to the right answer. Here are few more informal guidelines I have observed nonprofit leaders use with success:

- Does it conform to the Model Standards of Practice for the Charitable Gift Planner? A copy is reprinted in the Resources section. Additional guidelines on the reporting and counting of charitable gifts can be found on the website of the Partnership for Philanthropic Planning at http://www.pppnet.org.

- Is it really a gift? (The first answer the voice in your head blurts out is the one that counts the most: yes or no?) A gift is intended to be a gift. It has cost. Of course, there are a number of tax incentives specifically created to encourage or subsidize giving, and no one wants to miss out on those along the way.

- We don't want to ignore the tax benefits, but when an arrangement is driven primarily by tax considerations and not philanthropy, is there something underneath that requires examination?

- If it's "easy money," what are the assumptions that underlie the plan? Is there a hidden assumption that could topple everything?

- When there is a clear lack of philanthropic intent on the part of the prospective donor, I notice the gift is rarely, if ever, completed. Thus, if you suspect low intent, ask yourself if it is still worth investing scarce staff and volunteer time to explore the details. I have found that most volunteer board members or nonprofit staff can readily answer yes or no to this question. It is difficult to say no to a large potential gift—but are you saying no to the gift or to your dream of what you might do if you got such a gift? They are not the same thing. Saying no to the specific possibility of a gift is not saying no to the dream.

- Is the proposed arrangement or gift an example of creativity and a solution to a sticky problem or situation? Or is it a scheme for someone else's benefit?

- When does the charity have an actual gift in hand? The IRS defines the date of a gift at the point at which a nonprofit has full control over the gift. Some financial arrangements place that control at a distant point in the future. Is that fair? Appropriate?

- How will the gift be used? Will it be used to further the mission? Or is it severely restricted? If restricted, can the restrictions be accommodated or will they cost you to accept them?

- Are there any special arrangements that benefit the people making the gift arrangements (such as special use or access to land or a house, scholarships for family members, "complimentary" tickets to special events, and so on)?

- What are the motivations of the parties involved? I recall the owner of a former battery shop trying to "donate" the land on which the business had operated for many years. An inspection revealed many unlabeled drums filled with foul-smelling liquids. Was this a gift, or an escape strategy for the donor?

- Who benefits and how? This is a simple question, but the answer can be powerful if the questions is carefully considered.
- What are the transaction costs involved? In the past, businessmen who were used to being hard negotiators insisted charities pick up all sorts of transaction costs. Although this may be appropriate, even expected, in business transactions, in effect they benefit the donor. If they benefit the donor, the IRS says it counts as income or reduces the value of any tax deduction. At what point do transaction costs benefit the donor? At what point is it in the best interests of the nonprofit to incur costs?
- How are the parties compensated?
- Does it feel like a gift or a negotiated deal?
- What part of the transaction is in the form of a gift to charity? (Some family limited partnerships were structured with a tiny sliver given to charity as a way to enable a heavily discounted ownership share to heirs. Is this a gift or a scheme?)
- If you were asked by a news reporter, how would you describe the role of philanthropic intent in the gift?
- If the gift were described in detail, perhaps accompanied by a picture in the local newspaper, would you be pleased to read about it? Would all of your board members be pleased? Why, or why not?

IMPORTANT POINTS TO CONSIDER

- The phrase "too good to be true" has been around since at least the year 1580 for good reason. If a proposed gift sounds too good to be true, it probably is, and it's time to ask some hard questions before you invest too much time or effort.
- Donor interest in greater transparency will only increase. How will your donors be able to track how their gift is used and the impact it makes? Accountability and ethical issues will continue to become more important to boards of nonprofits, to donors, and to outside observers such as states' attorneys general. How will you respond?
- Trust = transparency + record of accomplishments + leadership
- Trust is a cornerstone of the process donors use to make legacy gift decisions.

Trust
+ Answers to Hidden Questions
+ Vision
+ Plans
= Donor Confidence
Donor Confidence = Gifts

AFTERWORD

For many years during my fundraising career, I thought that bequests and legacy gifts were all about elderly widows. It took me a long time to discover that this was the fundraising equivalent of an urban myth.

Consider the opportunity gap between the 8 percent to 9 percent of Americans who have named a charity in their will or estate plan, and the 30 percent to 40 percent who are willing to do so. Or the fact that one of the more important factors in bequest giving is to be named in the first will, which is often written between the ages of 40 and 60. It is true that, ultimately, bequests come from predominantly older donors, often women, but focusing primarily on them using transaction-based sales and marketing tactics is an approach doomed to fail for many small and mid-size nonprofits.

Researcher Adrian Sargeant, the Robert F. Hartsook Professor of Fundraising at the Center on Philanthropy at Indiana University, uses the word *abysmal* to describe how nonprofits are faring today with regard to building a stream of bequest and legacy gifts. Too often nonprofits focus their strategies on "transactional" strategies and tactics of raising money, rather than on the givers and the causes they care about. "Best practices" practiced out of context, scale, and decade—reinforced more by habit than by evidence and research—will take time to change. More and more research demonstrates that donors care less and less for artificial nonprofit campaigns and deadlines; instead, they focus on the impact of the gift and the difference it could make in the world. Often their focus is on helping those who have less than they do.

For small and mid-size groups, the social context of giving can also make a profound difference. When people of all ages, incomes, and social statuses come together to declare that your nonprofit's work has an important place in the future, the results can be powerful. Using the four steps—setting the stage, building trust and credibility, reaching a tipping point, and going public—will help you build that social context for giving and inspire gifts both today and in the future.

As a nonprofit leader, you can focus on bequests like transactions and ask donors to "make a bequest today." Or, you can choose to focus on the donor's legacy that manifests the link between their values, resources, and dreams, and the impact their gift will help your nonprofit to make in the many years to come.

Imagine the dreams you can help make come true.

READING LIST

Many of the books and "best practices" on this topic are based on larger institutional models of operation. These models can still work for the biggest groups with long-established programs. This short selection of books may be helpful to staff and volunteers at small and mid-size groups as they expand their knowledge about legacy giving. (*Note:* Detailed references for each book follow at the end of the narrative.)

Robert Sharpe's *Planned Giving Simplified* (1999, revised) was an excellent introductory book for its time. Although it still has value and relevance, notable parts of it have become less relevant as demographics, donor attitudes, and non-profit trends evolved in the decade after it was printed (and two economic/political shocks later).

Similarly, Doug White's *The Art of Planned Giving* (1995) contains some excellent discussion about the processes of making a gift, although significant portions of it are no longer applicable due to changes in tax law and the marketplace.

Linda S. Moerschbaecher's *Start at Square One* (1998), like *Planned Giving for Small Nonprofits* (2002) and *Planned Giving Workbook* (2002) by Ronald Jordan and Katelyn Quinn, are useful for "small" nonprofits if you define *small* as an organization with 5 to 10 dedicated development staff. For example, one of the implicit assumptions of *Planned Giving for Small Nonprofits* is that the organization be able to hire its own attorney/planned giving officer for planned giving work.

As a technical reference, no book matches Debra Ashton's The *Complete Guide to Planned Giving* (2004, revised 3rd edition). It is an excellent reference book, and one I highly recommend to anyone who want lots of easy-to-access information about many technical topics.

An endowment is one of the tools used in fundraising. Books on endowment funds might be likened to books about how to do a capital campaign or a major gifts campaign—that is, they focus on a project. *Endowment* is a term used to describe when a gift might be used. Many different fundraising approaches can be combined to build up an endowment fund. Current gifts, direct mail, planned gifts, bequests, monthly gifts, and so on can all be used. Often people equate endowment with bequests more as a stereotype, recognizing that larger, more public bequests are sometimes directed to be spent over time as part of an endowment fund.

There are several books on building endowments, including *Nonprofit Essentials: Endowment Building* (2005) by Diana Newman and *Building Your Endowment* (2003) by Edward Schumacher.

Notes

Ashton, Debra. *The Complete Guide to Planned Giving: Everything You Need to Know to Compete Successfully for Major Gifts.* Rev. 3rd ed. Quincy, MA: Ashton Associates, 2004.

Jordan, Ronald R., and Katelyn L. Quinn. *Planned Giving for Small Nonprofits.* New York: Wiley, 2002.

Jordan, Ronald R., and Katelyn L. Quinn. *Planned Giving Workbook.* New York: Wiley, 2002.

Moerschbaecher, Linda S. *Start at Square One: Starting and Managing the Planned Gift Program.* Chicago: Precept Press, 1998.

Newman, Diana S. *Nonprofit Essentials: Endowment Building.* New York: Wiley, 2005.

Schumacher, Edward C. *Building Your Endowment.* New York: Wiley, 2003.

Sharp, Robert F., Sr. *Planned Giving Simplified: The Gift, The Giver, and the Gift Planner.* New York: Wiley, 1999.

White, Douglas E. *The Art of Planned Giving: Understanding Donors and the Culture of Giving.* New York: Wiley, 1995.

BOOKS FOCUSED ON UNDERSTANDING DONORS

Hillman, James. *The Force of Character and the Lasting Life.* New York: Random House, 1999. An exploration of psychological and spiritual aspects of aging. Many planned giving officers are one, two, or three generations distant from their clients. This book may help bridge that gap.

Pollan, Stephen, and Mark Levine. *Die Broke.* New York: HarperBusiness, 1997. You will be surprised at how many unquestioned financial assumptions run your life. Understand your financial decisions and those of your donors in a new way.

Stanley, Thomas, and William Danko. *The Millionaire Next Door.* Athens, GA: Longstreet Press, 1996. A stereotype-breaking view and a must-read book. How many donors have you missed or inadvertently ignored?

Willis, Thayer. *Navigating the Dark Side of Wealth*. Nashport, OH: New Concord Press, 2003. A wealth therapist (and heiress) provides insights about the emotional aspects of wealth to help you professionally (and personally).

BOOKS FOCUSED ON VALUES

Grace, Kay Sprinkel. *Beyond Fundraising*. New York: Wiley, 1997. A focus on relationships with donor-investors and how a request for a gift is less an appeal for money than an invitation to join and invest in a process that will pay dividends in a stronger community.

Prince, Russ Alan, and Karen Maru File. *Seven Faces of Philanthropy*. New York: Jossey-Bass, 1994. People give for different reasons. That's not news, but we often forget and then fail to effectively make our case for a gift as result. I have to admit my biggest fundraising mistakes were the result of assuming people made charitable gifts for the same reason I did. This book will disabuse you of many inaccurate assumptions. It's a must-read for fundraisers and board members. If you read it long ago, it is worth exploring again. You may be pleasantly surprised at how it reading it again may recast (positively) some of your hard-earned fundraising lessons.

Sturdevant, William. *The Artful Journal: Cultivating and Soliciting the Major Gift*. Santa Monica, CA: Bonus Books, 1997. A step-by-step guide through the process of cultivation, solicitation, and stewardship.

CHAPTER 4

A Word document file of this example is included in premium web content.

Preparing for Estate Planning with Your Attorney

In preparing for an estate planning meeting with your attorney, you will need the following documents and information:

Personal Information

Date this form was completed:			
Legal Name	First	Middle	Last
Spouse	First	Middle	Last
Permanent Address			
Street			

City	State	Zip
Date of Birth (Self)	(Spouse)	
Telephone (Home)	(Work)	
Soc. Sec. # (Self)	(Spouse)	
Birth Certificate Location	Copy Location	
Date of Marriage	Place of Marriage	

If divorced or separated: Include names and dates of previous marriages, whether the marriage ended by divorce or legal separation, and the location of papers.

If spouse is deceased, include these details:

Name of spouse:	Date of marriage:
Date of death:	
Location of will:	
Location of federal estate tax return:	
Location of gift tax returns:	

There ☐ is ☐ is not a prenuptial agreement.

Location of prenuptial agreement

U.S. citizen? ☐ Yes ☐ No

If not a U.S. citizen by birth, indicate date and place of naturalization

Naturalization Date	Place
Naturalization Papers Located	
Other Citizenship	

Spouse: U.S. citizen? ☐ Yes ☐ No

If not a U.S. citizen by birth, indicate date and place of naturalization

Naturalization Date	Place
Naturalization Papers Located	
Other Citizenship	

Nearest Relatives List in this order:

1. Children

2. Grandchildren

3. Brothers and/or sisters

4. Parents

5. Nieces and/or nephews

Name	Relationship	Date of Birth	Address

Property and Personal Property Include personal effects, art or other collections, automobile(s), jewelry, household effects, furniture, artifacts, etc.

Item	Location	Approximate Value if Sold Today
		$
	Total	$

Cash (Checking, Savings, and Money Market)

Bank and Address	Title[a]	Account Number	Amount
			$

[a]"Title" refers to who owns title to the account. Options include husband, wife, jointly (indicate joint tenant if not spouse).

Certificates of Deposit

Bank and Address	Certificate Number	Maturity Date	Title[a]	Amount
				$

[a]"Title" refers to who owns title to the account. Options include husband, wife, jointly (indicate joint tenant if not spouse).

Stocks, Bonds, Mutual Funds Held in Brokerage Accounts

Name of Broker/Account	Number of Shares	Company	Title[a]	Value
				$
				$

[a]"Title" refers to who owns title to the account. Options include husband, wife, jointly (indicate joint tenant if not spouse).

Securities Not Held in a Brokerage Account

Type of Security	Title[a]	Serial Number	Date of Purchase	Amount
				$

[a]"Title" refers to who owns title to the account. Options include husband, wife, jointly (indicate joint tenant if not spouse).

Location of Any Stock Certificates, Bonds, Options, etc., That Are Not Held in Brokerage Accounts

Money Invested in Mortgages, Personal Loans, Trust Deeds (that is, money owed to you)

With Whom and Address	Cost when Acquired	Title[a]	Current Value
			$

[a]"Title" refers to who owns title to the account. Options include husband, wife, jointly (indicate joint tenant if not spouse).

Real Estate Owned

Type of Property and Location	Cost when Acquired	Title[a]	Current Value	Debt/Lender
			$	
			$	

[a]"Title" refers to who owns title to the account. Options include husband, wife, jointly (indicate joint tenant if not spouse).

Other Assets

Type of Property	Title[a]	Cost Basis	Date of Investment	Current Value
				$
				$

[a]"Title" refers to who owns title to the account. Options include husband, wife, jointly (indicate joint tenant if not spouse).

Life Insurance You Own (on Your Own Life)

Company	Type of Policy	Beneficiary	Amount
			$
		Total	$

Companies or Organizations That Own Insurance Policies on Your Life

Company	Type of Policy	Beneficiary	Amount
			$

Insurance Owned by You on the Lives of Others

Company	Type of Policy	Insured	Beneficiary	Amount
				$

Location of Life Insurance Policies

Other Insurance

Company	Type of Policy	Policy Number	Coverage

Individual Retirement Accounts, Pensions, Retirement or Death Benefit Plans

Fund Name and Company	Account Number	Beneficiary	Telephone	Amounts
				$
			Total	$

Safe Deposit Boxes

Box Location	Box Number	Key location	Name of Others with Access

☐ I am currently ☐ I expect to be the beneficiary of a bequest

Testator's name_____

Approximate value $_____

Total approximate value of estate $_____

☐ I am currently ☐ I expect to be the beneficiary of other income or assets

Source's name_____

Approximate value $_____

Location of Any Employment Contracts or Business Agreements Relating to Interests In Corporations, Partnerships, and Sole Proprietorships

What You Owe

Loans

To Whom Debt or Mortgage Is Owed	Address	Payment Date	Amount
			$
			$
Total Approximate Indebtedness			$

Trusts

Location of any Trusts That You Have Created, or under Which You Are a Beneficiary:

Tax Records

Location of Tax Records:

Persons

Persons, Other Than Nearest Relatives, Whom You Wish to Include in Your Estate Planning:

Name	Relationship
Address	
Name	Relationship
Address	
Name	Relationship
Address	

Religious/Spiritual Organization(s)

Religious/Spiritual Advisor(s)

Executor

Name/Telephone _____

Address____ _____

_____

Alternative Executor

Name/Telephone _____

Address _____

_____

Guardian for Your Children

Name/Telephone _____

Address _____

_____

Alternative Guardian for Your Children

Name/Telephone _____

Address _____

_____

Trustee for Children's Interests

Name/Telephone _____

Address _____

_____

Your Accountant

Name/Telephone _____

Address _____

_____

Your Attorney

Name/Telephone _____

Address _____

_____

Your Financial Planner

Name/Telephone _____

Address _____

_____

_____

Plan Your Estate Distribution Describe every specific asset that you want to go to a certain individual or nonprofit group here. Also, if you wish to give a specific sum of money to a person or charity, state the amount and the name.

Asset Designation

Person or Nonprofit	Address	Item, Property, or Sum of Money	Location of Asset

Information for Charities

Charity or Nonprofit Name	Address and Federal Tax ID Number	Telephone	Amounts ($ or % of estate)

After the specific bequests (if any), the simplest way to divide the rest of your estate is by percentages. Name the person or charity you wish to remember, and then state what percentage of the total remaining amount of your estate each is to receive.

	%
	%

Arrangements Location of Living Will or Medical Directives Order
My Preferred Funeral and Burial Instructions Are:

Letter of Last Instructions You may wish to write a letter of last instructions to your surviving spouse or other persons. Although it is not legally binding, it can enable you to communicate, in an informal and loving way, personal expressions, helpful information, or specific instructions, such as:

- The reason you made gifts to charities in your will and estate plan
- Location of your will, safe deposit boxes, important papers, and records
- Names and addresses of persons to help surviving spouse
- Names, addresses, and telephone numbers of individuals you wish to be notified of your death
- Funeral and burial instructions

TAXES: SAME SONG, DIFFERENT DAY

What Is the Estate Tax? Today, the Internal Revenue Code levies taxes on transfers of property at death (the estate tax), during life (gift tax), and to grandchildren or other descendants (the generation-skipping tax). Currently, the federal estate tax starts at 37 percent and rises to 55 percent.

The estate tax is levied on everything you own at death. It often includes assets on which no tax has ever been paid. This tax can be postponed until the death of your spouse. While tax is owed on the first dollar of the estate, the unified credit (or "exemption") allowed cancels out any tax owed until the estate reaches $7,000,000 for a married couple or $3,500,000 for a single person. In effect, an estate of a married couple of up to $7,000,000 would probably pay no tax at all but may pay income on other assets in the estate. As of publication (early 2010), changes were expected.

Does the Federal Estate Tax Affect You? Probably not. Tax law changes in the past decade have increased the threshold level for federal estate taxes. At current levels, 99.7 percent of the households in the United States will *not* be subject to such a tax.

Viewed another way, under 2009 law, only about 140 businesses and farms in the entire United States will be subject to paying estate tax in 2011. Even though the vast majority of estates will not be subject to actually paying any federal estate taxes, it is still prudent to plan, as every situation is different. Also, many states collect some sort of estate tax, depending on what is owned and who inherits it. Tax thresholds for state estate taxes vary.

In Oregon, for example, only 3 in 1,000 estates will likely be subject to the federal tax under the 2009 rules. That compares with 13 per 1,000 in 2000.[1] "'If you go to six funerals every single week in 2009, odds are you might attend one the entire year where the deceased's estate would pay any federal tax,' said [Policy Analyst Janet] Bauer. 'Even the busiest funeral parlor director won't see many individuals subject to the federal estate tax.'"[2]

A Relevant History of the Federal Estate Tax The first estate tax was enacted in 1797 as a way for our young nation to build a navy to police our shores. It was repealed in 1802. It returned during times, of national emergency during the Civil War and Spanish–American War; each time it was repealed after the war.

President Theodore Roosevelt and industrialist Andrew Carnegie were among many others who advocated for an inheritance tax. Their advocacy "came out of a tradition—a very American tradition—of concern about the dangers of concentration of wealth and power. Then, we rejected aristocracy, we rejected the notion of inherited wealth and power. That is very much a defining part of our identity, along with the desire for freedom and economic liberty and opportunity."[3] The estate tax became a permanent part of the tax code in 1916 and has remained basically unchanged since the 1930s.

> What kind of society do we want to become? Do we want to have a society as we did before the estate tax, with great concentrations of wealth and power? Because wealth is power . . . Supreme Court Justice Lewis Brandeis (he wasn't a Supreme Court Justice yet) said, "We can have concentrated wealth in the hands of a few or we can have democracy, but we cannot have both."[4]

Other Taxes to Know About   As you know, the IRS was not born yesterday. Over the years, there have been many attempts to avoid tax by shifting the ownership of assets. As a result, several other types of tax were created to prevent creative or disingenuous shifting of assets. There are two that are particularly important to know about as you plan your estate: gift tax and generation-skipping taxes.

Gift Tax   In 2009, gift tax was levied on taxable gifts greater than $13,000. For virtually everyone, the tax is not actually paid at the time of the gift. Instead, a gift tax form must be filed and when the estate is eventually administered—usually many years in the future—the amounts over $13,000 are factored in, with the result that your estate tax credit (the exemption amount) is reduced by the same amount as your gifts *over* $13,000 per person per year. Sounds detailed? It is. But the key point is that you can still give away gifts larger than $13,000; just make sure you file the gift tax return and keep records.

Note: About that $13,000 annual gift amount. This is the amount that you can give someone each year without needing to file a gift tax return. A married couple can each give $13,000. For example, if a couple gave their daughter and son-in-law a gift, they could give them up to $52,000 tax-free (mom and dad each give daughter and son-in-law $13,000 each; $4 \times \$13,000 = \$52,000$). This annual gift amount is a movable number, and the IRS adjusts it periodically based on inflation.

Generation-Skipping Tax   If you give away large gifts to grandchildren, you might be subject to generation-skipping taxes. The generation-skipping tax was designed to prevent creative means to avoid estate taxes, and it imposes a high percentage tax on transfers to someone who is two or more generations younger. (Avoid it by regularly using your tax-free annual gift opportunities.) As with the gift tax, relatively large amounts of money have to be involved before it becomes a factor in planning.

CHAPTER 5

The Donor Bill of Rights was created by the American Association of Fund Raising Counsel (AAFRC), Association for Healthcare Philanthropy (AHP), the Association of Fundraising Professionals (AFP), and the Council for Advancement and Support of Education (CASE). It has been endorsed by numerous organizations.

The Donor Bill of Rights

Philanthropy is based on voluntary action for the common good. It is a tradition of giving and sharing that is primary to the quality of life. To ensure that philanthropy merits the respect and trust of the general public, and that donors and prospective donors can have full confidence in the nonprofit organizations and causes they are asked to support, we declare that all donors have these rights:

I. To be informed of the organization's mission, of the way the organization intends to use donated resources, and of its capacity to use donations effectively for their intended purposes.

II. To be informed of the identity of those serving on the organization's governing board, and to expect the board to exercise prudent judgment in its stewardship responsibilities.

III. To have access to the organization's most recent financial statements.

IV. To be assured their gifts will be used for the purposes for which they were given.

V. To receive appropriate acknowledgement and recognition.

VI. To be assured that information about their donation is handled with respect and with confidentiality to the extent provided by law.

VII. To expect that all relationships with individuals representing organizations of interest to the donor will be professional in nature.

VIII. To be informed whether those seeking donations are volunteers, employees of the organization or hired solicitors.

IX. To have the opportunity for their names to be deleted from mailing lists that an organization may intend to share.

X. To feel free to ask questions when making a donation and to receive prompt, truthful and forthright answers.

CHAPTER 7

Format of the Case: Tried and Tested Methods

I urge groups to use PowerPoint, or another kind of presentation software, to create their case for support. Although you will rarely use a projector or a laptop to show it, the format lends itself to pithy, meaningful statements combined with images and charts. In addition, using larger fonts means that everyone will be able to read it.

Tips

- Print in color.
- Even though it saves paper (and I am very much in favor of that), please don't print on two sides. This will result in a confusing shuffling of paper, awkward page turning, and distractions in your meetings. Remember that coordination and vision are affected by age; keeping it simple will help. (If you wish, make a point of reducing paper use throughout your office in other ways to make up for single-sided presentations. For even more meaningful impact, you could also shift your office purchasing policies to using recycled and sustainable certified paper sources.)
- Some groups have inexpensive binding machines and use those to assemble the statements used for personal interviews. Others use a three-hole punch and put it in a small binder with plastic sleeves.
- Print in full-size pages (using one slide per page; don't use the two or four screens/slides to a page printing options). Older eyes need to read the large font for optimal reading comprehension.
- Use dark print on light backgrounds. Don't use reverse type (such as white type on a black or blue background) since eye research shows older eyes have difficulty reading reverse type. The same goes for type on colored background or printed over pictures.

SAMPLE INTERVIEW QUESTIONS

Here is a selection of questions you might use as a guideline in creating your own list of questions to test out your case.

How did you first get involved with ABC Charity?

What was your first impression of ABC Charity?

If ABC Charity came up in a conversation, what would you say about it to add to the conversation?

When you think about ABC Charity, how important is it to the community, on a scale of 1 to 10, with 1 being a waste of money and 10 being invaluable.

How important will ABC Charity be in ten years on that same 1 to 10 scale?

What is this organization's image among your friends and peers?

Do you support other organizations similar to this one?

Please name some: _____

Approximately how many nonprofits do you contribute to in a year?

Have you ever been asked to give to endowments before?

By what type of groups?

Have you ever given to an endowment before?

Do you think there is a clear case for the financial needs of this organization?

What important facts must this organization communicate in order to succeed in raising planned gifts/endowments?

From what you know now about this group, would you consider giving an endowment gift?

Is any nonprofit or community organization named as a beneficiary in your will?

Have you ever considered including ABC Charity in your will or estate plans?

Would you be willing to tell your story or work with others to help them discover the value and impact of completing legacy gifts?

Can you think of other people who would be interested in this work?

If you could offer the president (or executive director) some confidential advice, what would you whisper in his or her ear?

Is there anything you wish you had known before you became a board member (or become involved with ABC Charity)?

What do you feel is important for me to know or a question that I should have asked, but did not?

CHAPTER 11

Legacy Gift Confirmation and File Form

Keeping good records is vital. Use this form to confirm gifts and to ensure you have basic information about each gift and its intended use.

I strongly suggest that you fill this out in person with the donor. View it as a service: It's something that a family member would do without giving it a second thought. *Do not* mail this or otherwise send it to the donor. Donors may not fill it out, and the result will be an awkward situation. If you make a personal visit, you will build your relationship, offer a service, impress the donor with your concern, and most likely will learn more about the gift than you thought possible. That will *not* happen if you focus on "efficiency" and consider your convenience of higher value than deepening donor trust.

Sample Script of Introduction

Thank you for your gift. It must be exciting to reach that decision!

We want to make sure that we do everything you want done when the time comes.

Do you have a few moments to help me make sure we have all the right information exactly the way you would like it?

This information is confidential, of course. We keep it in a locked file in our office. When the time comes it will help us make sure we do exactly what you want done. (*Note:* Although you have already said this, it's useful to say it two, three, or even four times during your call. It will be appreciated each and every time.)

When I see you I will ask a few basic questions about your plans and how you want your gift used. I want to make sure we can do everything you want us to do with your gift. Of course, this is not a binding pledge; that's your choice.

Would it be possible to have a copy of the page from your will or a copy of the IRA designation form that names _____ [name of group; don't use "our" here and create an artificial division of ownership in thinking]? Please don't give me copies of the whole will or living trust— we don't need that. Keep that private. Just the page that names _____.

That way we can represent your interests when the time comes.

This Tuesday? That would be great. I'll see you at your house then.

Legacy Society

CONFIDENTIAL

Thank you for notifying us that you have included NONPROFIT in your estate plans. You can be proud of planning a lasting gift to the well-being of vulnerable children. Unless other arrangements are made, all gifts will be placed in the _____ endowment.

You are now a member of the Legacy Society. (Membership in the Legacy Society is without obligation). With your permission, we would like to recognize you in NONPROFIT's publications and on a beautiful plaque located in our boardroom. Please let us know how you prefer to be listed by checking one of the boxes:

☐ List my/our name(s) as I/we have printed them here.

☐ _____

☐ List me/us as "Anonymous."

About My Future Gift

(The following questions are optional.) We have included these questions to help us ensure that your wishes are accomplished when the time comes. This information will also help our Board of Directors to better plan for the future.

I have made the following charitable gift plans to NONPROFIT in my: (Please check all that apply.)

☐ Will (dated _____)

☐ Living trust (dated _____)

☐ Life insurance policy

☐ IRA or other pension plan

☐ Real estate

☐ Charitable trust

☐ Trust created in my will

☐ Other (please describe) _____

(The following two questions are also optional.) Answering the question regarding the current value of your gift will help the Board of Directors in long-range planning for children's programs.

Description of Gift _____

_____

_____

(Continued)

Approximate Current Value of Gift _____

    All information about your plans will be retained in the NONPROFIT's confidential files. Please note that this is *not* a legal document or binding pledge.

Donor's Signature(s) _____

Donor Birth Date(s) _____

Address _____

_____

Phone _____ E-mail _____

    Thank you and welcome to membership in the Legacy Society!

Nonprofit's Tax ID number: XX-XXXXXX

If you have questions about this form or would like to discuss your plans, we would be glad to assist you. Please call _____

Advisors Referral Form

Date

Name

Dear _____,

    We often receive requests from donors and prospective donors for the names of legal and financial professionals who understand charitable and planned giving techniques. Many times the advisors of these donors have retired or moved away; or our donors have moved and are no longer close to past advisors.

    It is our policy never to recommend any particular advisor; that choice must be the donor's alone. However, we realize how critical it is to have competent assistance in charitable, legal, and tax planning in this specialized area. As a result, we are creating a referral list that we will provide to prospective donors upon request.

    If you would like your name and the name of your firm to be included in this list we would appreciate it if you would take a few moments to complete the short questionnaire attached.

    We would also welcome your suggestions about others who should be on this list.

Thank you.

Sincerely yours,

_____

Your Name: **Fax:**

Business Name: **E-mail:**

Address: **Web:**

Phone:

In what category would you like your services to be listed?

☐ Attorney

☐ Broker, investment advisor

☐ CPA and tax advisor

☐ Financial advisors/planners

☐ Trust officers

☐ Insurance professional

☐ Other: _____

Areas of specialization and proportion of practice:

☐ Estate planning (__ % of practice)

☐ Charitable trusts (__ % of practice)

☐ Financial planning for those already retired (__ % of practice)

☐ Financial planning for those about to retire (__ % of practice)

☐ Other financial planning (__ % of practice)

☐ Insurance (__ % of practice)

☐ Investments (__ % of practice)

☐ _____ (__ % of practice)

What can a donor expect to happen their first visit with you?

☐ Yes, please send me a copy of this list when it is compiled.

☐ Please add me to your professional advisors newsletter.

☐ I would like to be invited to events at NONPROFIT.

☐ I would like information about volunteer activities at NONPROFIT.

CHAPTER 14

Model Standards of Practice for the Charitable Gift Planner

PREAMBLE

The purpose of this statement is to encourage responsible gift planning by urging the adoption of the following standards of practice by all individuals who work in the charitable gift planning process, gift planning officers, fundraising consultants, attorneys, accountants, financial planners, life insurance agents, and other financial services professionals (collectively referred to hereafter as "Gift Planners") and by the institutions that these persons represent.

This statement recognizes that the solicitation, planning, and administration of a charitable gift is a complex process involving philanthropic, personal, financial, and tax considerations, and often involves professionals from various disciplines whose goals should include working together to structure a gift that achieves a fair and proper balance between the interests of the donor and the purposes of the charitable institution.

I. Primacy of Philanthropic Motivation

The principal basis for making a charitable gift should be a desire on the part of the donor to support the work of charitable institutions.

II. Explanation of Tax Implications

Congress has provided tax incentives for charitable giving, and the emphasis in this statement on philanthropic motivation in no way minimizes the necessity and appropriateness of a full and accurate explanation by the Gift Planner of those incentives and their implications.

III. Full Disclosure

It is essential to the gift planning process that the role and relationships of all parties involved, including how and by whom each is compensated, be fully disclosed to the donor. A Gift Planner shall not act or purport to act as a representative of any charity without the express knowledge and approval of the charity, and shall not, while employed by the charity, act or purport to act as a representative of the donor, without the express consent of both the charity and the donor.

IV. Compensation

Compensation paid to Gift Planners shall be reasonable and proportionate to the services provided. Payment of finder's fees, commissions, or other fees by a donee organization to an independent Gift Planner as a condition for the delivery of a gift is never appropriate. Such payments lead to abusive practices and may violate certain state and federal regulations. Likewise, commission-based compensation for Gift Planners who are employed by a charitable institution is never appropriate.

V. Competence and Professionalism

The Gift Planner should strive to achieve and maintain a high degree of competence in his or her chosen area and shall advise donors only in areas in which he or she is professionally qualified. It is a hallmark of professionalism for Gift Planners that they realize when they have reached the limits of their knowledge and expertise and, as a result, should include other professionals in the process. Such relationships should be characterized by courtesy, tact, and mutual respect.

VI. Consultation with Independent Advisors

A Gift Planner acting on behalf of a charity shall in all cases strongly encourage the donor to discuss the proposed gift with competent independent legal and tax advisors of the donor's choice.

VII. Consultation with Charities

Although Gift Planners frequently and properly counsel donors concerning specific charitable gifts without the prior knowledge or approval of the donee organization, the Gift Planner, in order to ensure that the gift will accomplish the donor's objectives, should encourage the donor, early in the gift planning process, to discuss the proposed gift with the charity to whom the gift is to be made. In cases in which the donor desires anonymity, the Gift Planner shall endeavor, on behalf of the undisclosed donor, to obtain the charity's input in the gift planning process.

VIII. Description and Representation of Gift

The Gift Planner shall make every effort to ensure that the donor receives a full description and an accurate representation of all aspects of any proposed charitable gift plan. The consequences for the charity, the donor, and where applicable, the donor's family, should be apparent, and the assumptions underlying any financial illustrations should be realistic.

IX. Full Compliance

A Gift Planner shall fully comply with and shall encourage other parties in the gift planning process to fully comply with both the letter and the spirit of all applicable federal and state laws and regulations.

X. Public Trust

Gift Planners shall, in all dealings with donors, institutions, and other professionals, act with fairness, honesty, integrity, and openness. Except for compensation received for services, the terms of which have been disclosed to the donor, they shall have no vested interest that could result in personal gain.

Source: Partnership for Philanthropic Planning (formerly National Committee on Planned Giving), Model Standards of Practice for the Charitable Gift Planner. Revised April 1999. Reprinted with permission.

SAMPLE HIGHLIGHTS OF A NONPROFIT'S GIFT ACCEPTANCE POLICY

Note: This summary was prepared to accompany the sample policy that follows. The nonprofit used the summary for wider distribution. It also made both available on its website. For another set of sample policies, you can download model documents at the Partnership for Philanthropy website: http://www.pppnet.org/resource/model_docs.html.

Protection of Donor Interests

The Board and its volunteers and staff representative shall always consider the **interest of our prospective donors as the first priority** in planning gifts. This may include, for example, the donor's financial situation and philanthropic interests, as discovered by our representatives while planning for a gift. A donor shall not be encouraged to make a gift if it appears inappropriate. Donors shall be advised of the importance of seeking independent professional counsel.

What Are Gifts? For tax purposes, a *gift* is defined as a voluntary transfer of assets to ABC Nonprofit for which no forthcoming goods or services are expected for the donor. Gifts usually take the form of cash, securities, real property, or personal property. Once the Board has accepted a gift, it becomes the property of ABC Nonprofit. From this point, the donor has no direct decision-making power regarding the disposition of the gift. ABC Nonprofit will usually sell all gifts of stock or property so that it can invest the proceeds in accordance with the Board's investment policies.

Types of Gifts Gifts can be either outright or deferred. The most common outright gifts to ABC Nonprofit are those such as cash or publicly traded securities. Deferred gifts, also called "planned gifts," are arranged with ABC Nonprofit during the donor's lifetime, but the benefits do not accrue until a later time, usually after the death of the donor or his/her beneficiaries. *Bequests are the most common deferred gift.*

Restricted Gifts A donor's gift may be either unrestricted or restricted to a general area of use. Unrestricted gifts are preferable, and restricted gifts may be accepted at the discretion of the Board. The Board will accept only gifts and grants that are:

- Compatible with the mission of ABC Nonprofit and its programs,
- In compliance with the current Internal Revenue Code and other federal regulations,
- Compatible with ABC Nonprofit's tax-exempt status.

Finder's Fees or Commissions

Consistent with the codes of ethics of professional organizations, no finder's fee or commission of any type will be paid by the Board to any party in connection with the completion of a gift to ABC Nonprofit. No person in our employ may accept any compensation or material benefit from a donor as a result of the gift planning process.

Professional Fees Reasonable costs of gift acquisition, such as transaction costs and professional fees, will be borne by the donor.

Donor's Use of Professional Advisors When possible, all prospective donors will be encouraged to seek their own counsel in matters of estate planning, taxes, and planned gifts. It is not the province of the Board to give legal advice. This function is reserved for the donor's counsel, who alone must bear responsibility for all legal or tax conclusions and advice.

Confidentiality of Information Information learned by any representative of the Board about a donor or the donor's assets or philanthropic intentions shall be held in strict confidence.

For a complete copy, please call _____ (name of nonprofit staff person).

SAMPLE GIFT ACCEPTANCE POLICIES AND GUIDELINES

Note: This policy can be used as a starting point for your discussion with board members, volunteers, and prospective donors. It will be in your best interests to make this a robust and involved discussion to make sure the final policy truly reflects the needs and interests of both your donors and organization.

Gift Acceptance Policy for NONPROFIT

The _____, a not-for-profit organization organized under the laws of the State of _____, encourages the solicitation and acceptance of gifts to the NONPROFIT (hereinafter referred to as NONPROFIT) for purposes that will help further and fulfill its mission.

The following policies and guidelines govern acceptance of gifts made to NONPROFIT or for the benefit of any of its programs.

Mission: (Insert your mission statement here.) *Sample:* NONPROFIT is an independent, community-based organization that mobilizes the ideas, leadership, political support, and money to ensure a first-rate education for every child, in every school, in every neighborhood.

I. Purpose of Policies and Guidelines

The board of directors of NONPROFIT and its staff seek current and future gifts from individuals, corporations, and foundations to secure the future growth and mission of NONPROFIT. These policies and guidelines govern the acceptance of gifts by NONPROFIT and provide guidance to prospective donors and their advisors when making gifts to NONPROFIT. The provisions of these policies shall apply to all gifts received by NONPROFIT for any of its programs or services.

II. Use of Legal Counsel

NONPROFIT shall seek the advice of legal counsel in matters relating to acceptance of gifts when appropriate. Review by counsel is recommended for:

- Closely held stock transfers that are subject to restrictions or buy–sell agreements.
- Documents naming NONPROFIT as Trustee.

- Gifts involving contracts, such as bargain sales or other documents requiring the NONPROFIT to assume an obligation.

- Transactions with potential conflict of interest that may invoke IRS sanctions.

- Other instances in which use of counsel is deemed appropriate by the Finance Committee.

III. Conflict of Interest

NONPROFIT will urge all prospective donors to seek the assistance of personal legal and financial advisors in matters relating to their gifts and the resulting tax and estate planning consequences. NONPROFIT will comply with the *Model Standards of Practice for the Charitable Gift Planner* promulgated by the National Committee on Planned Giving, shown as an appendix to this document.

IV. Restrictions on Gifts

NONPROFIT will accept unrestricted gifts, and gifts for specific programs and purposes, provided that such gifts are not inconsistent with its stated mission, purposes, and priorities. NONPROFIT will not accept gifts that are too restrictive in purpose. Gifts that are too restrictive are those that violate the terms of the corporate charter, gifts that are too difficult to administer, or gifts that are for purposes outside the mission of the NONPROFIT. All final decisions on the restrictive nature of a gift, and its acceptance or refusal, shall be made by the finance committee of NONPROFIT.

V. The Finance Committee

The finance committee is charged with the responsibility of reviewing any gifts that fall outside the parameters of standard gift transactions as determined by NONPROFIT Chief Development Officer, Chief Financial Officer, and Executive Director. The finance committee will screen and accept these gifts, and make recommendations to the board on gift acceptance issues when appropriate.

(Continued)

VI. Types of Gifts

The following gifts are acceptable:

- Cash
- Tangible personal property
- Securities
- Real estate
- Remainder interests in property
- Oil, gas, and mineral interests
- Bargain sales
- Life insurance
- Charitable remainder trusts
- Charitable lead trusts
- Retirement plan beneficiary designations
- Bequests
- Life insurance beneficiary designations
- As of the date of this plan, NONPROFIT does not have a license to offer charitable gift annuities

The following criteria govern the acceptance of each gift form:

Cash

Cash is acceptable in any form. Checks shall be made payable to NONPROFIT and shall be delivered to _____, (NONPROFIT's administrative offices).

Tangible Personal Property

All other gifts of tangible personal property shall be examined in light of the following criteria:

- Does the property fulfill the mission of NONPROFIT?
- Is the property marketable? (NONPROFIT has a relationship with the Charity Group for the marketing of tangible personal property, and with Volunteers of America for the marketing of automobiles.)
- Are there any undue restrictions on the use, display, or sale of the property?
- Are there any carrying costs for the property?

Securities

NONPROFIT can accept both publicly traded securities and closely held securities.

- **Publicly Traded Securities.** Marketable securities may be transferred to an account maintained at one or more brokerage firms or delivered physically with the transferor's signature or stock power attached. As a general rule, all marketable securities shall be sold upon receipt unless otherwise directed by the investment committee. In some cases marketable securities may be restricted by applicable securities laws; in such an instance, the final determination on the acceptance of the restricted securities shall be made by finance committee.

- **Closely Held Securities.** Closely held securities, which include not only debt and equity positions in nonpublicly traded companies but also interests in limited partnerships and limited liability companies, or other ownership forms, can be accepted subject to the approval of the finance committee. In addition, gifts must be reviewed prior to acceptance to determine:

- there are no restrictions on the security that would prevent NONPROFIT from ultimately converting those assets to cash;

- the security is marketable; and

- the security will not generate any undesirable tax consequences for NONPROFIT.

If potential problems arise on initial review of the security, further review and recommendation by an outside professional may be sought before making a final decision on acceptance of the gift. The finance committee and legal counsel shall make the final determination on the acceptance of closely held securities when necessary. Every effort will be made to sell nonmarketable securities as quickly as possible.

Real Estate

Gifts of real estate may include developed property, undeveloped property, or gifts subject to a prior life interest. Prior to acceptance of

(Continued)

real estate, NONPROFIT shall require an initial environmental review of the property to ensure that the property has no environmental damage. In the event that the initial inspection reveals a potential problem, NONPROFIT shall retain a qualified inspection firm to conduct an environmental audit. The cost of the environmental audit shall generally be an expense of the donor. When appropriate, a title binder shall be obtained by NONPROFIT prior to the acceptance of the real property gift. The cost of this title binder shall generally be an expense of the donor. Prior to acceptance of the real property, the gift shall be approved by the finance committee and by NONPROFIT's legal counsel. Criteria for acceptance of the property shall include:

- Is the property useful for the purposes of NONPROFIT?
- Is the property marketable?
- Are there any restrictions, reservations, easements, or other limitations associated with the property?
- Are there carrying costs, which may include insurance, property taxes, mortgages, or notes, etc., associated with the property?
- Does the environmental audit reflect that the property is not damaged?

Remainder Interests in Property

NONPROFIT will accept a remainder interest in a personal residence, farm, or vacation property subject to the provisions of paragraph 4 above. The donor or other occupants may continue to occupy the real property for the duration of the stated life. At the death of the donor, NONPROFIT may use the property or reduce it to cash. Where NONPROFIT receives a gift of a remainder interest, expenses for maintenance, real estate taxes, and any property indebtedness are to be paid by the donor or primary beneficiary.

Oil, Gas, and Mineral Interests

NONPROFIT may accept oil and gas property interests, when appropriate. Prior to acceptance of an oil and gas interest, the gift shall be approved by the finance committee, and if necessary, by NONPROFIT's legal counsel. Criteria for acceptance of the property shall include:

- Gifts of surface rights should have a value of $20,000 or greater.

- Gifts of oil, gas, and mineral interests should generate at least $3,000 per year in royalties or other income (as determined by the average of the there years prior to the gift).

- The property should not have extended liabilities or other considerations that make receipt of the gift inappropriate

- A working interest is rarely accepted. A working interest may be accepted only when there is a plan to minimize potential liability and tax consequences.

- The property should undergo an environmental review to ensure that NONPROFIT has no current or potential exposure to environmental liability.

Bargain Sales

NONPROFIT will enter into a bargain sale arrangement in instances in which the bargain sale furthers the mission and purposes of NONPROFIT. All bargain sales must be reviewed and recommended by the finance committee and approved by the board of directors. Factors used in determining the appropriateness of the transaction include:

- NONPROFIT must obtain an independent appraisal substantiating the value of the property.

- If NONPROFIT assumes debt with the property, the debt ratio must be less than 50 percent of the appraised market value.

- NONPROFIT must determine that it will use the property, or that there is a market for sale of the property, allowing sale within 12 months of receipt.

- NONPROFIT must calculate the costs to safeguard, insure, and expense the property (including property tax, if applicable) during the holding period.

(Continued)

Life Insurance

NONPROFIT must be named as both beneficiary and irrevocable owner of an insurance policy before a life insurance policy can be recorded as a gift. The gift is valued at its interpolated terminal reserve value, or cash surrender value, upon receipt. If the donor contributes future premium payments, NONPROFIT will include the entire amount of the additional premium payment as a gift in the year that it is made.

If the donor does not elect to continue to make gifts to cover premium payments on the life insurance policy, NONPROFIT may:

- Continue to pay the premiums,
- Convert the policy to paid up insurance, or
- Surrender the policy for its current cash value.

Charitable Gift Annuities

Currently, NONPROFIT does not hold a license to offer charitable gift annuities.

Charitable Remainder Trusts

NONPROFIT may accept designation as remainder beneficiary of a charitable remainder trust with the approval of the finance committee. NONPROFIT will not accept appointment as trustee of a charitable remainder trust.

Charitable Lead Trusts

NONPROFIT may accept a designation as income beneficiary of a charitable lead trust. NONPROFIT will not accept an appointment as Trustee of a charitable lead trust.

Retirement Plan Beneficiary Designations

Donors and supporters of NONPROFIT will be encouraged to name NONPROFIT as beneficiary of their retirement plans. Such designations will not be recorded as gifts to NONPROFIT until such time as the gift is irrevocable. When the gift is irrevocable, but is not due until a future date, the present value of that gift may be recorded at the time the gift becomes irrevocable.

Bequests

Donors and supporters of NONPROFIT will be encouraged to make bequests to NONPROFIT under their wills and trusts. Such bequests will not be recorded as gifts to NONPROFIT until such time as the gift is irrevocable. When the gift is irrevocable, but is not due until a future date, the present value of that gift may be recorded at the time the gift becomes irrevocable.

Life Insurance Beneficiary Designations

Donors and supporters of NONPROFIT will be encouraged to name NONPROFIT as beneficiary or NONPROFIT beneficiary of their life insurance policies. Such designations shall not be recorded as gifts to NONPROFIT until such time as the gift is irrevocable. When the gift is irrevocable, but is not due until a future date, the present value of that gift may be recorded at the time the gift becomes irrevocable.

VII. Miscellaneous Provisions

- **Securing appraisals and legal fees for gifts to NONPROFIT.** It will be the responsibility of the donor to secure an appraisal (when required) and independent legal counsel for all gifts made to NONPROFIT.

- **Valuation of gifts for development purposes.** NONPROFIT will record a gift received by NONPROFIT at its valuation for gift purposes on the date of gift.

- **Responsibility for IRS filings upon sale of gift items.** NONPROFIT's Chief Financial Officer is responsible for filing IRS Form 8282 upon the sale or disposition of any asset sold within two years of receipt by NONPROFIT when the charitable deduction value of the item is

(Continued)

more than $5,000. NONPROFIT must file this form within 125 days of the date of sale or disposition of the asset. Form 8282 with Filing Instructions is attached as an appendix to these policies.

- Acknowledgment of all gifts made to NONPROFIT and compliance with the current IRS requirements in acknowledgement of such gifts shall be the responsibility of the board of NONPROFIT. IRS Publication 561 *Determining the Value of Donated Property* and IRS Publication 526 *Charitable Contributions* are attached to these policies as an Appendix.

VIII. Changes to Gift Acceptance Policies

These policies and guidelines have been reviewed and accepted by the finance committee of the ABC Nonprofit. The finance committee of the must approve any changes to, or deviations from, these policies.

Approved on the _____ day of _____, 20XX. _____

President, Board of Directors _____

IX. Attachments

(*Note:* These are not included in this book but are readily available via the Web at http://www.IRS.gov and http://pppnet.org.)

- Model Standards of Practice of the Charitable Gift Planner
- IRS Form 8282 and Instructions
- IRS Publication 561, Determining the Value of Donated Property
- IRS Publication 526, Charitable Contributions

GLOSSARY

Sometimes it's a challenge to communicate. With that in mind, the following are definitions to commonly used words in the world of legacy gifts. These definitions originate from the perspective of practical understanding and are not intended to be precise legal definitions.

In a conversation, it is a continuing challenge to use the technical language of legacy gifts, as well as knowing the level of vocabulary that should be used, when a variety of interests, professions, and levels of understanding come together in gift planning. It's been my experience that simple, plain language results in donor decisions that get completed and implemented.

When discussions veer off into dense and technical language, I notice the donor loses the emotional impact, or vision, for the gift. When this happens, gifts are often not completed, resulting in a loss to both the donor and the nonprofit.

It's been my experience that the more often legal or tax advisors use technically loaded language, the less they feel comfortable with, or understand the charitable dynamics of the transaction. As the facilitator of the gift, this could be considered a warning sign. Returning the focus to the charitable impact of the gift, and the vision that the donor has for the change she would like to see in the world, is important. In some cases, involving different professional advisors, with a better understanding of the role charitable giving plays in legal or tax planning, can be a good suggestion.

WORDS GROUPED IN RELATED CATEGORIES

The glossary is grouped by area or topic so that you could read the section and have related words grouped together for better understanding:

1. *Charitable gift terms:* Words used in relationship to completing charitable gifts

2. *Nonprofit insider terms:* Phrases nonprofit staff might use talking with other fundraising professionals

3. *Charitable gift tools:* A short description of the alphabet soup of charitable gift tools, primarily life income gifts

4. *Other estate, tax, and legal terms:* Words you may likely hear in the course of talking about legacy and bequest gifts

5. *Assets used to make gifts:* Sometimes the form of the gift has a specific name or term of art. Here are a few you may encounter

6. *Nonprofit terms:* Words related the business of nonprofit operations

1. CHARITABLE GIFTS

Beneficiary Designation: Often used in reference to retirement or pension plans and life insurance. A beneficiary designation form is a standard form available on the website of many mutual funds, IRAs, and other retirement plan administrators. Your designation recorded with the plan administrator determines to whom they write the check when you are gone. From a tax perspective, making a charity the beneficiary usually results in 100 cents on the dollar going to work for a good cause. If you direct it to a person or to your estate in general, all of the income tax you never had to pay on the contributions and appreciation and estate taxes may be due. *Important note:* For many plan administrators it will be critical to include the nonprofit's tax ID number in your designation.

Deferred Gift: This phrase describes the array of gift plans that are also called "planned gifts" or "legacy gifts." From the charity's perspective, the benefit from the gift is "deferred," and the nonprofit will not benefit from the gift until a later time—when the donor is deceased. This is in contrast to "current gifts," which immediately provide dollars to benefit the charity. Recognizing this term has a ring of insider jargon to it, many nonprofit leaders most often use the term *planned gift* or *legacy gift.*

Charitable Bequest: Both a legal and common phrase to describe a provision in a will, living trust, or estate plan that designates a gift to a nonprofit. Bequests can be specific assets (such as a painting, a house, or securities). Gifts can also be a specific dollar amount or a percentage of the estate. Gifts might also be described as the "residue" or what remains after other bequests have been completed. A charitable bequest is the most common kind of estate or planned gift. *Example of a bequest provision:* "I give, bequeath, and devise the sum of $100,000 to the ABC Nonprofit, with the current business address of 123 Main Street, Portland, Oregon, and Federal Tax ID Number of 94-12345."

Contingent Bequest: A provision in a will or estate plan that provides for an alternative gift. For example, a charity might receive a gift if all members of the immediate family pass away first.

Example of a contingent bequest provision: "In the event that _____ (insert name of family member or friend) predeceases me, I give ABC Nonprofit, with the current business address of 345 Main Street and Federal Tax ID Number of 94-78901, 50 percent of the residue of my estate to be used. In the future, should the board of directors of ABC Nonprofit determine that it has become impossible or impractical to apply effectively the gift made for this restricted purpose (for example, if the program or service no longer exists), the gift shall be used where the need is greatest as determined by the board of directors."

Leave A Legacy: A national bequest-awareness program initiated by the National Committee on Planned Giving (now renamed as the Partnership for Philanthropic Planning, website: http://www.pppnet.org).

Legacy Gift: As the focus of the gift planning field moves from the needs of the institution and counting gifts to donor needs and their interest in making an impact with their giving, this term is more often used. It reflects that shift in perspective. For the purposes of this book, I often use the terms *legacy gift* and *bequest* interchangeably.

Planned Gift: As defined by the Partnership for Philanthropic Planning, "Planned gifts are a variety of charitable giving methods that allow you to express your personal values by integrating your charitable, family, and financial goals. Making a planned charitable gift usually requires the assistance of the charity's development professional and/or a knowledgeable advisor such as an attorney, financial planner, or CPA to help structure the gift. Planned gifts can be made with cash, but many planned gifts are made by donating assets such as stocks, real estate, art pieces, or business interests—the possibilities are endless. Planned gifts can provide valuable tax benefits and/or lifetime income for you and your spouse or other loved one. *The most frequently made planned gifts are bequests* to charities, made through your will. Other popular planned gifts include charitable trusts and charitable gift annuities."

Restricted or Directed Gift: A gift that must be used for a particular purpose. "Restricted" is also an accounting reference to note that certain requirements must be met before the money can be spent. Example will language for a directed or restricted gift:

"I give and bequeath to the ABC Charity _____ (insert description of what you are giving), to _____ (describe the purpose of your gift)."

Unrestricted Gift: A gift that can be used however the board of the organization sees fit. Example will language for an unrestricted gift:

"I give and bequeath to the ABC Charity _____ (insert description of what you are giving), to be used in furtherance of its exempt charitable purposes, in such a manner as its Board of Trustees deems best."

Variance Clause: Sometimes by the time a bequest is received or some years after a bequest was received, circumstances change. Many legal advisors suggest their clients provide some flexibility to accommodate for a changing future and include a phrase in their gift directions to enable a charitable organization to adapt to circumstances. Here's an example of such a phrase to follow a bequest designation:

"If at some future time the Board of Directors of ABC Nonprofit determines that it has become impossible or impractical to apply effectively the gift made hereunder to the restricted purpose specified (e.g., because a specified department, service, or program no longer exists or its operation has been substantially reduced or changed), the gift made hereunder shall be used where the need is greatest at ABC Nonprofit as determined by the Board of Directors."

Here's another version of such a variance clause that can help ensure a gift has impact for many years to come:

"If this purpose becomes obsolete, inappropriate, or impractical, this gift may be used for purposes related, to the extent possible, to the original purposes of the gift after approval by the Board of Trustees."

2. NONPROFIT INSIDER PHRASES

Phrases Nonprofit Staff May Use

Bequest Expectancy: Used to describe an expected gift of a bequest. Not a great phrase to use out loud with donors.

Bequest Intention: A donor has informed you that your organization is included in his estate plan in some way. Some groups require a certain level of internal documentation before they count this as a gift.

Bequest Notification: A phone call or letter from an attorney or the executor of an estate to inform you that your organization has been included in the will or trust of someone who has recently passed away. Depending on state law, if you are included in the will, you have certain rights to see the documents and be included in the processes of settling the estate.

Cultivation: The process of building relationships with prospective donors. Cultivation can focus on groups of donors such as a group of annual fund donors. Or it may be focused on individual prospective or current donors.

Gift Planner, Gift Counselor, Planned Giving Officer: All are titles used to describe the somewhat specialized position focused on estate gifts in larger organizations.

Matured: A gift has "matured" when the donor or the beneficiary of a life income gift has passed away and the gift has been transferred to charity.

Stewardship: The process of acknowledging gifts, recognizing donors, and continuing to strengthen the relationship with donors following the receipt of gifts. Most often, nonprofit staff use the word *cultivation* to refer to advance work or preparation to a solicitation or "ask," and the word *stewardship* to refer to activities that take place after a gift has been completed or pledged.

3. CHARITABLE GIFT TOOLS

Annuitant: A person entitled to receive benefits from an annuity.

Annuity: A contract to pay income from a specific date until either the death of a person (the "annuitant") or a date in the future. Many commercial companies offer annuities as investments. Commercial annuities often have higher payout rates, though no charity will ultimately benefit.

Bargain Sale: Imagine if someone wanted to use a piece of real estate to make a gift but did not want to give 100 percent of the value of property. A bargain sale is the purchase of real estate by a nonprofit from a seller for less than its fair market value. The donor receives an immediate payment for the sale amount and a charitable tax deduction for the difference between the cash payment and the fair market value. The donor avoids the capital gains tax on a portion of the capital gain—the same proportion as the gift divided by the fair market value.

Charitable Gift Annuity: A charitable gift annuity is a contract between the donor and the charity. The donor transfers property—often cash or securities—and in return, the charity promises to pay the annuitant a set amount for the rest of her life. The American Council on Gift Annuities regularly reviews rates and suggests rates that charities could use that will provide for fixed payments and about half of the initial gift value to the charity at the end of the contract. The contract ends when the annuitant passes away. Since this is a contract, all the assets of the nonprofit are obligated for payment of the contract, unlike that of, for example, a charitable trust, in which the obligations are limited to the assets of only the trust.

Charitable Lead Trust: Not common. But like many tools, if your situation fits, it's a great tool even though it has a number of complex working parts. When used, it is done primarily for estate and gift tax purposes, rarely for income tax reasons. From the point of view of a small group, simply knowing the name might be all you need.

Charitable Remainder Trust: Also called CRT, CRUT, charitable remainder unitrust, retirement trust, or charitable remainder annuity trust (CRAT), among others. The charitable trust is specifically established in law. There are specific regulations that describe the payout, length of time, and structure of trusts. Variations include NICRUT/NIMCRUT, Flip Trust, and net income, the variations which primarily vary how and when payments to the beneficiary are structured. There are excellent discussions of the details of charitable trusts and their variations on the web at the Planned Giving Design Center (http://www.pgdc.com).

Sometimes these trusts are given interesting names as a way to make them appear to be special or unique in their application or as way for professional advisors to market their services in new ways.

A charitable trust is a separate legal entity. The textbook example of a trust might look something like this. The donor has appreciated real estate and wishes to make a gift, needs income, and wishes to bypass capital gains taxes. The solution: a charitable trust. The trust is created, the property transferred to the trust, the trust sells the property and then pays the donor or other beneficiaries income for a number of years or lifetime. The donor bypasses capital gains, gets a current tax deduction, and gets income, too. When the trust period ends, the charity gets the remainder in the trust.

Community Foundations: Charitable organizations that may administer a number of endowed funds generally for local or regional purposes. They may offer donors a variety of gift vehicles including charitable trusts, donor advised funds, gift annuities, pooled income funds, and field-of-interest funds. Some offer nonprofit services as well, acting as administrator for endowment funds or designated purpose funds or as trustee for charitable trusts. The foundations are administered by a board or distribution committee. Community foundations are sometimes seen as alternatives to private or family foundations, especially when total amounts to be managed may be less than $5 million.

Donor Advised Fund (DAF): These funds have been the fastest-growing tool or vehicle for charitable giving in the past 20 years. In essence, the donor can make a gift to a fund today, receive a deduction for the current tax year, and then to give all or part of that amount to charitable groups later in the future. More than 100,000 funds hold more than $17 billion in assets today.[1] Fidelity Investments is the largest of the funds; Charles Schwab and Vanguard Investments are also national funds with substantial assets in DAFs. Community foundations, major universities, and larger charities throughout the United States also offer donor advised funds.

Income Beneficiary: Who gets the income from a trust or annuity.

Irrevocable Trust: A trust that cannot be changed, hence "irrevocable." A charitable trust is irrevocable in that once assets are transferred to the trust, the transaction cannot be undone. But provisions of the trust document can provide a wide range of latitude or restrictions on how the trust will operate and who will benefit. Trust documents can also give the right to change charitable beneficiaries.

Life Estate or Retained Life Estate: A donor may make a gift of his house to charity and retain the right to live in the house for the remainder of his life. The donor receives an immediate income tax deduction for the gift. Defined in federal tax law, the donor irrevocably deeds his or her home to a nonprofit but retains the right to live in it or use it for the rest of his or her life or a term of years, or both. In return, the donor receives an immediate tax deduction. The life estate gift plan can also be used with a vacation home or farm.

Life Income Gifts: Another word for the larger category of the alphabet soup of trusts, annuities, pooled income funds, and the like. So named because they provide income over the lifetime of the donor or beneficiary. This label is applied from the perspective of the donor. The label *split interest gift* describes the same set of gift vehicles but from the technical perspective of an accountant or lawyer.

Split Interest Gifts: Technically, many charitable gift vehicles are split interest gifts in that the interest is split among the donor or beneficiary and a charitable beneficiary. Charitable trusts of all shapes and forms are defined as split interest gifts, as are other vehicles such as pooled income funds and gift annuities.

4. OTHER ESTATE, TAX, AND LEGAL TERMS

Beneficiary: The person or nonprofit organization you designate to receive ownership or income.

Capital Gain/Loss: Assets may increase in value (gain) or decline in value (loss) over time. This term is most often used in reference to real estate and other kinds of investments.

Capital Gains Tax: The capital gains tax is a federal and/or state tax assessed on the asset's appreciation over the donor's basis (amount paid for the asset by the donor). When an asset is sold that has been owned less than one year, ordinary income tax rates apply. If the asset has been held for more than one year, long term capital gains rates apply (generally a lower tax rate applies). When an appreciated asset is contributed to charity, the donor generally avoids the capital gains tax that would be due if he sold the property. If the property has declined in value, it is generally best to sell the property, claim a loss on one's taxes, and donate cash for a larger income tax deduction.

Codicil: A supplement to a will that may modify, add to, subtract from, or otherwise alter existing provisions of a will.

Community Property: Laws vary among states that recognize community property. In brief the concept is that the husband and wife each acquire an equal interest in property acquired during marriage. When one spouse dies, half the property is inherited, since the other half is already owned by the surviving spouse.

Competence (or Capacity): The ability to make the decision about whether to make a gift and to understand the circumstances and information related to making the gift. Capacity might be affected by, for example, dementia, Alzheimer's disease and related disorders, or other mental incapacities. There are various legal definitions about what *capacity* or *ability to make decisions* means, and they vary by state. Charitable fundraisers have an ethical responsibility to be open and honest and to put the interests of donors first.

Cost Basis: What did it cost? That is the common-sense definition of the phrase. This definition will come into play when donors determine the value of their deduction after a gift of securities or other kind of property. Real estate used in a business or rental property may be depreciated over time for tax purposes. This will reduce the cost basis and increase the potential for added capital gains when the property is sold.

Devise: An older legal term generally used to refer to real estate left to someone under a will. In some states, the word *devise* now applies to any kind of property given to another by will, making it the same as the term bequest.

Executor: The person appointed in the will to carry out the provisions of the will. This person might also be called a "personal representative."

Estate: Your estate is made up of all of your property, including land, houses, bank accounts, investments, and everything you own by yourself or with someone else. Also included are retirement plans and insurance.

Estate Tax: A federal and/or state tax paid on the transfer of a dead person's assets to heirs and beneficiaries. Estate tax is generally levied on the assets accumulated during a lifetime, including a house, savings, and other assets. While estate tax law and rates have been in flux for a number of years, the amount exempt from estate tax continues to increase. In 2009, for example, a couple would have to have an estate valued at more than $7 million before the first dollar of federal estate tax would be have to be paid. Individual state estate tax thresholds vary and may differ from federal levels. Though it is sometimes referred to as the "death tax,"[2] a phrase that is a misnomer since it is not a tax on death, rather, it is often a tax primarily on parts of the estate that have never been taxed and have often appreciated in value over time. Continue to expect change regarding the estate tax at both the federal and state levels.

Fair Market Value (FMV): The price that a knowledgeable and willing buyer would pay for the asset to a knowledgeable and willing seller, assuming both buyer and seller have full knowledge of all facts relevant to the property's value. FMV is established by different means for different assets. For publicly traded stock, FMV is the mean (average) of the high and low trading price on the day ownership is effectively transferred to the charity. For real estate, nonpublicly traded stock, tangible personal property, and other types of assets, an independent appraisal is used to determine FMV. An appraisal will determine an estimated value, but the actual return or benefit to the charity will depend on the sale price, commissions, and expenses incurred by the sale.

Generation Skipping Tax: A federal transfer tax assessed when an individual transfers assets to a "skipped generation." A "skipped person" is defined as someone who is two or more generations younger than the donor.

Gift Tax: If you give a lot to friends and family, you might have to file a gift tax return. Gift tax is something to be aware of, and your professional advisors can help you. In general, however, it is an overrated concern—don't let this scare you or stop you from making gifts (at least until you pass gifts of $1 million). In 2009, you could give $13,000 to any number of friends and family without facing gift taxes and without the recipient of your gifts owing any income tax.

Grantor: A person who transfers property. Sometimes you will see reference to a grantor trust, which is a trust in which the grantor keeps enough control over the asset that the IRS considers the asset to belong to him (in contrast to any charitable trust).

Holographic Will: A handwritten will. Some states limit the validity of these documents.

Inheritance Tax: *See* Estate Tax.

Inter vivos trust: Latin for "between the living" and is often referred to in plain language as a living trust. (*See* Living Trust.)

Intestate: Dying without a will. Without at least a simple will, state law determines who gets your property, and a judge may decide who will raise any children. With a will, one can make these decisions for oneself.

Life Insurance Trust, or Irrevocable Life Insurance Trust (ILIT): A trust that contains a life insurance policy on the life of the settler/trustor. Proceeds from the life insurance policy pass to beneficiaries outside the estate and are not subject to estate tax.

Living Trust: A trust established while the person is living. It is *not* to be confused with a charitable trust. A couple might establish a living trust in order to make the transfer of assets easier when the first passes away. It is an estate planning or asset management tool sometimes used as a will substitute—it may or may not include any charitable bequest provisions. A more proper definition of a trust is a legal relationship in which property is transferred to and managed by a person or institution for the benefit of another.

Predecease: Pass away first. For example, "Should Peter predecease me, then the house goes to my favorite charitable organization."

Present Value: A mathematical formula to assess the value today or at present of an amount to be received in the future. *Example:* Assuming long-term interest rates will be about 3 percent, the value of $100,000 to be received in 10 years is worth today, or at present, about $74,409. Such calculations often play a role in how the IRS forms its regulations about tax deductions allowed when people make life income gifts.

Probate: The court supervised process that determines ownership of property previously owned by a deceased person and passes that property on to the rightful recipients. Probate court is a court with the power to settle wills and estates. A personal representative is appointed to pay outstanding expenses, taxes, and to distribute the property to those who are legally entitled. Some forms of property (nonprobate) will pass directly to heirs without going through this process, such as a bank account or stock account owned jointly with another person. Some people wish to avoid probate for reasons of privacy. Some lawyers suggest the concern for privacy is overrated and not worth the trouble and expense to create a living trust.

QTIP, or Qualified Terminal Interest Property: A type of interest in property passed from one spouse to the other that qualifies for the marital estate tax deduction.

Remainder Beneficiary (or Remainderman): This is a term for who gets what's left or what "remains" when the time comes. In the case of a charitable trust, the charity gets whatever remains in the charitable trust when the donor passes away or the term of years of the trust is reached.

Residue, or Residual Estate: What's left over in the estate after all debts and other bequests have been paid.

Settlor/Trustor: The person who establishes the trust. *Trustor* is a term no longer in favor; the preferred term is now *settler* in many state statutes.

Simple Will: Most people need only a simple will, not complex trusts or other legal arrangements in order to complete basic estate planning.

Testamentary trust: A trust established by a will after the testator (or person who made the will) has passed. A trust established as part of a last will and "testament."

Testator: The person who made the will.

Trust: A legal entity in which property is transferred into and managed by a person or institution for the benefit of another. There are many forms, both taxable and charitable.

Trustee: The trustee is the legal owner and must manage the trust for the benefit of the beneficiary(ies). A trustee must follow the instructions of the trust. A beneficiary gets the benefits of the trust. In the case of a charitable trust, the charitable organization is also included in the definition of beneficiary.

Unified Credit: A federal tax credit that offsets estate and gift tax liability. When someone says the first $3.5 million of an estate is exempt from tax, in effect the "unified credit amount" is a tax credit that is the equivalent to paying tax on up to $3.5 million in assets (as of 2009).

Will: A legally executed document that describes how and where a person wants her property distributed after death.

5. ASSETS USED TO MAKE GIFTS

Closely Held Stock: Sometimes called "thinly traded stock." Unlike stock that could be sold, for example, on the NYSE, this stock will have a limited market. Due diligence should be applied before accepting it because it may have limited marketability or other restrictions.

Noncash Asset: An asset other than cash, such as real estate, securities, or other property. Gifts of currency, checks, or via credit card are considered cash gifts.

Personal Property (Tangible Personal Property): In terms of gifts to nonprofits, this category of property might include art, jewelry, and things that are tangible. It does not include cash. There are specific IRS rules about the donation of tangible personal property. The IRS publishes several publications that detail how to make a gift and how to determine the value of any tax deduction.

Real Estate: A significant portion of wealth in the United States is held in the form of real estate. While due diligence is required, especially with regard to environmental liability concerns, real estate can be an excellent gift. After exercising appropriate due diligence and accepting a gift of real estate, most nonprofits choose to sell the property as soon as possible.

Real Property: A general term including land, improvements on the land such as buildings, and the rights associated with that site. If there is a mortgage on the property and the property has been used as collateral, the claim on the property is described as encumbered.

Securities: A generic word used to include common stock, mutual funds, and bonds. Most often these are publicly traded and there is a ready market to sell them.

6. NONPROFIT TERMS

Endowment: From the perspective of a donor, it is a permanent fund, a portion of which is used each year by the nonprofit group. The accounting definition describes an endowment as a fund that is "permanently restricted." For donor clarity, I recommend using this word to mean exactly that and not to mix and match technical accounting labels. Accounting standards regarding endowments: Standards are set out by the Financial Accounting Standards Board. They define three types of endowments: (1) true endowment, (2) term endowment, and (3) quasi-endowment. FASB Staff Position 117-1 sets forth proposed guidelines for reporting endowments governed by UPMIFA. It states that a charity should classify "all or a portion" of an endowment as permanently restricted net assets, based on explicit donor restrictions (if any) or what the Board determines must retained permanently. FASB's website is http://www.fasb.org.

FASB: Financial Accounting Standards Board (FASB, often pronounced fahz'-bee) is a private, nongovernmental group providing generally accepted accounting standards.

Nonprofits: An organization that does not distribute funds to shareholders and instead uses them for its social purposes.

"The nonprofit sector in the United States has mushroomed over the past 20 years. It is now immense. There are 1.5 million organizations incorporated under the Internal Revenue Service 501(c)(3) law. The total income of the sector is about $1 trillion per year; if it were a single industry, it would be our nation's largest. The nonprofit sector employs 10 percent of the workforce and is, in general, an enormous economic driver."[3]

The nonprofit sector is often referred to as the third sector, independent sector, voluntary sector, philanthropic sector, social sector, tax-exempt sector, or charitable sector. An increasing number of people are beginning to use the phrase "social profit" to describe these kinds of groups.

Operating Reserve: A fund set aside to stabilize a nonprofit's finances—a savings account. Operating reserves or unrestricted fund balances are similar to retained earnings or equity in a business. Reserves can provide the flexibility and financial cushion to survive lean periods and unexpected events. Nonprofit revenue can be quite fickle and cyclical. An operating reserve can enable it to survive, if not thrive, having the financial flexibility to also take on new opportunities. How much is enough of a reserve? This will vary by type and size of group. Some groups use a rule of thumb of three to six months of operating expenses; recently, in the face of changes in the economy, some are considering increases of up to a year's worth of reserve.

Quasi-Endowment: A fund the board of directors has decided to retain; it may vote to spend the fund at any time. Practically speaking, it has nothing to do with the concept of "permanent." If used, it often confuses donors. Consider avoiding it and using a more truthful label instead.

Social Profit: A word to describe the community of groups long described as charities or nonprofits. The phrase better recognizes the value these groups contribute to our society. "Such a term would also give us a new way to name the people who support organizations that promote the public good: social investors. . . . Today's social investors seek and expect a return on their efforts, in the form of an increase in the greater good."[4]

UPMIFA and UMIFA: Many states adopted the Uniform Management of Institutional Funds Act (UMIFA, often pronounced "you-miff′-ah") that sets out rules for how nonprofits handle endowments. More than half the states have adopted the newer version of this set of model laws called the Uniform Prudent Management of Institutional Funds Act (UPMIFA, pronounced "up′-miff-ah").

Working Capital: Positive working capital means the organization can pay off its short-term liabilities. With private businesses, investors look at working capital as a measure of efficiency. Working capital = current assets − current liabilities.

DISCLAIMER

While this glossary provides general educational information, it cannot give you legal or tax advice on a specific matter or about the laws in the state in which you reside. In planning your personal and organizational affairs, please consult an attorney or tax expert about your own specific situation.

PREFACE

1. "Yale to increase endowment payout to expand access and advance science." Yale University Office of Public Affairs, January 7, 2008. Accessed at http://opa.yale.edu/news/article.aspx?id=2327 on October 1, 2009. As of September 2009, the endowment value was estimated at $16.3 billion.

2. *Source:* Year-end 2008 AFP national survey.

INTRODUCTION

1. Bersi, Robert M. "History, philosophy, standards." Long Beach, CA: American Institute for Philanthropic Studies, California State University, 1999.

2. James, Russell N., III. "Research unveiled: What every fundraiser needs to know about bequest giving." Presented at the AFP International Conference on Fundraising, March 29–April 1, 2009.

3. Sargeant, Adrian. "Research unveiled: What every fundraiser needs to know about bequest giving." Presented at the AFP International Conference on Fundraising, March 29–April 1, 2009.

4. *Op. cit.,* Bersi, p. 13.

5. "The future of charitable gift planning: a report of the NCPG Strategic Directions Taskforce." *Journal of Gift Planning,* 11(2):16–26.

6. There is an array of philanthropic products ranging from donor advised funds, trust administration, and specialized foundations that prospective donors can use.

CHAPTER 1

1. GivingUSA Foundation. www.givingusa.org.

2. Boston College Center on Wealth and Philanthropy. http://www.bc.edu/research/cwp.

3. Schervish, Paul G., and John J. Havens. *Millionaires and the Millennium: New Estimates of the Forthcoming Wealth Transfer and the Prospects for a Golden Age of Philanthropy.* Chestnut Hill, MA: Social Welfare Institute, Boston College, October 1999.

4. Robert Avery's 1990 Cornell Wealth Transfer Study suggested a transfer of $10.4 trillion, of which $1.4 trillion would be directed to charity over a 55-year period. Over a 20-year period, a Cornell study projected $2.8 trillion and $0.4 trillion to charity. Using slightly different methods, John J. Havens and Paul G. Schervisch's Boston College Wealth Transfer Study suggested a transfer of $41 trillion transferred, with $6 trillion to charity. Boston College projected $12 trillion and $1.7 trillion to charity over 20 years.

5. Holman, Margaret M., and Barlow T. Mann. "Gift Planning Boom(ers) or bust?" Presented at the National Conference on Planned Giving, Denver, CO, October 25, 2008.

6. Strauss, William, and Neil Howe. *The Fourth Turning.* New York: Broadway Books, 1997, pp. 221–222.

7. Gates, Bill, Sr., and Chuck Collins. "Estate Tax is Fairest Means of Building Revenue." *The Politico,* November 14, 2007. http://www.businessforsharedprosperity.org/node/65.

8. *Op. cit.,* Gates and Collins.

9. When pressed repeatedly for examples that the estate tax harmed family farmers, none were forthcoming. Tom Buis, president of the quarter-million-member National Farmers Union, has said, "Family farmers and ranchers

are insulted by those who use farmers as the reason for eliminating estate taxes, when the real beneficiaries are the nation's multimillionaires." *Op. cit.*, Gates and Collins.

10. Congressional Budget Office. "Estate Tax and Charitable Giving." July 2004. http://www.cbo.gov/ftpdocs/56xx/doc5650/07–15-CharitableGiving.pdf.

12. For an insightful perspective on the question, see the book by Bill Gates, Sr., and Chuck Collins, entitled *Wealth and Our Commonwealth: Why America Should Tax Accumulated Fortunes* (Boston: Beacon Press, 2003).

13. "The Future of Charitable Gift Planning: A Report of the NCPG Strategic Directions Taskforce." *Journal of Gift Planning.* http://www.pgdc.com/ncpgarticle/the-future-of-charitable-gift-planning-a-report-ncpg-strategic-directions-taskforce (available only to members).

14. Kramer, Mark. "Donors Learn How to be Effective by Seeing a Charity's Real Challenges." *Chronicle of Philanthropy,* November 23, 2006, p. 39. A number of donors were interviewed. These donors were viewed by other donors as "highly effective" in their philanthropy. Kramer is part of FSG Social Impact Advisors.

15. *Ibid.*

CHAPTER 2

1. Drucker, Peter F. *The Daily Drucker: 366 Days of Insight and Motivation for Getting the Right Things Done,* New York: HarperBusiness, 2004.

2. Sargeant, Adrian, Walter Wymer, and Toni Hilton. "Marketing Bequest Club Membership: An Exploratory Study of Legacy Pledgers." *Nonprofit and Voluntary Sector Quarterly,* 35(3):384 404.

3. *Ibid.*

CHAPTER 3

1. Prince, Russ Alan, and Karen Maru File. *The Seven Faces of Philanthropy: A New Approach to Cultivating Major Donors.* San Francisco: Jossey-Bass, 1994.

2. Ramsay, Ken. "Correcting a Market Inefficiency." *Gift Planning in Canada,* 13(1):4–5 and *Planned Giving in the United States 2000: A Survey of Donors.* Indianapolis, IN: National Committee on Planned Giving, 2001.

3. Sargeant, Adrian (Robert Hartook Professor of Fundraising). "Legacy Fundraising: Lessons from Research." Presented at the Institute of Fundraising National Convention, July 6, 2009.

4. *Planned Giving in the United States 2000: A Survey of Donors.* Indianapolis, IN: National Committee on Planned Giving, 2001.

5. Dean, Laura Hansen. "Lessons from *Planned Giving in the US 2000: A Survey of Donors* for Planning and Managing Planned Giving Programs." Presented at the National Conference on Planned Giving, October 3, 2001.

6. Ramsay, Ken. "Correcting a Market Inefficiency." *Gift Planning in Canada,* 13(1).

7. *Op. cit.,* Dean.

8. Bequest numbers from "Executive Briefing: Gift Planners and Their Work. Selected Data from a National Survey of Gift Planners." *The Journal of Gift Planning,* 12(1).

9. *GivingUSA.* Indianapolis: GivingUSA Foundation, 2008.

10. Henze, Lawrence, and Katherine Swank. *Creating a Legacy: Building a Planned Giving Program from the Ground Up.* Charleston, SC: Blackbaud Desk Reference, pp. 3–4.

11. Henze, Lawrence, Target Analytics. "How to Identify Planned Giving Prospects." Presentation at the Northern California Planned Giving Conference, April 2009.

CHAPTER 4

1. Johnson, Rees C. *Wills & Estate Planning.* Oregon Handbook, Revised Edition. Seattle, WA: Hara Publishing, 2003, p. 1.

2. Nearing, Helen. *Light on Aging and Dying: Wise Words.* Gardiner, ME: Tilbury House, 1995, p. viii.

3. *Ibid.,* p. 15, referencing an article in the *New York Times,* April 1990.

CHAPTER 5

1. "Survey: Giving Softened in 2006." *Non Profit Times,* January 2007. Story regarding a *Wall Street Journal* Online/Harris Interactive survey.

2. James, Russell N., III. "Wills, Trusts, and Charitable Estate Planning: An Analysis of Document Effectiveness Using Panel Data. *Journal of Financial Counseling and Planning* 20(1).

3. Konar, Ellen, Sheryl Sandberg, and Melissa Brown. "Destination unknown, donors' money isn't going where they think it is." *Stanford Social Innovation Review,* Winter 2008

4. *Op. cit.,* Kramer.

5. A copy of his well-written pledge letter is on the Berkshire Hathaway website: http://www.berkshirehathaway.com.

6. Loomis, Carol J. "Conversation with Warren Buffett." *Fortune,* June 25, 2006.

7. See note 5 above.

8. *Op. cit.,* Kramer.

9. Some of these questions were inspired by the writings of Claude Rosenberg's New Tithing Group and the book *Robin Hood Was Right: A Guide to Giving Your Money for Social Change,* by Chuck Collins, Pam Roger, with Joan P. Garner, The Haymarket People's Fund, 2000.

10. Beatty, Sally. "Philanthropy (A Special Report). How Charities Can Make Themselves More Open." *Wall Street Journal,* December 10, 2007, p. R.1.

11. Gose, Ben. "To Identify Stellar Groups, Authors Tell Foundations to Look Beyond Results" *Chronicle of Philanthropy,* October 4, 2007.

CHAPTER 6

1. Henze, Lawrence, and Katherine Swank. *Creating a Legacy: Building a Planned Giving Program from the Ground Up.* Charleston, SC: Blackbaud Desk Reference, 2008.

2. Gladwell, Malcolm. *The Tipping Point: How Little Things Can Make a Big Difference.* New York: Back Bay Books, 2002.

CHAPTER 7

1. Henze, Lawrence. Blackbaud Analytics (then Target Analytics). Presentation at the Northern California Planned Giving Conference, San Francisco, CA, March 21, 2007.

2. Wasley, Paula. "New Research Sheds Light on Bequest Giving." *Chronicle of Philanthropy*, April 1, 2009.

CHAPTER 8

1. Most states have adopted the Uniform Management of Institutional Funds Act (UMIFA, often pronounced "you-miff'-ah"), which sets out rules for how nonprofits handle endowments. More than half the states have adopted the newer version of this set of model laws, called the Uniform Prudent Management of Institutional Funds Act (often referred to in shorthand as "up'-miff-ah"). Accounting standards regarding endowments are set out by the Financial Accounting Standards Board, a private, non-governmental group providing generally accepted standards. The Financial Accounting Standards Boards (FASB, often pronounced fahz,'-bee) defines three types of endowments: (1) true endowments, (2) term endowments, and (3) quasi-endowments. FASB Staff Position 117-1 sets forth proposed guidelines for reporting endowments governed by UPMIFA. It states that a charity should classify "all or a portion" of an endowment as permanently restricted net assets, based upon explicit donor restrictions (if any), or what the Board determines must retained permanently. FASB's website is http://www.fasb.org.

2. Covey, Stephen M.R. *The Speed of Trust: The One Thing That Changes Everything*. New York: Free Press, 2006, p. xxv.

CHAPTER 9

1. Gladwell, Malcolm. *The Tipping Point: How Little Things Can Make a Big Difference*. New York: Back Bay Books, 2002.

2. Rogers, Everett M. *Diffusion of Innovations*. Glencoe, NY: Free Press, 1964.

3. For more about storytelling, several articles and resource materials, see: http://www.agoodmanonline.com.

4. *Ibid.*

5. Lagasse, Paul. "Measure for Measure: How Measuring Performance Can Transform Fundraising." *Advancing Philanthropy,* September 2007. Published by the Association of Fundraising Professionals, http://www.afp.org.

6. Sawhill, John, and David Williamson. "Measuring What Matters." *The McKinsey Quarterly,* (2001):98–107. This article can also be viewed on the McKinsey & Company website: http://www.mckinseyquarterly.com/Measuring_what_matters_in_nonprofits_1053.

7. *Planned Giving in the United States 2000: A Survey of Donors.* Indianapolis, IN: National Committee on Planned Giving, 2001.

8. For an expanded discussion of metrics, see "Asking the Right Questions: The Mysteries and Metrics of Planned Giving Programs," by Kathryn Miree. Presentation at the National Planned Giving Conference, Oct. 11, 2007. See the National Committee on Planned Giving website for access to the paper at http://www.ncpg.org.

9. A detailed overview of using a logic model approach is included in the presentation at: http://www.exinfm.com/workshop_files/logic_model.ppt.

10. W.K. Kellogg Foundation. "Using Logic Models to Bring Together Planning, Evaluation, and Action: Logic Model Development Guide" Updated January 2004. http://www.wkkf.org. (To receive additional copies of the Logic Model Development Guide, call 1-800-819–9997 and request item number 1209.)

CHAPTER 11

1. Burke, Penelope. *Donor Centered Fundraising: How to Hold on to Your Donors and Raise Much More Money.* Chicago: Cygnus Applied Research/ Burk & Associates, 2003. This research was updated in 2009 with a survey of more than 17,000 donors. For a report on the update, see: http://www.cygresearch.com.

2. *Ibid.*

3. *Ibid.,* pp. 132–133.

4. *Ibid.,* pp. 132–133

5. Our population is rapidly aging and becoming an even larger share of the philanthropic marketplace. With age comes sensory and cognitive changes. Some examples of how vision is affected appear in an article prepared for the American Institute for Graphic Design. You can see for yourself what a 20-year-old, a 60-year-old, and a 70-year-old person would see. (Personally, I was little depressed.) The results, I suspect, will be cause to reconsider how to design annual reports, newsletters, and brochures intended for prospective donors. Read the article and see the examples at: http://www.aiga.org/content.cfm/typography-and-the-aging-eye#. In other research, a report titled "Research-Based Web Design and Usability Guidelines," issued by the U.S. Department of Health and Human Services, states: "Research has shown that fonts smaller than 12 points elicit slower reading performance from users. For users over age 65, it may be better to use at least 14-point fonts. Never use less than a 9-point font on a Web site." (See: http://www.usability.gov/pdfs/guidelines.html.) The purpose of good design is to communicate to the people most likely to make the biggest difference to your work. Make sure your design meets that objective. For another interesting take on your own visual "eye-Q," see the self-test and online course on design on Andy Goodman's site at: http://www.agoodmanonline.com/red.html.

6. Nichols, Judith E. *Pinpointing Affluence in the 21st Century.* Chicago: Bonus Books, 2001.

CHAPTER 13

1. *Bank of America Study of High Net-Worth Philanthropy: Initial Report.* Researched and written by the Center on Philanthropy at Indiana University, October 2006. Figure 23. The report was based on a survey of 30,000 households in high net worth neighborhoods in the United States. *The 2008 Study of High Net Worth Philanthropy: Issues Driving Charitable Activities among Affluent Households.* Indianapolis, IN: The Center on Philanthropy at Indiana University, March 2009, pp. 7, 61.

2. *Bank of America Study of High Net-Worth Philanthropy: Initial Report.* Indianapolis, IN: The Center on Philanthropy at Indiana University, 2006.

3. *The 2008 Study of High Net-Worth Philanthropy: Issues Driving Charitable Activities among Affluent Households.* Indianapolis, IN: The Center on Philanthropy at Indiana University, 2008.

4. While circumstances are real, names used are fictional.

5. Johnson, Steve. "Best Practices: Asking the Philanthropic Question." *Journal of Gift Planning,* 9(1):16–23.

6. *Die Broke* (1997) and *Live Rich* (1998) are two books by Stephen M. Pollan and Mark Levine. Both are published by HarperBusiness Books.

7. Thompson, Gregg, and Susanne Biro. *Unleashed: Expecting Greatness and Other Secrets of Coaching for Exceptional Performance.* New York: Select Books, 2006. This book contains many good suggestions about conversations and questions you may be able to put to work with clients and donors.

RESOURCES

1. Bauer, Janet. "New Year Kicks in Generous Federal Estate Tax Rules." Oregon Center for Public Policy. December 30, 2008. http://www.ocpp.org/cgi-bin/display.cgi?page=nr20081230EstTax.

2. *Ibid.*

3. Chuck Collins quoted in Johnson, Kevin. "Philanthropy and Estate Tax Repeal: An Interview with William Gates, Sr." *Journal of Gift Planning,* 7(2).

4. *Ibid.*

GLOSSARY

1. Hastings, Andrew W., and the National Philanthropic Trust. "Philanthropic Statistics." *Donor Advised Fund Market Report 2008.* Jenkintown, PA: National Philanthropic Trust, 2008.

2. Alvarez, Lizette. "Capitol Hill memo: In 2 parties' war of words, shibboleths emerge as clear winner." *New York Times* April 27, 2001: "It took five years to get Republican lawmakers and lobbyists to use the words 'death tax' consistently. Jack Faris, the president and chief executive officer of the

National Federation of Independent Business, said he remembered his Rotary Club members complaining five years ago that the estate tax felt more like a tax on death. Mr. Faris took the phrase 'death tax' back to his trade group and made everyone in the office use it. Those who slipped paid $1 into a pizza fund, he said, adding, 'The fund grew pretty large.' The pizza fund idea spread to Capitol Hill, where Mr. Gingrich and others instituted it. Soon, everyone was using the term. 'Whoever the father is or was, God bless them,' Mr. Faris said, 'because it has really helped us shape the debate on the unfairness of the whole tax, not who is paying it.'"

3. Klein, Kim. "Mobilizing the nonprofit sector." *Kim Klein and the Commons.* Accessed July 30, 2009, at http://kimkleinandthecommons.blogspot.com/2009/06/mobilizing-nonprofit-sector.html.

4. Gaudiani, Claire. "What about 'social profit.'" *Alliance Magazine,* September 1, 2007.

ACKNOWLEDGMENTS

If I were to name everyone who has helped with this book, I would have to name several hundred people. There are many nonprofit executives, board members, foundation leaders, and volunteers with whom I have had the privilege of working and who have shared their experiences and helped contribute to the making of this book.

A few people really helped make this book into what it is. Joan Flanagan asked me a question that prompted me to think more about the need in the nonprofit world for a book like this. She also provided useful, early advice about the outline. A comment from Suki Molina at a meeting held along the banks of the Snake River stuck with me for a long time and helped catalyze some of my other experiences about what legacy gift techniques really worked and didn't work for small and mid-size nonprofits. Sharon Harmon, Gary Kish, and Mary McLain graciously provided me with places to get away from the office and focus on writing at critical junctures.

Kim Klein, Martha Richards, Donna Bandelloni, Glenn Lamb, Alan Horton, Evie Lamb, Krista Larson, Peter Jurncy, Lawrence Henze, Amy Brown, Keith Thomajan, and Kristen Trainor all helped with early comments and insight about what a book like this should look like. A special thanks to Sarah Conley for providing some peace of mind at the right moment.

Stephanie Debner read the first draft and tactfully suggested it needed a complete rewrite; she was correct. Later, Ken Margolis, Roger Ellison, and Ann Barden spent hours providing comments and catching some real blunders on my part. Thanks to both Al Zimmerman and Richard Ely for detailed comments on a key section, too. There were also a number of trusted colleagues who made a host of suggestions about content and the title. Thanks to Cynthia Guyer and Jennifer Schmidt who helped frame the title. A special thanks to Tamara Ryan who carved time out of her busy schedule to attend to many last-minute editing and continuity tasks. As I write this on a rainy Oregon afternoon, I know I have forgotten more than one person. I apologize in advance for this oversight.

Allison Bruner and Dani Scoville at Jossey-Bass deserve a special thanks for moving the book along. Thank you for your patience with this first-time book author.

And, of course, thanks to my partner Stephanie Debner, who tolerated me writing evenings and weekends more often than I can count. Though she won't be reading this, Mollie the yellow Labrador dutifully did her job, reminding me that not all was writing and that the great outdoors beckoned—frequently. (FYI, Mollie's favorite hike is Wahkeena Falls in the Columbia Gorge.)

Thanks to all of you!

ABOUT THE AUTHOR

Kevin Johnson is a nonprofit consultant whose work focuses on helping non-profits be more effective in strategy and fundraising. A principal of Retriever Development Counsel, LLC, he works on a regular basis providing training, coaching, and strategic planning for nonprofit executives, boards, and volunteers located throughout western North America. He has had the opportunity to serve a wide range of nonprofit groups, ranging from humane societies to land trusts, private colleges, regional hospitals, arts organizations, and advocacy groups. His experience includes a variety of roles with public service organizations, including college vice president, director of development for a national environmental organization, acting executive director for a large children's service organization, vice president and manager of consulting group focused on executive training, and a planned giving officer for a national conservation organization.

INDEX

Trust, in nonprofit organizations, 66; description of, 81–82; donor control and, 151–152; fundraising tools to build, 164; gift acceptance policies and, 122–130; hidden questions regarding, 106–107, 108, 119, 120, 138; importance of, 153

Trust, in professional advisors, 217

Trustees, 210, 285

Trusts: assumptions about, 38; definition of, 285; example of, 279; gift tool selection and, 209, 210

Type size, in newsletter, 197, 198

U

Unified credit, 285

Uniform Management of Institutional Funds Act (UMIFA), 287–288

Unrestricted gifts, 276

U.S. News & World Report, xxiii

V

Values, 22, 108

Variance clause, 276–277

Visibility, of organization, 84

Vision: of donors, 23–25; donors' hidden questions regarding, 119, 120, 139; in long-term sustainability, 108–109

Visits, with donors, 199–201

Visual presentations: of case statements, 92–93, 97, 100; of newsletters, 198; software for, 253–254

Volunteers, 88; campaigns involving, 182; donor suggestions regarding, 181, 182; gift acceptance policy and, 122–123, 127–130; opportunities to secure gifts from, 201–202; professional advisors as, 128–129, 220

W

Wealthy and Wise: How You and America Can Get the Most Out of Your Giving (Rosenberg), 71

Wealthy donors: assumptions about, 37–38; capital campaigns and, 187; estate tax changes for, 8–9; historical bequests of, xxi–xxiii; stereotypes of, 29

Websites, of nonprofits, 166

White, D., 239

Williamson, D., 167, 174

Willis, T., 241

Wills: board selection and, 113; common questions related to, 56–58; definition of, xviii, 52, 285; donor trust and, 81–82; drafting and signing process, 49, 54–56; emotions related to, 51; importance of, 48; multiple nonprofits named in, 62; of nonprofit leaders, 48–60; purpose of, 51, 55–56; resources for, 48; revisions to, 55; seminars about, 164

Women, bequests from, xxii

Working capital, 149, 288

Working Woman Magazine, xxiii

Y

Yale University, xv